Jewish American and Holocaust Literature

SUNY series in Modern Jewish Literature and Culture
Sarah Blacher Cohen, editor

Jewish American and Holocaust Literature

Representation in the Postmodern World

Edited by
Alan L. Berger
and
Gloria L. Cronin

State University of New York Press

Published by
State University of New York Press, Albany

© 2004 State University of New York

All rights reserved

Printed in the United States of America

For information, address State University of New York Press,
90 State Street, Suite 700, Albany, NY 12207

Production by Judith Block
Marketing by Susan Petrie

Library of Congress Cataloging-in-Publication Data

Jewish American and Holocaust literature ; representation in the postmodern
    world / edited by Alan L. Berger and Gloria L. Cronin
        p. cm.
    Includes bibliographical references and index.
    ISBN 0-7914-6209-9 (alk. paper) — ISBN 0-7914-6210-2 (pbk. : alk. paper)
        1. American literature—Jewish authors—History and criticism. 2. World War,
    1939–1945—United States—Literature and the war. 3. American literature—20th
    century—History and criticism. 4. Holocaust, Jewish (1939–1945), in literature. 5.
    Postmodernism (Literature)—United States. 6. Jews—United States—Intellectual
    life. 7. Holocaust survivors in literature. 8. Judaism in literature. 9. Jews in
    literature. I. Berger, Alan L., 1939–   II. Cronin, Gloria L., 1947–

    PS153.J4J47 2004
    810.9'8924—dc22   2004041626

            10 9 8 7 6 5 4 3 2 1

*This book is dedicated to the memory of
Jay J. Raddock and Irving Botnick.*

Contents

Acknowledgments

The editors acknowledge with thanks the following people. Sarah Anne Bylund, Professor Cronin's research/technical assistant, worked hard on source checking, typing, preliminary editing and formatting, and communication with all the contributors to this volume. Currently, she is pursuing an M.A. in American literature at Brigham Young University. She is also the *Saul Bellow Journal* intern. Bonnie Lander, Professor Berger's secretary, diligently kept the project in order and on track. Ms. Martha Zubrow, his graduate assistant, was tenacious and skillful in tracking footnote references; these traits approached legendary proportion. Ana Johnson rendered valuable assistance in identifying certain sources. We are pleased to acknowledge the support of the FAU Foundation for help in bringing this book to fruition. We are also grateful to the anonymous referees who read and commented on this book when it was in manuscript. It has been a delight working with James Peltz, editor-in chief of SUNY Press, and Judith Block, senior production editor.

Introduction

ALAN L. BERGER AND
GLORIA L. CRONIN

New beginnings always occasion reflection on the past. This inexorable rule of human behavior applies especially to the cultural realm where innovation is in constant, and frequently creative, tension with what has gone before. Thus, the dawn of the new millennium is an appropriate moment to view two related literary genres, which have to a large extent shaped twentieth-century literature. Jewish American and Holocaust literature together have confronted, and reflected on, the meaning of being human, the place of tradition in modernity, the content of Jewish identity, the issue of memory, the nature of evil, and the role of God in history. Further, the questions raised by these genres have both particular and universal resonance. Composed against a tumultuous background of great cultural transition and unprecedented state-sponsored systematic murder, this literature addresses the concerns of human existence in extremis.

Despite frequent rumors of its demise, the Jewish American literary tradition shows every sign of healthy continuation at the turn of the new millennium. While Malamud is gone, Bellow's career is closing, and Roth seems to be at the peak of his powers, the grandchildren of the great twentieth-century "Bellow Malamudroth" nevertheless continue the tradition. Despite its ambivalent relation to the multicultural movement of the past thirty years, and recent academic critical preoccupation with various postmodernisms, young Jewish American writers have recently been the subject of an annual American Literature Association Symposium devoted to rereading the established tradition from new scholarly perspectives, as well as exploring contemporary writers. The 1997 November/December issue of *Tikkun* was devoted to the Jewish literary revival, while Andrew Furman reminds us in his *Contemporary Jewish American Writers and the Multicultural Dilemma* (2001) that "we should rejoice that we had a Bellow, but read and enjoy young Jewish novelists on their own terms" (B9). In his feature article in *The Chronicle of Higher Education* (July 2001), "The Exaggerated Demise of the Jewish American Writer," Furman argues that Jews are still writing about their experiences in America. Most important, the vitality of Jewish

1

American letters has finally been acknowledged by the appearance of the new *Norton Anthology of Jewish American Literature* (2001).

The first phase of Jewish American presence in American literature begins with the arrival of Jewish immigrants on American shores in the eighteenth century. This literature of arrival continues up to the 1880s, to be followed by what the editors of the *Norton Anthology* call the "The Great Tide" from 1880 to 1924, which ends with the xenophobic slamming shut of the gates at Ellis Island. What follows is the steady advance of Jewish American writers on Broadway, in Hollywood, in radio, in the television industry, and into the American literary mainstream. In the eyes of the literary establishment, the Jewish American tradition comes of age with Roth, Malamud, and the awarding of the Nobel Prize to Saul Bellow in 1976. Around this culminating achievement, a rich scholarly critical discussion emerged regarding the phenomenon of self-meditation about Jewish identity in America. It includes a significant tradition of humor writing, scholarly commentary, literary criticism, contemporary religious commentary, Holocaust literature, post-Holocaust literature, and second-generation Holocaust literature.

The Holocaust is a watershed event that divides culture into a before and an after. Moreover, the Shoah stands as the defining mark of the twentieth century. Elie Wiesel observes that every age has produced a distinctive literary form. "If," he writes, "the Greeks invented tragedy, the Romans the epistle, and the Renaissance the sonnet, our generation invented a new literature, that of testimony."[1] Holocaust literature, which for Wiesel is itself an oxymoron, is paradigmatic. Written in many languages, this literature underscores the fact that no field of human endeavor remains untouched by the extermination of the Jewish people. The flames of the Shoah revealed in a stark and irrefutable manner the fact that culture is no shield against murder. At first, in the early 1960s, a few survivors wrote about their experience. With the passage of time and the increase in historical documentation, novelists increasingly turned their attention to the manifold implications of the Holocaust. Literary critics then began discussing Holocaust literature and its radical challenges to assumptions about God, the meaning of language itself, and its impact on traditional teachings. As the essays in this volume reveal, the discussion of the meaning and message of testimonial is continuing and deepening.

Linking the Genres

Jewish American and Holocaust literature share several attributes that link them in surprising ways. For example, they share the misperception of being exhausted forms. The argument runs that not much of importance has appeared since Bellow, Malamud, and Roth. Or, conversely, what has appeared is simply a reworking of the past. In terms of Holocaust literature, one frequently hears that too much attention has been paid the Shoah—that it is time to move on. Accusations, some well intended, others mean-spirited and self-serving, warn against remembering the Holocaust as the watershed event of Jewish and human history.

The second shared characteristic is that both genres are experiencing a renewal. Among the significant names that come to mind here are writers such as Max Apple, Gina Berriault, Rosellen Brown, Melvin Jules Bukiet, Helen Epstein, Ruth Feldman, Rebecca Goldstein, Allegra Goodman, Hugh Nissenson, Jacqueline Osherow, Marge Piercy, Tova Reich, Adrienne Rich, Jonathan Rosen, Thane Rosenbaum, Art Spiegelman, Steve Stern, and a host of others. These writers extend and enrich the genres in important ways.

Writing Our Way Home: Contemporary Stories by American Jewish Writers, the 1992 anthology edited by Ted Solotaroff and Nessa Rapoport, reveals the breadth and depth of both Jewish American and Holocaust literature. For example, the editors observe that "in rescuing the Holocaust from the banality of repetition, these stories from writers of diverse background provide another indication of the fresh winds of imagination that blow from various sectors of the Jewish scene" (xxiii).

Concerning the Holocaust, Yosef Hayim Yerushalmi notes in *Zakhor* (1996) that more has been written on the Shoah than on any other historical event in Judaism. However, the image of the Holocaust, he writes, "is being shaped, not at the historian's anvil, but in the novelist's crucible" (98).[2] Memoirs, novels, poetry, and short stories dealing with the event and its aftermath continue to appear with great frequency. These literary works treat the experiences of survivors ranging from the theologically shattering writings of Elie Wiesel to the psychologically overwhelming stories of Ida Fink. Additionally, the memoirs of hidden children have begun to emerge with increasing frequency. These works raise crucial ethical, philosophical, societal, and theological issues. Moreover, novels by and about the second generation, that is, children of Holocaust survivors, form their own distinctive subgenre and are the subject of several scholarly studies including Alan L. Berger's *Children of Job: American Second-Generation Witnesses to the Holocaust* (1997), the first systematic study of American second-generation Holocaust novels and films. Berger observes that the writings of the present children of Job continue "to shape both contemporary memory of the Holocaust and late twentieth-century Jewish ritual" (190). Additional works dealing with second-generation witnesses include Alan L. and Naomi Berger (editors), *Second-Generation Voices: Reflections by Children of Holocaust Survivors and Perpetrators* (2001); Efraim Sicher (editor), *Breaking Crystal: Writing and Memory After Auschwitz* (1998), and Dina Wardi, *Memorial Candles:*

Children of the Holocaust, translated by Naomi Goldblum (1992). Their Holocaust legacy plays a vital role in the psychosocial lives and the imagistic realm of the second generation. Moreover, these works point the way to a reworking of old Judaic myths and to new rituals of post-Auschwitz Jewish identity.

The third resemblance between these genres is that, frequently, the works of a single author represent both types of writings. For example, one thinks of the writings of Nathan Englander, Allegra Goodman, Marge Piercy, Lynne Sharon Schwartz, Joseph Skibell, and Areyh Lev Stollman, among others. The extraordinary events of twentieth-century Jewish history continue to compel the literary imagination as literary critics and writers seek to confront the possible meanings of the bloodiest century in human history. Writers of second-generation Holocaust literature reveal both a means of coping with the enormity of the Shoah and a refusal to permit its becoming merely literature. Furthermore, this work displays the deep wellsprings of the Jewish imaginative capacity. These are challenges that will only deepen and mature in the new century.

Mainstream scholarly articles, journals, national newspapers, weeklies, and a variety of Jewish publications have published literally thousands of book reviews and articles devoted to the subjects of Jewishness in America and what constituted Jewish American literature in the twentieth century. This literature's principal lines of inquiry have always been celebration, self-recognition, and cultural self-awareness. However, new cultural assessments of the conditions of Jewish life for second-generation Holocaust witnesses and American Jews in the midst of plenty seem to have supplanted those dealing with Zionist politics, economic deprivation, and social alienation. In the postalienation era we find renewed emphasis on the life of a demographically dwindling generation of American Jews. This generation is largely unschooled in Jewish traditions, as a consequence of the returnee or *ba'al t'shuvah* phenomenon, renewed concern over the meaning and aftermath of the Holocaust for second- and now third-generation witnesses, and the resurgence of traditional orthodox Judaism. Critical assessments, biographical investigation, bibliographical mapping, theological commentary, and historiography continue apace. The liberal humanist critical perspective celebrating primarily the values of Jewish humanism is now joined by feminism, postcolonialism, postmodernism multiculturalism, men's studies, gay studies, and a newly reconstituted cultural studies. Hence, the current critical discussion on Jewish American and Holocaust literature negotiates the ethical issues emerging from the postmodern moment and the multicultural debate with their emphasis on identity.

This volume of essays is intended to further this critical metanarrative by showing how traditionally canonized Jewish American writers are being reread and reassessed through the lenses of contemporary critical theory, and by extending critical assessment to the works of current Jewish American writers who comprise an ongoing vibrant contemporary tradition in the new millennium, and who continue to grapple with the legacy of the unmasterable trauma of the Holocaust.

Part One: Holocaust Literature

The essays dealing with the Holocaust are far-reaching and include a discussion of the writings of those who perished as well as a post-9/11 meditation on the relationship between aesthetics and grief by a son of Holocaust survivors. International in scope, three themes emerge from these studies: a focus on hiding, narrative strategies for remembering, and the emergence of the genre of Holocaust literature itself. Alan L. Berger's study of the literature of hidden children notes the complex psychosocial and theological legacy of their hiding experience, which constitutes an assault on their core identity. Were they Jews? Were they Christians? Whom could they trust? Why were they separated first from their Jewish birth parents and then from their Christian foster families? Berger cites the poignant comment of Robert Krell, himself a hidden child, who observes, "Liberation was not altogether liberating." During the war, hidden children had to embrace silence to survive. After the war, they had to learn to overcome this silence in order to bear witness and to begin working through their experiences. Among the lessons to be learned from the experience of hidden children, Berger writes, "perhaps the most important legacy will occur when people who hear their testimony seek to build a moral society which cherishes, rather than murders, children."

Ellen Fine's lucid analysis of Ida Fink's writing discusses the intimate connection between the survivor's focus on the "hidden witnesses" in *A Scrap of Time* and the subtext of relationships, especially those between parents and children. Fink's stories tell of the Germans' continuing attempt to sever intimate bonds. The Polish survivor seeks to bring the reader, who is an outsider, inside the event. "Fink's stories themselves," writes Fine, provide a "connection between the inner and outer, allowing the reader (the outsider) to gain an inside glimpse into the impact of the hiding experience upon ordinary men, women and children." Fink's tales offer "chinks" or points of contrast between inner and outer, reader and event, life and death, the living and the dead, author and reader. In spite of the limits of representation, Fink's work insightfully "creates narratives out of the lives [of the victims] and the dark universe they inhabited, the terror they courageously faced on a daily basis." Inevitably and tragically, the survivors feel guilty for having lived. Fink's narratives, Fine attests, "assure us that the traces [of their lives] will not vanish."

The late Harry James Cargas writes perceptively about a different dimension of hiding. Responding to a newspaper attack which claimed that

Jerzy Kosinski, the enigmatic Polish writer and Holocaust survivor, was not really the author of his own works, Cargas addresses the issues raised by the ensuing scandal. His conclusion? Kosinski was indeed the author of his own works. One of the major themes in Kosinski's books is the "attempt to hide identity." This is a type of hiding that evokes important questions for Holocaust literature. What, for example, is the nature of memory? What kind of identity do survivors possess? What constitutes truth in literature?

Hugh Nissenson's articulate piece discusses the works of six major European writers who experienced the Holocaust. Linking aesthetics to content, Nissenson writes that these six—Tadeusz Borowski, Anne Frank, Etty Hillesum, Jacob Presser, Primo Levi, and Emmanuel Ringelblum—are the best stylists on the Shoah. Further, these writers shared a common theme, a "vision of the Holocaust as a new historical reality." Nissenson pursues his thesis in contending that these writings, for all their emphasis on bearing witness, are also important because their authors had a love of both language and of the specific form being worked—frequently the diary or literary journal. Nissenson concludes his essay by observing that the enduring prose of these writers marks a major contribution to twentieth-century European literature, the genre of "Holocaust literature—with its unprecedented subject matter, modern Europe's volitional descent, back through its own Dark Ages and the chaos preceding its creation—into the pit."

Gerhard Bach's concern is with narrative strategies against forgetting employed by both older and younger writers. He discusses how American writers Cynthia Ozick and Saul Bellow, and European authors Martin Amis and Irene Dische, reveal a different way of communicating the Holocaust. Ozick's *The Shawl*, attests Bach, exemplifies Irving Howe's demand that "Holocaust fiction communicate to the reader both the external Auschwitz (factual events and experiences) and the internal Auschwitz (individual suffering, coping with memories)." Bellow's *The Bellarosa Connection* shifts from story to storyteller. Bach notes that this "implies a shift from objectifying testimony to subjectified witness." Amis and Dische, for their part, reflect the postmodernist impetus by deconstructing the historicity of the Holocaust. Their narratives in, respectively, *Time's Arrow* and *Pious Secrets*, Bach argues, "make an appeal to the reader to serve as implicit—and to a certain extent even complicit—*collaborateurs* in the mental reconstruction of Holocaust realities." Consequently, for second-generation writers the demand is not for empathy. Rather, the writer—and reader—are called upon to activate their own strategies against forgetting and to construct meaning out of memory. Bach asserts that contemporary strategies against forgetting are "stringently forceful antidotes to an otherwise rampant culture of obliviousness."

Marianne M. Friedrich, Gila Safran Naveh, and Susan E. Nowak deal with specific case studies of Holocaust memory, images of the Shoah, and the role of fiction in representing the Holocaust. Friedrich discusses Ozick's *The Shawl*. Unlike Bach, however, she views the novella as exemplifying both an ancient and a modern form of literature. Thus, Ozick's work simultaneously establishes a "midrashic intertextuality in particular . . . based on an ancient oral tradition" and addresses "a very avant-garde international trend in fiction pointing toward an increased emphasis on 'secondary orality' in an Ongian sense." Further, Friedrich sees a connection between *The Shawl* and Paul Celan's *Todesfugue* in that both works treat a "deeply troubled mother-child relationship, overshadowed by the problem of Jewish identity." Friedrich views both works as embodying Ozick's vision of haggadic fiction as "liturgical literature." Consequently, and in the face of the destruction of the European Jewish community, this fiction recalls—even as it relates the horrific loss of—European Judaism.

Gila Safran Naveh focuses on the aesthetics of representation. How, she inquires, can the Holocaust be made real to us despite its "lack of presence"? Naveh asserts that rather than attempting to expunge the Shoah from ordinary life, writers and filmmakers such as Aharon Appelfeld, Isaac Bashevis Singer, and Claude Lanzmann bring the Holocaust into everyday life, creating what Ozick terms "a mind engraved with the Holocaust." For Lanzmann, the situation is one of antimemory; "the transmission is the knowledge." In the case of the writers, Appelfeld's use of the term a "grain of wheat" and Singer's "speck of dust" are, argues Naveh, unique signifiers that "cause the signified rather than being caused by it." "Grain" and "speck" are terms that resonate with the Jewish historical experience. For example, they conjure God, Jewish literature, biblical statements, and Jewish prayer. Annihilation is read as "turning into dust." God's promise to Abraham is to make the Jewish people more numerous than grains of sand on the shore.

Susan E. Nowak deals with the theological implications of the Holocaust on the writers Norma Rosen and Rebecca Goldstein. For both of these authors, explains Nowak, Holocaust fiction is a "self-reflexive, dynamic, and transformative genre." Rosen and Goldstein are therefore concerned not with simply mirroring the remains of a vanished world, but rather in engaging the insistent, haunting presence of the Shoah in a manner that seeks a *tikkun*—repair or mending of the world—even if in an imperfect and fragmented manner. Consequently, each of these writers is convinced that to glimpse a repaired world is simultaneously to "bear responsibility for creating it." Nowak thus views the task of the post-Holocaust writer as being morally responsible for creating a better world while instructing her readers on how we can live in a post-Holocaust universe.

Part One concludes with Thane Rosenbaum's profound meditation "Art and Atrocity in a Post-9/11 World." A second-generation Holocaust witness, Rosenbaum explores the complex relationship between art and aesthetics.

"Murder," he reminds his readers, "is not a work of art, but rather a moral crime." How is one to respond to this crime? On the one hand, it assumes the proportion of a gigantic struggle between the imagination of writers and the imagination of terrorists. Yet, on the other hand, silence—at least initially—may be the most appropriate response to the moral outrage of terrorist mass murder. Rosenbaum emphasizes the fact that September 11, 2001, was not the Holocaust. However, the attack revisits the question of the proper role of memory in the aftermath of atrocity. Both for the Holocaust victims and for the victims of 9/11, "sitting with the sadness and listening to the silence"—anathema in a culture seeking instant closure—are necessary preludes to any attempt at an aesthetic of atrocity. Let us listen, Rosenbaum pleads, to the ghosts.

Part Two: Jewish American Literature

Essays treating Jewish American literature in this volume range from a focus on particular authors such as Saul Bellow, Philip Roth, and Jonathan Rosen to an exploration of what constitutes a Jewish writer. The concluding three essays in this section specifically concern themselves with Jewish feminism and its contemporary challenges.

Gloria Cronin, using the "whiteness studies" theoretical model from postmodern postcolonial theory, urges renewed ethical consideration of how we read the work of canonized Jewish American authors. Examining the racial architecture of Saul Bellow's fiction, she points out that in Bellow's novels degeneracy, cultural collapse, barbarism, and the deterioration of Western culture are very often troped black and African, and that such tropes of African barbarity and moral corruption escalate with increasing animus throughout the Bellow canon until contemporary animality, urban desolation, and the inner city itself become a true heart of darkness or Africanized ancient forest. She also points out how Africanity becomes a device through which Bellow meditates on a forbidden and feared white shadow self, filled with physical terror and internal loneliness. Hence, it would appear that Bellow is recirculating Conradian tropes of blackness from the old colonial archive in a self-serving double move in which he conceives of himself as "civilized" and therefore "not nigger," while simultaneously reinforcing and perpetuating the "niggerhood" of those behind its veil.

Sarah Blacher Cohen revisits Bellow, now in the twilight of his career, and lauds his lavish talent as a comic writer who expresses a preference for the use of comedy rather than complaint as an antidote to despair. Throughout his career, she argues, he uses comedy to interrupt, resist, reinterpret, and transcend diversity. While in the earlier novels he uses comedy to stave off mistrust and melancholy, in the later novels it becomes a tonic, "a compassionate shield," "a flashing saber," "a balance and a barricade," "a counter to depression," "a satiric glass," and a "defiant even militant irony." In an analysis of several works, she demonstrates how he spans the full range of highbrow and lowbrow vaudevillian Jewish humor "to dull the progressive illness of mortality." Given how little has been published on humor in Jewish American literature in the last twenty years, this essay points to the need for further such humor studies.

Bonnie Lyons uses Philip Roth's *American Pastoral* as an illustration of how contemporary Jewish American writers increasingly draw upon European texts, American mythos, and Jewish preoccupations with time, memory, loss, and history as they develop their fiction. Through her explication of *American Pastoral*, she illustrates the sheer postmodern variety and complexity of Jewish life at the turn of the millennium in a rapidly evolving American culture.

Evelyn Avery addresses the issue of what distinguishes a Jewish writer by tracing the respect and interest Cynthia Ozick and Bernard Malamud shared for one another during Malamud's lifetime, as evidenced through their personal correspondence and interviews. Despite Malamud's secular orientation and Ozick's orthodox life, she argues, both writers shared the values of *Yiddishkeit*, compassion for the underdog and outrage against injustice. She compares several key works and characters by both authors, and concludes with a moving account of Cynthia Ozick's recognition of Malamud's essentially Jewish soul by her reciting of the *Shema*, the holiest prayer in the Jewish world, at his secular funeral.

Suzanne Lundquist provides a postmodern and ethnographic reading of Jonathan Rosen's *Eve's Apple*, which she reads as a disquisition on the relationship between the forbidden fruit of the book of Genesis and the contemporary human body, its mystery of hunger and denial, connection and acceptance. She describes Rosen's ability to connect the contemporary condition of anorexia to current spiritual hunger and a whole complex of Judeo-Christian cultural constructions of the human body, hunger, addiction, femininity, masculinity, human intimacy, family dysfunction, bodily malconception, and eternal hunger, and to our concept of God.

S. Lillian Kremer provides a comprehensive overview of the ideological shift in Jewish women's writing of the last thirty years. In opposition to the tendency of Jewish male writers to portray Jewish women as noisy and pushy, manipulative mothers or lovers, spoiled daughters, or castrators of husbands and sons, she demonstrates contemporary Jewish American women writers writing against this grain by portraying Jewish women with a concern for ethical, social, and political justice. Female protagonists are often more complex and show concern for the pull between Jewish languages, history, religious philosophy, and tradition. Intelligent, assertive women, strongly influenced by Judaism and feminism, are fashioning new paradigms, seeking entrée into religious life, reevaluating traditional Judaism, grappling with secular feminism, and generally displacing male experience as normative. This newest generation of Jewish American women writers are at ease with Judaism and Western high culture, portray the Holocaust from a female perspective, often use a midrashic narrative mode, and engage in text centeredness, redemptive writing, and *tikkun* (healing) themes.

Miriyam Glazer provides a valuable updated map of twentieth-century Jewish women writers by exploring (1) earlier fiction featuring pursuit of the American quest-romance of the prefeminist era; (2) more recent fiction describing the cracks in the overall structure, where Jewish women refuse to look for gentiles over their shoulders and become assertively Jewish; and (3) a mostly secular fiction in which Jewish women fail to find their places. Provocatively, she invokes postmodern hybridity theory, in asking whether Jews are white or not, and at what point Jews do or do not become what Homi Bhabha calls a "reformed, recognizable Other" who embodies an "authorized version of Otherness." Are Jews half-breeds who understand everyone because they belong completely to no larger society, she asks? Such questions take the twentieth-century debate on issues of Jewish identity and the identity of the Jewish writer into the twenty-first century.

Janet Burstein focuses intensively on women's filial narratives of parents, children, and women, which sidestep the typically male Harold Bloom–style "anxiety of influence" filial narrative of priority, competitiveness, and status. She traces the Oedipal family romance with all its aggressive scenarios through fiction and criticism and shows how filial stories written since the late 1960s by Jewish American women transform these parental stories through staging patterns of engagement rather than rupture, continuing dialogue rather than guilt and nostalgia. She also examines fiction that reveals the mixed effects upon daughters of the frustrations of their mothers' lives, and what they carry forth of the precursor's story even as their own narratives reverse it. She credits this new generation of Jewish women writers with producing a "matrix of generous influence" which Harold Bloom called "illusory," instead of the usual masculine agonistic androcentric model.

Notes

1. Wiesel, Elie, "The Holocaust as Literary Inspiration," in *Dimensions of the Holocaust.* (Evanston: Northwestern University Press, 1977), 9.

2. One now needs to expand Yerushalmi's observation to include cinematic representations of the Holocaust. For insightful studies of Holocaust films and their societal impact, see Judith E. Doneson, *The Holocaust in American Film*, Second Edition, Syracuse University Press (2002), and Annette Insdorf, *Indelible Shadows: Film and the Holocaust* Third Edition. Cambridge University Press (2002).

1

Holocaust Literature

1

Hidden Children:
The Literature of Hiding

Alan L. Berger

Of all the voices from the Holocaust we [hidden children]
have been the most silent and the least noticed.

Robert Krell[1]

Speaking of his experience as a hidden child during the Holocaust, the
Israeli psychologist Shlomo Breznitz recalls his father's comment that "hiding at best only delays the final outcome." The elder Breznitz believed that
hiding was pointless because "sooner or later the Germans would find everybody; their hunting of Jews was too systematic to be derailed by a temporary
disappearance."[2] His assessment was chillingly accurate. Approximately 1.5
million of the 1.6 million prewar Jewish child population in Nazi-occupied
Europe were murdered. This means that only 6 to 7 percent of Jewish
children lived through the Shoah. Hidden in a variety of places including
farms, barns, cellars, pigsties, convents, and monasteries, their hiding experience invariably robbed them of their childhood; indeed, André Stein speaks
of hidden children being *"evicted from our childhood"* (emphasis added).[3]
Although many of the child survivors have led successful lives, their hiding
experience left them a complex psychosocial and theological legacy that had
a profound impact on their sense of identity and consequently, for a long
time, left them uncertain as to what exactly they were bearing witness.

In this chapter, I first present an overview of the issues of Jewish identity and bearing witness among hidden children in the Holocaust. I then
focus on three works: two memoirs of Jewish children hidden in different
parts of Europe, Ruth Kapp Hartz's *Your Name Is Renée*, as told to and
written by Stacy Cretzmeyer, and Nechama Tec's *Dry Tears: The Story of a
Lost Childhood*; and a novel, Elisabeth Gille's *Shadows of a Childhood*.[4]
Four themes emerge from these written works: fear of abandonment by

parents and by God; the psychic disorientation imposed by a new identity necessitated by the invention of a life history in order to survive; silence and a lack of understanding of why this happened to them; and a search for justice. While these themes do not receive equal weight in the works under discussion, each forms a part of the mosaic of the legacy of hiding. In addition, I note two types of motives for rescue, including the theological ambivalence of "responder" altruism in the accounts of Tec and Gille and the "idealist" altruism portrayed in the story of Hartz.[5] I conclude with possible lessons learned from the writings of hidden children.

The Crisis of Identity: Religious and Psychosocial Dimensions

The question of identity among hidden children is profoundly complex, involving memory of trauma and embracing both their Jewish affiliation and their identity as survivors. Concerning religion, for children old enough to have a memory of Jewish ritual and family life, being forced to hide led in many cases to a fundamental confusion about their Jewish selves. For example, it was typical for hidden Jewish children to be exposed to the religious beliefs and attitudes of their Christian foster parents. Some of these children did not wish to leave the safe haven provided them during the war. The religious dimension of this issue is twofold. On the one hand, there was an outright rejection of Judaism, as in the case of the nine-year-old girl who proclaimed, "The Jewish God killed my parents. He burned my home. Jesus Christ saved me."[6] On the other hand, Christianity was embraced as salvific. Viewed through the lens of a young child, Judaism was "bad"; it caused the child to be separated from his or her parents. Christianity, for its part, was "good" because being Christian meant being protected.

What can be said is that for many of the children who emerged from hiding, their Christian identities were far better formed than their Jewish selfhoods. The path back to Judaism frequently was strewn with many psychic and theological obstacles. Robert Krell, hidden in Holland at age two, emphasizes the psychic dislocation experienced by hidden children, noting, "I had been torn from my parents twice. Once at age two from my Jewish family, once at age five from my Christian family."[7] Furthermore, the postwar situation of hidden children was itself fraught with peril. Many remained with their Christian hiding parents. Jewish agencies and organizations disputed their future. Moreover, a biological parent or parents who survived the camps had also undergone trauma; they themselves were now orphans who were physically and psychologically scarred. Nevertheless, Holland required that these Jewish people obtain a document certifying that they were fit parents. While this requirement was based on a concern for the welfare of the hidden children and was not motivated by anti-Semitism, postwar reunions were frequently more traumatic than therapeutic. In Krell's words, "Liberation was not altogether liberating."

Initially, questions were raised concerning whether hidden children should even be considered survivors. Some older survivors as well as many in the nonwitnessing population expressed skepticism on this issue. For instance, Krell reports that since the war he has been told the following: "You couldn't possibly remember, you were too young." "You're so lucky, I was in a concentration camp." "Don't talk about it. Get on with your life."[8] Furthermore, the hidden children had to deal with a paradoxical situation for which they bore no responsibility. For example, they were hidden not because of any wrong that they had done, but rather because of the enormous moral wrongs committed by the adult world. Consequently, hidden children had to embrace silence, seek memory, and comprehend their identity in a morally distorted and chaotic world bent on their destruction. Discouraged from speaking about their experiences after the war, the hidden children continued their silence.

Many hidden children have an understandably ambivalent relationship to Jewish identity. Being Jewish during the Holocaust meant being a target of murderers and being deprived of elemental happiness. Being driven into hiding because of their Jewish birth meant concealing their true identity. Consequently, the question for hidden children is this: "Can one be proud of one's elemental Jewish identity after the trauma induced by shame and confusion about that identity?" The hidden child's postwar search for memory illuminates the painful conflict experienced by those whose core identity had been obliterated so that they could survive. Yet, as we shall discover, the hidden children in our study found their way back to some type of postwar Jewish identity. Although this identification may not have embraced traditional Jewish ritual, it did focus on bearing witness to the Shoah.

Furthermore, if a name is a destiny, consider the situation Saul Friedländer describes in his haunting memoir, *When Memory Comes*. Following his baptism in the Church of Notre-Dame, Friedländer recalls the difficulty he had at age nine getting used to his Christian name of Paul-Henri:

> At home I had been called Pavel, or rather Pavlicek, the usual Czech diminutive, or else Gagl, not to mention a whole string of affectionate nicknames. Then from Paris to Neris I had become Paul, which for a child was something quite different. As Paul I didn't feel like Pavlicek any more, but Paul-Henri was worse still: I had crossed a line and was now on the other side. Paul could have been Czech and Jewish; Paul-Henri could be nothing but French and resolutely Catholic, and I was not yet naturally so.

What was more, that was not the last of the name changes: I subsequently became Shaul on disembarking in Israel, and then Saul, a compromise between the Saül that French requires and the Paul that I had been. *In short, it is impossible to know which name I am, and that in the final analysis seems to me sufficient expression of a real and profound confusion.* [Emphasis added][9]

But the situation of hidden children was further complicated by tensions within the Jewish community itself. For example, Friedländer, who came from an assimilated Jewish family, recalls the absolute despair he felt when, at age six, his parents placed him in a "home" for Jewish children in Montmorency. Many of the children in the home were pious. Among them was a boy named Jacob who, writes the author, "noticed immediately that his prayers were as foreign to me as his Yiddish, his yarmulka, and his earlocks" (44). Friedländer was termed a "goy," a negative term for a non-Jew. He was tied to a tree and beaten. Writing of this episode many years later, the author observed that he was "beaten by Jewish children because they thought I was different from them. So I belonged nowhere" (45). Consequently, in reaction to this trauma, the young boy began wetting his bed and was transferred to the "baby" section. He refers to his time at the "home" as a "period of continual suffering" because of being separated from his parents. Following the war, Friedländer went to Israel, where he became a professor and a distinguished author.

Overcoming Silence: Bearing Witness

To help save their own lives, hidden children had to embrace silence: silence about their Jewish identity; silence about their very presence in a particular hiding location; and silence in the form of controlling spontaneity, which is itself the defining trait of children. What contributed to their survival during the war, however, became destructive after the Shoah. Continuing to conceal their experience, hidden children remained silent well into middle age. For example, Friedländer's memoir, among the earliest of those written by hidden children, appeared thirty-three years after the Holocaust. This was followed by several stunning memoirs: Nechama Tec's *Dry Tears* (1982), Frida Scheps Weinstein's *A Hidden Childhood, 1942–1945* (1985), Yehuda Nir's *The Lost Childhood* (1989), and Shlomo Breznitz's *Memory Fields* (1992).

At least part of the reason for this very silence is the necessity of reconstructing fragments of memory which, while bringing cohesion to their experience, also causes great pain as the hidden children remember parents and other relatives who were murdered in the Holocaust. Furthermore, public ignorance of, and silence about, hidden children meant nonvalidation of the experience of the youngest survivors of the Shoah. It was as if they had been expelled from the history of the Holocaust. While hidden child testimonies began to be recorded in Vancouver as early as 1978, and hidden children have been meeting since the 1980s,[10] thereby beginning the process of unlocking the unconscious, the youngest survivors of the Shoah are now beginning to emerge from the shadows and to receive public validation owing to widespread attention paid to the 1991 Hidden Children Gathering in New York City.

The Literature of Hiding: Your Name Is Renée

Ruth Kapp Hartz recounts her story of being hidden in a convent in Sorèze in the south of France. Divided into three parts, the memoir traces the author's terror when she goes into hiding at age five. The German-born Kapp family escapes to France, where four-year-old Ruth learns a twofold lesson: it is dangerous to be Jewish, and she must not use her real name. Ruth's older cousin admonishes the child, "Remember, your name is Renée and you are French." When Pétain's Vichy government begins rounding up Jews, the family flees to the south of France. Although they are helped by the righteous, there are also many collaborators. Told from a child's point of view, Ruth's story evokes the trauma of confusion, danger, fear, and uncertainty she experiences in the convent. Unlike other young Jewish children, however, Ruth has a stronger grasp of her Jewish identity. Like Friedländer, Ruth Kapp Hartz is seeking her lost childhood and gratefully acknowledges the help of her former student, Stacy Cretzmeyer, who is Catholic, for putting her experience into narrative form (xx).

Your Name Is Renée sheds light on the complex and ever-shifting situation of hidden children. For example, Ruth/Renée is *both* "in hiding and visible," and "in hiding and hidden."[11] She attends a village school in southwestern France, but because informers are omnipresent, she is denied the normal events of childhood such as playing outside with friends. To a small child the question was simple: "Why do we have to hide while others do not?" Furthermore, the young girl receives training in being a hidden child. She must never admit to being Jewish, and she must not tell anyone of her parents' whereabouts. As Jews in hiding, she observes, "we always had to be on the alert" (99). This hypervigilance exacts an enormous psychic toll on the five-year-old. For example, a Protestant minister helps her father escape but, she remembers, "I hated him for trying to take Papa away from us, and I began to cry" (117).

Memory and Identity

Ruth's metamorphosis into a hidden child necessitates mastery of various rituals. There is, on the one hand, the ritual of the escape route, which requires that she learn when and how to hide in a coal cellar. Additionally, false papers are necessary. Old identities must be obliterated. From her experience of hiding, the young girl draws a lesson about Jewish identity. Renée/Ruth decides it is better *not* to be a Jew. She muses that the "Jewish people got into trouble and were taken away. First Haman, now Hitler, thus, there must be something terribly wrong with being Jewish" (126). This negative self-evaluation has significant ramifications for the hidden child. For instance, Moskovitz and Krell note that feelings of shame "further [sap] the child's confidence, initiative and freedom to act."[12]

Renée/Ruth is in hiding and hidden in the convent/orphanage at Sorèze. The young girl, separated from her parents, is further traumatized at her first sight of a black-garbed nun. Rénee thinks, "I've never seen anyone dressed like this. I don't know what to do" (131). Amid the chaos of assuming a new identity, Ruth remembers bits and pieces of biblical tales concerning King David, Ruth and Naomi, and the Purim tale of Queen Esther, which sustain her during the time she spends in the convent. Moreover, the young girl discovers that there are several other Jewish children at the convent, but, because "they had to fit in" and were afraid of being reported to Sister Marie Louise, they could not speak to each other about being Jewish. For Renée/Ruth the problem is even more complex. She is terrified upon being told that her parents are dead, which is untrue, and that she is an orphan. She cries that she does not know what an orphan is. Told to bathe before dinner, Ruth weeps as she remembers that her mother used to bathe her at home. The youngster wonders, *"who will look after me?"* (135, emphasis added). In short, she is denied the sense of security to which every child is entitled.

The advent of the Jewish holiday of Hanukkah precipitates a psychoreligious crisis for Ruth. Owing to the extreme danger of the situation, Ruth's mother could not visit her daughter at Sorèze. Instead, she sends a piece of Hanukkah candy via her friend as a signal to Ruth that she is alive. Elated by the news, the youngster soon faces yet another trauma of hiding. Asked by one of the nuns where she got the candy, Ruth truthfully replies that it is from her mother. The nun responds that the child's mother is in heaven. Consequently, Ruth is compelled to admit that she stole the candy. That night, the young girl confesses to God that she had lied, but she did not confess to having stolen. Thus, the youngster retains a sense of her true identity.

The psychological wounds inflicted by Ruth's stay at the convent are great. She recalls waking every morning with a "sickening sensation in [her] stomach." Furthermore, she remembers imagining that her parents were dead. "Why else," she wonders, "had they abandoned me, split up our family, and left me in the hands of strangers" (169). But the mother superior at Sorèze is one of the Hasidei Umot HaOlam (Righteous Among the Nations). Not only does she consistently outwit the Nazis; she provides asylum to many Jews, including a rabbi. Moreover, the mother superior is an idealist, one whose altruistic behavior is autonomous and who has empathy for the plight of Jewish children. She works closely with Jewish organizations in protecting youngsters. In fact, the memoir singles out the OSE (Oeuvre de Secours aux Enfants) for the vital job they did in safely placing Jewish youth. Moreover, the mother superior reads both Jewish and Christian penitential prayers to the children shortly before they leave the convent.

Post-Holocaust Testimony

Silence continues to play a major role after Ruth is reunited with her parents. Each party believes that they are protecting the other by not speaking of their experience. Ruth is convinced that her mother would never understand the "nightmarish thoughts" she had during her five months in the convent. The mother, for her part, feels that it was "too difficult" for her to talk about the time they had been separated. Like many hidden children, Ruth feels abandoned by her parents. After their reunification, she asks, "Why didn't you come to see me, Maman?" (175). Following the war, Ruth experiences continued anti-Semitism on the part of her classmates and her teacher. Nevertheless, she affirms her Jewish identity in a variety of ways. For example, she joins a Jewish scout organization and has only Jewish friends. Furthermore, she remembers that her mother wants her to learn about Judaism and "not be afraid of it any longer." Nevertheless, shortly after being reunited with her parents, Ruth reveals strong elements of the Christian identity she was compelled to embrace when she prays the rosary and thanks Christ for bringing her home.

It is both enraging and pathetic to note at this point that the lack of official acknowledgment of hidden children as Holocaust survivors continues. France provides a heartbreaking illustration. Hidden children are seeking justice in the area of restitution. Let us bracket out the prior question of what could possibly constitute a proper compensation for losing one's childhood and ask instead about the official response to the quest for restitution. Moskovitz and Krell (2001) report in their study that "French officials . . . tell Child Survivors that since they were young children and too young to work, there is nothing to compensate them for, since they lost no work." The study also notes that certain Jewish agencies "treat [the now adult hidden children] like a beggar and stall and delay for years just like the Germans."[13] Is it any wonder that the sense of rage among hidden children continues?

Dry Tears

Nechama Tec was born in Lublin in Poland to Roman and Estera Bawnik. She and her older sister were raised with a strong sense of Jewish identity. Her memoir, *Dry Tears*, is a searing tale of a family whose lives were rent by the Nazi persecution. The family's experience is a microcosm of the fate of those in hiding. In the first place, it reveals that even in one family there were different types of hiding. Owing to their Aryan looks—light hair, blue eyes, and unaccented Polish—Nechama and her sister are in hiding but visible; they are able to move about with false papers. The parents, however, are in hiding and hidden. They "look Jewish"—have dark hair and speak Polish with a "Jewish accent." Second, secretiveness was the leitmotif of her wartime existence. "All my life," she writes, "revolved around hiding; hiding thoughts, hiding feelings, hiding my activities, hiding information. Sometimes I felt like a sort of fearful automaton, always on the alert, always dreading that something fatal might be revealed" (109). The family was reunited in Kielce during the war, at which time Nechama momentarily recaptured the joy of the childhood she had lost. Smothered in her parents' embrace, the young girl muses: "It was good to feel like a child again, to *be* a child, loved, protected, and not to have to talk about anything serious or upsetting" (115).

Passing as a Christian eventuates in Tec becoming a "double person." She recalls growing "oddly accustomed to anti-Semitic remarks" (144). One consequence of hiding is that a "slow transformation" took place in the young girl. In certain circumstances, she "began to see herself as a Pole" (144). Imbibing the "diffuse cultural anti-Semitism" of Poland, Tec is nonetheless able to remember and retain her Jewish identity.[14]

For many far younger children this task was unattainable. Poignantly subtitled *The Story of a Lost Childhood*, Tec's memoir recalls the innocent joy that she and her sister experience as they skip home from work. Briefly recapturing childhood, Tec is nonetheless aware that this was "a luxury Jewish children could no longer afford" (159).

Memory and Identity

Dry Tears provides a detailed account of Tec's transformation from a young Jewish girl, Helka Bawnik, to a Christian youngster named, variously, Pelagia Pawlowska and Christina (Krysia) Bloch. Moreover, there were definite codes and strictures of hiding. The process of assuming a new identity involved various changes. These ranged from new names to acquiring an intimate familiarity with the practices of Catholicism. "To remain a stranger to Catholicism," writes Tec, "was dangerous" (71). Rituals and rites had to be correctly observed. Those in hiding repeatedly tested each other; if one did not genuflect properly or know the proper way to cross oneself, the error could easily be fatal. Additionally, the young girl had to memorize a new date and place of birth, as well as obtain the correct type of identification papers.

Before going into hiding, Tec's parents impressed on their daughters the fact that there would be an "after the war" (1). Far more than adherence to any specific or traditional Jewish religious practice, this assurance of a future played a vital role in Nechama's survival. In fact, both parents had abandoned belief in normative Jewish theological teachings. Her father became disillusioned with religion long before the war. Tec's mother, an observant Jew prior to the Holocaust, believed that the Shoah proves there is no God. Before the Holocaust, Tec and her sister attended a Jewish private school, which downplayed the religious dimension of Judaism and de-emphasized Jewish particularity. In place of religion, the parents taught their daughters the vital importance of survival strategies, emphasizing to the girls that "if you are going to survive you must use your wits and you must know what it is all about. You must grow up fast" (8). A key part of surviving involved knowing about money, which in various forms—jewelry, gold, and American dollars—was sewn into their clothes.

Tec's dual identity—as both Christian and Jewish—exacts a heavy psychological toll. On the one hand, her father admonishes the eight-year-old, "Never, never, admit to anyone you are Jewish" (93). Yet, as noted, the young girl feels as though she is a "double person." This dichotomous self is deeply troubling. For example, her Polish friend Janka once tells Nechama/Krysia about the infamous "blood libel," that is, Jews murder Christian children and use their blood to bake matzo. Krysia enquires if Janka has ever personally seen this. Although the query could have been fatal, Janka—two years older than Krysia—replies that Jews "do it secretly." The older girl then chides her younger friend, calling her "young and dumb."

In yet another example of the tension between passing as a Christian and deep feelings of allegiance to her core Jewish identity, Tec writes of seeing a group of Jewish prisoners. Guarded by heavily armed German soldiers, the hapless Jewish workers walk in the middle of a road. Nechama/Krysia thinks to herself, "If dead people could walk, I would expect them to walk that way" (143). The young girl's Polish friend was indifferent to the situation and criticized the Jewish prisoners. Although Nechama did not respond at the time, that night she "cried tears of helplessness" when describing the scene to her parents (143). She grows keenly aware of her Polish friends' distorted and stereotypical view of Jews. Not interested in Jews as "living and suffering beings," the young Polish children referred instead to "imaginary Jews" who symbolized "greediness, dishonesty, and guile" (143). The author is struck by the fact that those whom she thought of as "kind, considerate, and helpful, were often the most vehement in their remarks about Jews" (143).

Post-Holocaust Testimony

Tec's memoir bears witness to the complexity of Polish Catholic response to the Jewish plight during the Shoah. For example, the Homar family agreed, for a price, to hide the Bawniks. The youngster is puzzled by the Homars' frequent expressions of anti-Semitism. Moreover, the hiding family frequently refers to what they term "real Jews." Mr. Bawnik explains to Nechama that the Homars' "real Jew" is not real at all. The family "hated an abstraction, the stereotype of the Jew, but not actual people like us who happened to be Jewish" (121–122). This account does little to assuage the young girl's confusion.

Hiding imposed an additional obligation on the twelve-year-old Krysia. The young girl must remain hypervigilant in order to protect not only herself but her parents who, because they lacked documents, did not officially exist. Discovery of their hiding place would signal death for them all, including the family with whom they were staying. Consequently, she was constantly alert, especially at those times when unexpected guests would come to the house where she and her family were hiding. Furthermore, Tec underscores the omnipresent danger of hiding. She writes, "no matter how many precautions we took, the possibility of sudden disaster was a constant hovering presence" (182).

At war's end, Nechama receives another lesson in anti-Semitism. The Homars wanted the Bawnik family to "leave Kielce as Poles." Their hiding family wanted no one to know that they had helped a Jewish family survive. This greatly upset the Bawniks, because the Homars not only "failed to reassure us that they were glad we were alive," but they did not feel "gratified by the part they played in our rescue" (214).

Although the trauma of hiding has lasting psychosocial implications, at the end of the war Tec made a promise as she entered the American Zone in Berlin. "I promised myself," she writes, "never again to pretend to be someone else. This promise I kept" (241). As a distinguished Holocaust scholar, Tec has written many award–winning books and served both as senior research fellow at the Miles Lehrman Center for the Study of Jewish Resistance at the United States Holocaust Memorial Museum and as scholar-in-residence at Yad Vashem in Israel. However, *Dry Tears* is a memoir that reveals the complex matrix out of which a Polish-Jewish child miraculously emerged to bear witness to the world.

Shadows of a Childhood

Elisabeth Gille's *Shadows of a Childhood*, winner of the 1997 Grand Prix des Lectrices, focuses on the painful legacy of children hidden in convents.

When Gille was five her mother, the Russian writer Irène Némirovsky, was sent to Auschwitz, where she perished. Gille's novel is a fictionalized account of her and her sister's hiding experience in the French countryside. The author, an accomplished editor, died in Paris in 1996. Told from the perspective of an omniscient narrator, *Shadows of a Childhood* relates the intersecting story of two young girls and their protector in a convent school at Bordeaux. One of the girls, five-year-old Léa Lévy, a child of privilege, is Jewish. Her parents had had the resourceful and willful youngster baptized in hopes of saving her life. Bénédicte Gaillac, two years older than Léa, is the daughter of French resisters. Despite their intense friendship, which alienates their classmates and lies beyond the understanding of their teachers, both of the girls are silent concerning "the secrets of their real lives" (29). This silence is linked to memory of their parents and helps in making the absent parents present.

The novel also portrays the great dangers faced by rescuers. For example, Léa is brought to the convent school shortly after her parents are arrested and deported. The child's rescuer, Pierre, is himself the brother of Sister Marthe, one of the convent's nuns. Shortly after Léa's arrival, Pierre is murdered by Nazis. Additionally, the author underscores the hardships faced by all parties in the hiding situation. For example, both Léa and the nuns had meager food rations, inadequate clothing, and lived under constant stress owing to the omnipresent danger of raids and arrest.

But the ambiguity of Catholicism itself is portrayed in the person of Sister Saint-Gabriel, acting director of the convent school. That she responded to the plight of Jewish children is beyond question. She makes unauthorized decisions that save Léa's life and is protective of the child. Yet, owing to the Vatican's failure to send any clear official signal about the Jews, individual Catholics had to choose between normative Christianity, which advocated love for the Other, and official Church teachings, which supported anti-Semitism. Thus, it was possible to be a rescuer and simultaneously to internalize anti-Semitic feelings. For example, Léa's rebellious nature causes Sister Saint-Gabriel to muse: "Her race was said to be overbearing and sly. Was it true, then?" (20). Moreover, Sister Saint-Gabriel never associates the tradition of Christian anti-Semitism with the Holocaust. Further, given Léa's disheveled appearance, "she looked like a devil, . . . the nuns would stealthily cross themselves at the sight of her" (29). Léa, like many hidden children, thus receives a mixed message about the validity of her Jewish identity; she is hunted by the Nazis and shunned by the nuns. Commenting on the situation of the French Church and the Jews, Michael Marrus and Robert Paxton observe of Cardinal Gerlier, archbishop of Lyon, that he perhaps "best epitomizes the hesitations of much of the hierarchy, torn between charitable impulses and the pull of Pétainist loyalties and anti-Jewish stereotypes."[15]

Memory and Identity

Gille portrays the issue of identity and memory by focusing on Léa's life during and after the Shoah. While the outward manifestations of the child's Jewish identity can be concealed or destroyed—Sister Saint-Gabriel burns Léa's clothing and her doll, which had been a gift from her father, in the kitchen stove—the young girl struggles to retain her memory of the past. Thus, despite a name change, instruction in catechism, and thrice-weekly attendance at Mass, Léa idealizes her parents who are "very rich and very powerful." She also expresses her sense of rage in claiming that they will retrieve her, bring "lots of pretty things" and "kill everyone" who was mean to her. Léa's rage and anger are also expressed when she asks embarrassing theological questions such as, "What was God doing during this war? Was he blind. Or on vacation? If Christ was his son, why had he let him die?" (31).

Léa's struggle with the memory of her parents is emblematic of the difficulty faced by young Jewish children forced into hiding. For example, Gille observes that "extravagant details about the child's former life were the result of her growing amnesia: the more memories she lost, the more she invented" (39). This is an "invisible tragedy," one in which Léa's sense of identity is severely undermined.[16] Psychologically, Léa must deal with the paradoxical fact that her parents are present mainly through their absence. Following the war, Sister Saint-Gabriel, who had given no credence to reports of people being gassed, takes Léa to her parents' apartment. The anti-Semitic concierge complains to Sister Saint-Gabriel about the "swarm of Israelites" hiding in the apartment during the July roundups until the landlord had the locks changed. While Léa is upset because a box of colored beads has been usurped by the child currently living in the apartment, Sister Saint-Gabriel notices the exquisite silver service that had once belonged to the Lévys.

Léa learns the truth about her parents, and about the camps, in a vivid and horrific manner. Alone in a room in a hotel that had been converted into a reception center for survivors, she encounters a child survivor of the camps. The skeletal child, described as a "living corpse," fascinated by Léa's colored beads which she has taken from her former apartment, pours them over her head. She asks him about her parents who, she naively states, "went away on a trip three years ago, and have not come back yet." Intuitively, she queries the corpse: "My parents—you know, right? You know where they are, don't you?" (72).

The survivor "lifted up a lock of her hair, came so close that she could feel his feverish breath, and murmured in her ear, 'Gassed. Poisoned like rats. Burned in an oven. Turned into black smoke. Poof, your parents. Poof' " (72). This overwhelming news shatters Léa's illusions and eventuates in her subsequent demand for remembering Auschwitz and for bringing Nazi criminals and collaborators to justice.

Post-Holocaust Testimony

Léa's post-Shoah testimony is dominated by feelings of abandonment and by her search for justice. Bénédicte provides her only abiding sense of human connection. After Léa's adoption by the Gaillacs, Madame Gaillac seeks to reassure the young girl that her parents, wherever they are, think about her just as she thinks of them. In response, Léa announces, "I have no father or mother. I never had any parents" (82). Even several years later, Léa clings to her rage and fear, contending that she hates her parents because they abandoned her. Léa excels in school but rejects all efforts by teachers—or others—to get close to her. At age nine her one passion is to devour newspaper accounts and posters dealing with the arrest and trials of collaborators. Listening to a poem extolling the nobility of the French and their passion for liberty, Léa reminds Bénédicte that the same people who are being praised for kicking the Germans out of France had also rallied in support of the collaborationist Marshal Pétain.

The hidden child continues to hide after the war, concealing from the Gaillacs, who think she knows nothing of the Shoah, the fact that she knows a great many details about the extermination camps and the feeble postwar efforts of the French courts. The eight-year-old Léa clandestinely listens to the family radio. She is able to understand some of the news and relishes the announcement of Laval's execution. However, she doesn't know the meaning of the words "Jews" and "Israelites." Although hardly a theologian, Léa arrives at a conclusion about the relationship between God and the Holocaust. Like Nechama Tec's mother, she renounces belief in God, telling Bénédicte that "there couldn't be an almighty God mean and stupid enough to create men simply in order to exterminate them" (92). Attending a movie, Léa sees a documentary about Auschwitz, Bergen-Belsen, and the Little Camp at Buchenwald. The irony of Buchenwald's *kleine kamp* was that even in places of horror and extermination, the Jewish prisoners were kept separate from the rest. Expressing a type of survivor guilt, Léa believes that her body should have been among those bulldozed into the mass grave at Bergen-Belsen.

The hidden child's search for justice includes keeping detailed charts about the postwar trials of French Nazis. She makes elaborate plans to attend a military tribunal where she hopes to recognize the people who took away her parents. Angered by defense lawyer strategies that gain the defendants release, the petite Léa vaults over the benches and, planting herself in front of the defendants, yells out, "Hey! You! What did you do with my mother and father?" The accusation, writes Gille, "echoed around the crowded courtroom like divine thunder over Mount Sinai" (106). Bénédicte tells her parents of Léa's suicidal behavior; she frequently mutilates herself, withdraws into silence, and becomes increasingly obsessed with reading about the Holocaust.

Léa is portrayed as the perpetual rootless soul, at home nowhere. Madame Gaillac muses that she lacks family, memories, documents, a language, a culture, even an ancestral cemetery. Bénédicte views her friend as being both very light and very heavy. "Friendship made her feather-light" (132). But her presence "evoked so many memories of pain and fear that she weighed Bénédicte down" (133). On the physical level, at age eighteen Léa still has not menstruated. This serves to reinforce the idea that she is still, and always will remain, a child in hiding. Furthermore, the fact that at this point in her life she is attracted by the slogans of the French Communist Party also underscores her political immaturity.

As a university student, Léa equates her commitment to justice with her Jewish identity. She begins attending the Sorbonne lectures of Vladimir Jankelevitch, a professor of philosophy, a moralist and, like her, Jewish. Léa is elated when she reads his essay attacking Vichy France and the immorality of indifference and denial. Perhaps, she thinks, "being Jewish meant something after all" (135). Against the Sartrean view that Jewish identity is imposed from the outside, Léa imagines the possibility of assuming a voluntary Jewish identity, one free of the constraints of both the Orthodox and the Zionists. The possibility of loving one's fellow man without forgiving or forgetting exhilarates the young woman, as does the fact that "Janke" was, like her, Russian. She tells Bénédicte, who is firmly committed to Communism, that she prefers Janke's doubts to the "temporary absolute certainties of the Party" (137).

The psychic trauma of the hidden child is, however, never overcome. Gille makes it clear that hidden children find no permanent respite from the wounds inflicted by their experience. A fractured identity can never be made completely whole. Moreover, as the suicide of Holocaust writers such as Jean Améry, Taddeusz Borowski, Paul Celan, Jerzy Kosinski, Primo Levi, Piotr Rawicz, and others reveals, bearing witness to an indifferent world can be devastating. Bénédicte's death in an auto accident spells the end for Léa as well. Losing the last thread of her hope, Léa claws at her face and sinks into insanity. Gille writes of "the shower of beads [that] had changed to a rain of ashes, which covered her completely in a shadowy gray blanket that finally deadened all sound" (138).

Conclusion

What lessons can be taken from the experiences of the hidden children? One of the lessons comes from the very act of testimony itself. "It is," notes Krell, "a tremendous victory over years of behavioral training when a child survivor tells his/her story publicly or in print. It may mark the passage from *shamed victim to proud survivor* by conferring meaning on survival."[17] Thus, memoirs by hidden children attest to their determination to move out of the shadows and into the light of shared experience. Furthermore, these memoirs are an attempt to retrieve a fragment of their lost childhood in spite of the trauma that accompanies memory.

The passage to proud survivor implies four important lessons. First, the coping skills of hidden children in the face of an unprecedented assault are an indication of the miraculous human capacity for resilience. Learning rituals of a new identity, including name changes, rites of the Catholic religion, and deliberate suppression of their core identities were difficult tasks performed under conditions in which one false move could be fatal. Yet the children in our study, including the fictional Léa, move toward a post-Holocaust affirmation of their Jewish identity. Moreover, despite the rage resulting from their powerlessness, many hidden children entered the helping professions and determined to seek a *tikkun* or mending both of the self and of the post-Auschwitz human condition.

Second, because they were chosen for life and not selected for death, their testimony leads us to examine the actions of those whom Lawrence Baron terms "the moral minority," those who engaged in rescue behavior.[18] What prompted those who helped? Can their behavior be emulated? Is altruism an innate or a learned behavior? What of the religious ambiguity felt by certain of the helpers? As we have seen, Gille's Sister Saint-Gabriel is a "responder" who, nevertheless, has unresolved feelings of ambiguity toward the Jewish people. Furthermore, the Homar family—in Tec's memoir—while hiding the Bawniks, continue to express anti-Semitic feelings. On the other side, Kapp Hartz's portrait of the mother superior reveals that certain people were idealists, thoroughly committed to helping those in need no matter the danger to self. The action of the moral minority in the face of massive indifference requires a reexamination of the meaning of religion after Auschwitz.

The third point deals with *Hakarat haTov*, official recognition of good. This needs to be a moral centerpiece after the Shoah with its message of extermination. This is so *not* in terms of counterbalancing the evil; there is no way that can or should be done. Rather, one can demonstrate that moral behavior during the Holocaust was possible. Goodness is a greater mystery than evil. Recognizing that one person's actions can literally save a life prompts us to seek alternatives to following genocidal orders. Moreover, by recognizing goodness we develop a more genuine and far-reaching understanding of the nature of heroism and the heroic. Resisting evil may and must be accomplished by armed force. But as the mother superior of Sorèze demonstrated, resistance may also employ "weapons of the spirit." By recognizing goodness, those who study the Shoah provide a more complete history of the catastrophe and offer some small basis for hope, even in a deeply flawed and genocidal universe.

The fourth point has to do with the legacy of abuse. What greater abuse can be visited upon a youngster than murdering his or her parents and sending the child away from all that is familiar and nurturing? Nazism was in fact a deadly assault on the notions of parenting and childhood itself. It is important for hidden children to work through their Holocaust memories and thus learn how to mourn their losses. Further, it is also vital to acknowledge that children who were abused in their hiding homes do not necessarily become abusers themselves. Perhaps the most important legacy of hidden children will occur when people who hear their testimony seek to build a moral society that cherishes, rather than murders, children.

Notes

1. Robert Krell, "Hiding During and After the War: The Fate of Children Who Survived the Holocaust," in *Holocaust and Church Struggle: Religion, Power and the Politics of Resistance*, eds. H. G. Locke and M. S. Littell (Lanham, MD: University Press of America, 1996), 279.

2. Shlomo Breznitz, *Memory Fields* (New York: Alfred A. Knopf, 1993), 125.

3. André Stein, *Hidden Children: Forgotten Survivors of the Holocaust* (New York: Penguin Books, 1993), 272.

4. Stacy Cretzmeyer, *Your Name Is Renée: Ruth Kapp Hartz's Story as a Hidden Child in Nazi-Occupied France* (New York: Oxford University Press, 1999); Nechama Tec, *Dry Tears: The Story of a Lost Childhood* (New York: Oxford University Press, 1984); Elisabeth Gille, *Shadows of a Childhood*, trans. Linda Coverdale (New York: The New Press, 1998). Page numbers appear in parentheses.

5. For a discussion of "responder" and "idealist" altruism see Lawrence A. Blum, "Moral Exemplars: Reflections on Schindler, the Trocmes, and Others," *Midwest Studies in Philosophy* 13 (1988): 196-221. Responders are individuals who help owing to the circumstances. They are moral heroes. Idealists, for their part, are "moral saints" (exemplars) and moral heroes.

6. Ella Mahler, "About Jewish Children Who Survived WW II on the Aryan Side," *Yad Vashem Bulletin* 12 (1962): 49.

7. Robert Krell, "Psychological Reverberations of the Holocaust in the Lives of Child Survivors," The Mona and Otto Weinmann Lecture (Washington, DC: United States Holocaust Memorial Museum: Center for Advanced Holocaust Studies): 1.

8. Krell, "Hiding During and After the War," 279.

9. Saul Friedländer, *When Memory Comes*, trans. Helen R. Lane (New York: Farrar Straus Giroux, 1979), 94. Page numbers from this edition appear in parentheses in the text.

10. I am grateful to Professor Yehudi Lindeman, director of living testimonies at McGill University, for bringing this to my attention.

11. Deborah Dwork distinguishes between children who were "in hiding and hidden," and those who were "in hiding and visible." Anne Frank is perhaps the best known of children who were in hiding and hidden. Nechama Tec, who, thanks to her "Aryan" appearance, passed as a Christian in her native Poland, represents a child who was in hiding and visible. On this concept see Dwork, *Children with A Star: Jewish Youth in Nazi Europe* (New Haven: Yale University Press, 1991), xiii.

12. Sarah Moskovitz and Robert Krell, "Child Survivors of the Holocaust: Psychological Adaptations to Survival," *Israel Journal of Psychiatry and Related Sciences* 27, no. 2 (1990): 84.

13. Sarah Moskovitz and Robert Krell, with Itzik Moskovitz and Ariella Askren, "The Struggle for Justice: A Survey of Child Holocaust Survivors' Experience with Restitution," *Remembering for the Future: The Holocaust in an Age of Genocide, vol. 2. Ethics and Religion* (London: Palgrave, 2001), 935.

14. Tec coined the phrase "diffuse cultural anti-Semitism" to describe Polish attitudes toward the Jewish people, even among some of the Polish rescuers. See Nechama Tec, *When Light Pierced the Darkness: Christian Rescue of Jews in Nazi-Occupied Poland* (New York: Oxford University Press, 1986).

15. Michael R. Marrus and Robert O. Paxton, *Vichy France and the Jews* (Stanford: Stanford University Press, 1995), 199.

16. Susan E. Nowak employs the term "invisible tragedy" in her discussion of Gille's work. See Nowak, "In a World Stripped of Innocence: Rescue and Belief in Elisabeth Gille's *Shadows of a Childhood*," in *The Holocaust Rescuers*, special issue of *Literature and Belief*, ed. Alan L. Berger, 18, no. 1 (1998): 109.

17. Moskovitz and Krell, "Child Survivors of the Holocaust," 86.

18. Lawrence Baron utilizes the term "moral minority" to describe the rescuers. See his chapter "The Moral Minority: Psycho-Social Research on the Righteous Gentiles," in *What Have We Learned? Telling the Story and Teaching the Lessons of the Holocaust*, ed. Franklin H. Littell, Alan L. Berger, and Hubert Locke (Lewiston: The Edwin Mellon Press, 1993), 119–140.

Works Cited

Breznitz, Shlomo. *Memory Fields*. New York: Alfred A. Knopf, 1993.

Cretzmeyer, Stacy. *Your Name Is Renée: Ruth Kapp Hartz's Story as a Hidden Child in Nazi-Occupied France*. New York: Oxford University Press, 1999.

Friedländer, Saul. *When Memory Comes*. Trans. Helen R. Lane. New York: Farrar Straus Giroux, 1979.

Gille, Elisabeth. *Shadows of a Childhood*. Trans. Linda Coverdale. New York: The New Press, 1998.

Krell, Robert. "Hiding During and After the War: The Fate of Children Who Survived the Holocaust." In *Holocaust and Church Struggle: Religion, Power and the Politics of Resistance*. Ed. H. G. Locke and M. S. Littell. Lanham, MD: University Press of America, 1996.

Mahler, Ella. "About Jewish Children Who Survived WW II on the Aryan Side," in *Yad Vashem Bulletin* 12 (1962): 49.

Marrus, Michael R., and Robert O. Paxton. *Vichy France and the Jews*. Stanford: Stanford University Press, 1995.

Moskovitz, Sarah, and Robert Krell. "Child Survivors of the Holocaust: Psychological Adaptations to Survival." *Israel Journal of Psychiatry and Related Sciences* 27, no. 2 (1990): 84.

———, Itzik Moskovitz, and Ariella Askren, eds. "The Struggle for Justice: A Survey of Child Holocaust Survivors' Experience with Restitution." In *Remembering for the Future: The Holocaust in an Age of Genocide, vol. 2. Ethics and Religion*. London: Palgrave, 2001.

Nir, Yehuda. *The Lost Childhood: A Memoir*. New York: Harcourt, 1989.

Stein, André. *Hidden Children: Forgotten Survivors of the Holocaust*. New York: Penguin Books, 1993.

Tec, Nechama. *Dry Tears: The Story of a Lost Childhood*. New York: Oxford University Press, 1984.

Weinstein, Frida Scheps. *A Hidden Childhood, 1942–1945*. New York: Farrar Straus Giroux, 1985.

2

❧

An Eye on a Scrap of the World:
Ida Fink's Witnesses

ELLEN S. FINE

In an essay in the collected work, *Probing the Limits of Representation: Nazism and the Final Solution* titled, "German Memory, Judicial Interrogation, and Historical Reconstruction: Writing Perpetrator History from Postwar Testimony," Christopher Browning points to the limits inherent in writing the narrative of perpetrator history.[1] Despite the difficulties encountered, in his penetrating study *Ordinary Men: Reserve Police Batallion 101 and the Final Solution*, he succeeds in presenting a portrait of what he calls " 'the killers'—the 'little men' at the bottom of the hierarchy of the 'machinery of destruction' " (27), an expression coined by Raul Hilberg in *The Destruction of the European Jews*. These were middle-aged Germans from working-class backgrounds, haphazardly selected and drafted into reserve units for the purpose of murdering Jews from Polish villages. These "ordinary men" rounded up Jewish men, women, and children, assembled them in the town marketplace, and loaded them onto trucks which shuttled them to the forest where the victims were shot at point-blank range.

In his essay, Browning calls attention to the historian's problems in finding sources to document the participation of these itinerant units in which, as he states in his book, "mass murder and routine had become one."[2] Few reports were filed. The police themselves did not write about their experience in memoirs after the war, and not all were brought to trial. As for eyewitness accounts by victims, in the destructive wake of the battalions, there were virtually no survivors. The few Jews who did not die knew only that "unknown men arrived, carried out their murderous task, and left." "There can be no history of Reserve Police Batallion 101 from survivor testimony," Browning concludes ("German Memory," 28). Just as the experience of the death camps and gas chambers is considered "unrepresentable," "unpresentable," "unsayable," as demonstrated, for example, in Geoffrey Hartman's essay, "The Book of the Destruction,"[3] so, too, the massacres in the forests of Eastern Europe are even more circumscribed in their possibility or impossibility of representation. How then is it possible to create a narrative about these mass shootings from the point of view of the witness?

Christopher Browning's observations, in effect, attest to the Nazi intention to eradicate all evidence, all traces of their crimes, all eyewitnesses. This is corroborated by Shoshana Felman and Dori Laub, who claim in *Testimony: Crises of Witnessing in Literature, Psychoanalysis, and History* that the Holocaust is "an event without witness."[4] In discussing Claude Lanzmann's film, *Shoah*, Felman speaks of the impossibility of testifying both from inside and outside the event. The inside is untransmittable, the truth unable to be grasped, conceived, or articulated even to the ones already in, she argues. One has crossed over the threshold of the human; what one has lived through is rejected as alien.[5] "*The inside has no voice,*" Felman says, "and is *not present to itself.*"[6]

It is also impossible to bear witness from without. An outsider such as Jan Karski, the Polish courier whose mission was to secretly report on the Warsaw Ghetto to the Allies, could tell the world of the horror and the inhumanity that he saw in the ghetto, but he could never truly transmit the cries from the other side of the wall. While he journeyed with empathy into the universe of the Other, and observed how it felt to be an insider, he was also acutely aware, as Felman notes, that "there is a radical, unbreachable and horrifying difference between the two sides of the wall." The inside and outside are "irreconcilable," she says (Felman and Laub, *Testimony*, 236). Jan Karski's mission ultimately failed politically because his testimony was kept secret by the Western Allies and officially disbelieved (232–233). Like Karski, another example of an outsider with knowledge of the limits of witnessing is Claude Lanzmann, who during the war was a student Resistance leader. He attempts in his film, *Shoah*, to cross the boundary and testify from inside the gate. Through his art, Lanzmann is able to reach the spectators, to take "the inside outside" (242), as Felman puts it, and make its impact felt.

Ida Fink, through her writing, also forms a link between the interior and exterior of the event. Like the French writer Charlotte Delbo in *La mémoire et les jours*, Ida Fink in her collection of stories, A *Scrap of Time*, reaches into her *mémoire profonde*, that deep memory buried under multiple layers, to dig in "the ruins of memory" and reconstitute a narrative from that "other time,"[7] as she puts it— time arrested, fractured and broken at the moment that the German *Aktions* or roundups in the villages began. In a spare, elegant, poetic style, Ida Fink crafts her prose into dramatic tales constructed from the point of view of what we can call the hidden witness.

"Hidden witness" would appear to be a contradictory term. A witness signifies presence—I was there, I saw with my own eyes. In contrast, a person in hiding leaves no sign of his or her presence, and must "live without vestige of existence," as Deborah Dwork notes about hidden children in her book *Children with a Star: Jewish Youth in Nazi Europe*.[8] Hidden witnesses fall into a category of their own. They too are both inside and outside of the event. Whether they live under an assumed identity or in hiding places ranging from attics, haylofts, closets, and bunkers to sewers, cellars, and graveyards, they dwell on "the edge of catastrophe," as Saul Friedländer, who was hidden as a Catholic in a French monastery, expresses it in his memoir, *When Memory Comes*.[9] Yet while they did not actually experience the atrocities of the camps, hidden witnesses had to endure the trauma of the hunted, living in constant dread of being denounced, discovered, and eventually deported.

A fundamental question that Ida Fink faces as a writer is this: how can a witness in hiding see with his or her own eyes what is taking place and how can this be transmitted to the reader? How can the unrepresentable be presented, how can the unseen and the unheard become audible and visible? An example from Fink's story "The Pig" in *A Scrap of Time* briefly illustrates how the double life of the hidden witness is structured into a narrative.

An older man, a doctor, survivor of four Nazi *Aktions* in the region, is hiding in the hayloft of Polish peasants. The man makes a small opening in the wall of the barn in order to see and hear what is going on in the everyday existence outside of his confined space. "Through this chink he could keep an eye on the scrap of the world" (Fink, *A Scrap of Time*, 79), the author-narrator tells us. He becomes witness to the sounds of trucks rumbling down the road to transport the Jews, to the shots and screams in the distance, and to the silence. In effect, the refrain, "shots, screaming, silence" echoes throughout Fink's tales like a Greek chorus. Evidence of the roundups and executions is perceived from afar in her stories, from the dark interiors of apartments behind closed curtains, from an obscure corner between two buildings, from a hillside above the town, from a pigsty deep in the ground.

Spending entire days looking through the chink with one eye at a time, the man beholds only fragments, traces, scraps of what is taking place. "What kept him alive in this attic was the chink. He saw" (80). The chink in the wall of the barn becomes the critical link between the internal and external world, as viewed from the perspective of the victim who is, at the same time, a spectator. The chink affirms the possibility, albeit limited, of witnessing for those in hiding. It is representative of Ida Fink's stories themselves, which form a connection between the inner and the outer, allowing the reader (the outsider) to gain an inside glimpse into the impact of the hiding experience upon ordinary men, women, and children. The chink also exemplifies what Saul Friedländer in *Probing the Limits of Representation*

calls Fink's use of "allusive or distanced realism," which portrays the stark-
ness of reality, "perceived through a filter . . . a narrative margin which
leaves the unsayable unsaid."[10]

If Fink depicts diverse aspects of the hiding process, from the outset
she admits to what Jean-François Lyotard in *The Differend: Phrases in Dispute* calls "the impossibility of a *we*" as collective witness.[11] "It was right there
in front of the town hall, that we were ordered to form ranks. I should not
have written 'we' for I was not standing in the ranks," Fink states in her first
story, "A Scrap of Time" (4). Having broken ranks and not reported to the
town square, the author-narrator distinguishes between "we," the reprieved,
and "we," the condemned. Immersed in the event, she nonetheless establishes her distance from it. Within and without, she identifies with the victims but is the writer as observer. She is present and absent at the same time,
manifesting what the Israeli novelist Aharon Appelfeld has called "a sense
of . . . psychological hiddenness."[12]

Born in Zbaraz, Poland, in 1921, Ida Fink escaped from the ghetto in
1942 with her sister and went into hiding. With false identity papers, they
posed as Polish country girls and were sent to work in Germany as voluntary
laborers in a factory and then as farm workers until the end of the war. Their
harrowing trip through Nazi Germany where they barely escaped denunciation on several occasions is recounted in the novel *The Journey*, published
in 1990. In addition to the novel, Ida Fink has written the short story collection, *A Scrap of Time*, published in 1985 and translated into English in 1987
and into seven other languages as well. The book is the winner of several
literary prizes, including the Womens International Zionist Organization
(Wizo) in France and the Anne Frank Prize for Literature in the Netherlands. Fink, in 1997, also published a second collection of stories, *Traces*,
and has written radio plays dramatized on Israeli and German television.
After the war, she returned to Poland from Germany. In 1957, Fink immi-
grated from Poland to Israel with her husband and daughter.

In an interview, the author acknowledges that the narratives in *A
Scrap of Time* are based on remnants unearthed from the depths of her
memory and from accounts by friends and family. She believes that it is
important to be faithful to the actual experience in order to be authentic.[13]
Within the context of the stories themselves, Fink gives recognition to
those non-Jewish, nonhidden bystanders who are among the primary sources
of the evidence transmitted and who have helped her to overcome the
limits of the hidden witness.

In one tale, she calls attention to "the peasant who had not dared to
speak at the time, [who] came back after the war and told us everything"
(Fink, *Scrap of Time*, 10). In another, "A Spring Morning," on a peaceful,
sunny Sunday, a procession of Jews, "like a gloomy gray river flowing out to

sea" (47) is crossing the bridge, heading for the town square, and then on to the flat, green meadow that was soon to be "dug up like a fresh wound" (40). "A former secretary of the former town council . . . the possessor of an Aryan great-grandmother," as Fink describes him (39), is standing near the bridge, able to hear words that a man and wife say to each other, and which form the basis of the narrative. "Thanks to him and to people like him, there have survived to this day shreds of sentences, echoes of final laments, shadows of the sighs of the participants in the *marches funèbres*, so common in those times," the author-narrator notes.

Ida Fink has incorporated these precious shreds and shards of testimony into her writing, so that the reader, too, may "see" through the chink and share the last moments of shattered lives. In an artistic style filled with vivid details and images, the author describes various stages of the hiding process: the dreaded wait to be discovered for those without a hiding place ("A Spring Morning"); parents and a child practicing how to disappear behind the bathroom plumbing ("The Key Game"); the prostitution of a young girl in order to obtain false papers ("Aryan Papers"); exploitation by rescuers, a woman who has an affair with the husband of a couple she is sheltering ("A Conversation"). We observe the return—those who come back to the town from a bunker in the forest, or a hole beneath a cowshed, ragged, shrunken, and withered, and those who wait in vain at the railway station for their loved ones to return ("The Tenth Man"). Fink also reveals an aspect of the hidden condition not often discussed nor rendered into fiction: how survivors coped with their experience in the aftermath. Although they desperately tried to make known their stories, often their words were not listened to, and the hiding experience had to be repressed, blunted, kept secret ("The Splinter," "Night of Surrender").

Agafia, the Polish housekeeper of an elderly Polish woman invalid in the tale "Behind the Hedge" is one of the few characters in the book who is an eyewitness to the actual shootings. The old woman does not want to listen to the stories of Nazi atrocities, but Agafia insists: "We have to know about it. And look at it. And remember" (Fink, *Scrap of Time*, 17). The "we" here refers neither to the reprieved nor to the condemned, but to the world. Agafia is conscious of the importance of her role as witness. She recounts how early one morning she and her brother set out for a nearby town to buy some flour. Hearing shots from the road, they jumped down from their horse and wagon and sat at the grass at the edge of the woods. They then heard screaming, followed by silence. Agafia could see the Jews digging their own graves before the shooting began again. She wanted to run away but was compelled to look: "Something kept me there and said to me. 'Watch. Don't shut your eyes'" (Fink, *Scrap of Time*, 19). "I could see everything, every blessed thing," she says (18). Clearly, she wants others to see as well.

While the old woman, confined to her chair, hopes to be spared listening to these stories that Agafia has been telling daily over the course of twenty years, she confesses that they are "my only link to the outside world" (15), "my only way of participating—emotionally, passively—in the history of our days" (16). Here then is her chink—as it is ours—the reader's eye on a scrap of the world. The woman also observes, "These stories are very complex, although they are about simple matters, and are full of tiny details that at first seem extraneous but which by the end turn out to be what makes the stories vivid and complete" (15).

Ida Fink here seems to be giving the reader an insight into her own narrative technique. Restrained and concise, her style is at once textured with evocative images and similes, colors and aromas, profound and stark observations. Filled with irony, the tales often have unexpected endings. The author likes the use of contrasts. For example, the desperation of those in hiding, as well as anguished conversations after the war about the hiding experience, are often set against the beauty of nature. This technique has been compared to that of Claude Lanzmann, who in his film *Shoah* juxtaposes the voice-over of the survivor exposing the barbarity of the death camps with a panoramic view of the camps as they stand today, covered by a peacefully green, apparently innocent landscape.[14] It is up to the spectator to make the connection. In Ida Fink's writing, too, the reader must put the details, the scraps, together in order to grasp that which remains unsaid.

A close reading of the texts reveals that while the organizing principle of *A Scrap of Time* is the hidden witness, the subtext is relationships, in particular those between parents and children. The Nazis, or the Germans as Ida Fink refers to them mostly throughout her book, sought to sever intimate bonds. In Fink's stories, examples abound of the ultimate separation of parents and children in hiding, with the one not discovered suffering permanently from survival guilt.

One of the most poignant tales that demonstrates the intense feelings of the survivor's shame and self-condemnation is the story "Crazy." The narrator is a humpbacked dwarf, a garbageman who earns his living by sweeping the streets. Married, with three beautiful, blond, "normal" daughters ranging in age from three to seven, he and his family escape the first two *Aktions* in the ghetto. During the third *Aktion*, he squats in a corner between two houses and hides behind his broom. When someone knocks down his broom, he catches a glimpse of his daughters, who have been loaded onto the truck. They are the only ones to notice him in the corner, and the three-year-old cries out, "Papa, Papa, come to us!" (109). He gestures to them to be quiet. The oldest covers the mouths of the two youngest with her hand. The dwarf's instinct for survival is at odds with his paternal instinct, and he must live for the rest of his life with a sense of guilt for having failed to help his daughters, for having let them die, and, above all, for having failed to join them. Taken for crazy, he goes around shouting, "I'm coming! I'm coming!" but he knows he is not crazy, for he is acutely aware that "in any case they can't hear me anymore."

Elie Wiesel in *Legends of Our Time* describes this phenomenon: "I am alive, therefore I am guilty. If I am still here, it is because a friend, a comrade, a stranger, died in my place."[15] And Robert Jay Lifton in his book *Death in Life: Survivors of Hiroshima* studies in depth the guilty feeling of having cheated death. "To survive is perceived as improper, wrong, inexcusable, even hateful," he says.[16] "The survivor feels accused in the eyes of the dead for 'selfishly' remaining alive" (36).

While not as violently expressed as in "Crazy," survival guilt is implied in "A Spring Morning" as well. The rumbling of trucks, that telltale sign emblematic of imminent destruction throughout Fink's stories, breaks the silence and awakens the man in the story in the early hours on a Sunday morning. He has failed to hear the trucks as they came down from the hills; they are now too close and it is too late to hide his wife and young daughter. Fearful, resigned, despairing because he is unable to protect his family, marked by hunger and poverty, the pallor and grayness of the father is contrasted with the blond little girl, "round and large and rosy as an apple" as she wakes up (Fink, *Scrap of Time*, 41). Wise for her five years, she knows. "Are those trucks coming for us, Papa?" she asks (43). "If only we had a hiding place," his wife murmurs. "If we had a hiding place everything would be different" (42). We gain an insight into the feelings of vulnerability and terror of those having no place to hide. The wife wonders if they should hide down in the storeroom, or in the wardrobe or under the bed. The man contemplates hiding the child in the coalbox because she is so small. They finally just sit and wait without hope. Their choice is to stay together, not to be separated.

As dawn breaks, they find themselves herded with others through the town, marching toward the railroad station and those green pastures that await them. Feeling the life pulsating through his daughter's warm, young body as he carries her in his arms, he is compelled "to find some chink through which he could push his child back into the world of the living" (45). Here the chink is not between the inner and outer nor between the reader and the event, but more fundamentally between life and death, the living and the dead. As the group nears the churchyard, the father finds the chink: he puts the little girl down on the ground and tells her to run and join the crowd in front of the church with the idea that someone will eventually take her in. The man does not look back. Instead he softly prays as he walks straight ahead, gazing upward imploringly at the "pale spring sky in which the white threads of a cloud floated like a spider web," a web that has entangled him and his family (46). His prayers are cruelly answered by a shot that rings out. The rosy apple turns into a bloody rag. The Germans ask the parents to claim the body. The man picks it up and, to his surprise, is allowed to continue in what is a funeral procession—his daughter's, his wife's, his own. Carrying the dead child in his arms, he quietly begs her forgiveness. Unlike the dwarf-father in "Crazy," the father here does not abandon his daughter but bravely attempts to save her from his own fate. However, the Nazis have made him into a murderer, and he must live with that guilt until he reaches his own grave in the flat green meadow.[17]

If in "Crazy" and "A Spring Morning" the parents feel guilty for having survived, in other narratives it is the children who feel they have betrayed their parents by not accompanying them. In the tale "Splinter," for example, in the aftermath of the war, a boy is compelled to rid himself of his story, which he describes as "a deep splinter that has to be removed, so it won't fester" (Fink, A Scrap of Time, 123). He is speaking to a young girl he scarcely knows in an idyllic setting of lush meadows dotted with bright flowers where they are spending a day together.

Despite the girl's reluctance to listen, as they stretch out upon the soft pine needles of the forest, the boy recounts the story of his survival. Hearing the Germans stomp up the stairs, his mother threw open the heavy oak door of their apartment and pressed him into the corner behind it. With all of his strength, he held on to the handle of the door so that it would not close. Struck in the face, his mother was brutally taken away in her nightgown. "I would give a great deal to let go of that handle," the boy confesses. Clearly, he has never let go. He is ridden by guilt for having abandoned his mother, for not having joined her, and above all for having survived in her place. Looking over at the beautiful young girl lying beside him and imploringly asking her for forgiveness, he realizes that his listener is a nonlistener; the girl is fast asleep (126). What lies unsaid here exposes the wide gap between those who were there and those who were not, and the impossibility of bridging and/or representing that gap.

The last short story in A Scrap of Time, "Traces," does not depict the agonizing separation of parents and children, but rather pays homage to the quiet heroism of small children. The title refers, first of all, to traces of footprints in the snow, visible in the foreground of a copy of a blurred snapshot shown to the woman narrator, who is being questioned about its contents. Along the edges of the photograph are old wooden market stalls that had served as shelters for several families in the ghetto. The traces of footprints are memorial markers; they are all that remain of those people who lived in the stalls. Initially, the narrator resists the painful recollection of the event, but suddenly conscious of being the sole link—the chink, so to speak—between the present and those who have disappeared, she is pressed to bear witness, requesting that her words "be written down and preserved forever, because she wants a trace to remain" (136). The second traces, we discover, are those of the children.

Their parents had been rounded up from the market stalls and forced to stand in the courtyard. About eight children, the oldest of whom was seven years old, were hiding in the attic of the Judenrat, the Jewish Council, which was strictly forbidden, "because children no longer had the right to live," as the narrator puts it (137). Discovered by the SS, they were brought on a horse cart to the courtyard, where the Germans ordered them—shouted at them—to jump down and point out their mothers and fathers. "But none of the children moved," the woman tells us. "They were all silent." The unsayable is left unsaid. The fierce courage of these children who refused to denounce their parents will not be forgotten, nor will the inevitable conclusion be forgotten: they were all shot.

This tale leads us back to Christopher Browning's comments. It was the Nazi intention to obliterate all evidence of their crimes and to destroy all witnesses. But survivor-writers such as Ida Fink, with an extraordinary ability to create narratives out of the lives of ordinary men, women, and children and the dark universe they inhabited, the terror they courageously faced on a daily basis, assure us that the traces will not vanish. In effect, Ida Fink has written a second volume of stories, *Traces*, in which variations of the same themes are presented, thus affirming that she will continue to create a "chink" between author and reader. Despite the limits of witnessing and the limits of representation, Ida Fink has insightfully brought us inside the event. As a result, "what others suffer, we behold," as Terrence Des Pres puts it,[18] and the vital yet painful stories—the scraps—of the hidden witnesses will no longer be concealed from our own eyes nor from the "eye" of the world.

Notes

1. Christopher Browning, "German Memory, Judicial Interrogation, and Historical Reconstruction: Writing Perpetrator History from Postwar Testimony," in *Probing the Limits of Representation: Nazism and the "Final Solution,"* ed. Saul Friedländer (Cambridge, MA: Harvard University Press, 1992), 25–26.

2. Christopher Browning, *Ordinary Men: Reserve Police Batallion 101 and the Final Solution* (New York: Harper, 1992), xix. Daniel Jonah Goldhagen in *Hitler's Willing Executioners: Ordinary Germans and the Holocaust* (New York: Alfred A. Knopf, 1996) also points out that the material on these itinerant units is scattered throughout Germany's justice system and only a partial knowledge of their activities exists (529). While both historians attempt to show how "ordinary" Germans came to be willing agents of genocide, Goldhagen believes that the underlying German "eliminationist antisemitism" explains the actions of the perpetrators.

3. Geoffrey Hartman in "The Book of the Destruction" in *The Longest Shadow: In the Aftermath of the Holocaust* (Bloomington: Indiana University Press, 1996), 119, discusses Jean-François Lyotard's notion of presenting unrepresentable reality as formulated in his book *The Postmodern Condition: A Report on Knowledge* (Minneapolis: University of Minnesota Press, 1984).

4. Shoshana Felman and Dori Laub, *Testimony: Crises of Witnessing in Literature* (New York: Rutledge, 1992), 80, 224.

5. Geoffrey Hartman speaks of inconceivability with regard to the Shoah in *The Longest Shadow:* "what we have lived through, or what we have learned about, cannot be a part of us: the mind rejects it, casts it out—or it casts out the mind. We are forced to admit that something in human behavior is alien to us, yet that it could be species-related" (120).

6. Felman and Laub, *Testimony,* 231.

7. Ida Fink, *A Scrap of Time,* trans. Madeline Levine and Francine Prose (New York: Schocken, 1987), 3.

8. Deborah Dwork, *Children with a Star: Jewish Youth in Nazi Europe* (New Haven: Yale University Press, 1991), 71.

9. Saul Friedländer, *When Memory Comes,* trans. Helen R. Lane (New York: Noonday-Farrar Straus Giroux, 1991), 155. For a discussion of Frieldänders's Memoir see pages 15–16 in this volume.

10. Saul Friedländer, *Probing the Limits of Representation: Nazism and the "Final Solution"* (Cambridge, MA: Harvard University Press, 1992), 17.

11. Jean-Francois Lyotard, *The Differend: Phrases in Dispute,* trans. George Van Den Abbeelé (Minneapolis: University of Minnesota Press, 1988), 97–98.

12. Aharon Appelfeld, "On Being Hidden: Silence and the Creative Process: A Conversation with Aharon Appelfeld," *Dimension* 6, no. 3 (1992): 15.

13. Johanna Kaplan, Review of *A Scrap of Time* by Ida Fink. "Eva Hoffman: Interview," *New York Times Book Review* 12 (July 1987): 7.

14. Colette Baer, "Introduction to Ida Fink," *Les Nouveaux Cahiers* 101 (1990): 56.

15. Elie Wiesel, *Legends of Our Time* (New York: Schocken Books, 1968), 171.

16. Robert Jay Lifton, *Death in Life: Survivors of Hiroshima* (New York: Vintage Books, 1969), 56.

17. It is important to note that in "Description of a Morning," a story that appears in Ida Fink's second collection, *Traces,* a variation of the same theme occurs with a different ending. As parents and child are walking toward their death, this time the little girl runs out of line on her own when she spots a cat. She is shot, but the parents do not step forward to reclaim her. Having survived and hidden in an attic, they are obsessed by survival guilt and by the sacrifice of their child; they

try to justify "selfishly" remaining alive. "She was small, she couldn't run fast. . . . Isn't it true that if she had gone with us, we wouldn't have been able to get away?" the woman says to the man. *Traces*, trans. Philip Boehm and Francine Prose (New York: Metropolitan Books, 1997), 95.

18. Terrence Des Pres, *Praises and Dispraises: Poetry and Politics in the 20th Century* (New York: Viking, 1988), xv.

Works Cited

Appelfeld, Aharon. "On Being Hidden: Silence and the Creative Process: A Conversation with Aharon Appelfeld." *Dimension* 6, no. 3 (1992): 14–17.

Browning, Christopher. *Ordinary Men: Reserve Police Batallion 101 and the Final Solution*. New York: Harper, 1992.

———. "German Memory, Judicial Interrogation, and Historical Reconstruction: Writing Perpetrator History from Postwar Testimony." In *Probing the Limits of Representation: Nazism and the "Final Solution."* Ed. Saul Friedlander, 22–36. Cambridge, MA: Harvard University Press, 1992.

Delbo, Charlotte. *Days and Memory*. Trans. Rosette Lamont. Marlboro, VT: Marlboro Press, 1990.

———. *La mémoire et les jours*. Paris: Berg International, 1985.

Des Pres, Terrence. *Praises and Dispraises: Poetry and Politics in the 20th Century*. New York: Viking, 1988.

Dwork, Deborah. *Children with a Star: Jewish Youth in Nazi Europe*. New Haven: Yale University Press, 1991.

Felman, Shoshana, and Dori Laub. *Testimony: Crises of Witnessing in Literature, Psychoanalysis, and History*. New York: Rutledge, 1992.

Fink, Ida. *A Scrap of Time*. Trans. Madeline Levine and Francine Prose. New York: Schocken, 1987.

———. *The Journey*. Trans. Joanna Weschler. New York: Plume, 1990.

———. *Traces*. Trans. Philip Boehm and Francine Prose. New York: Metropolitan Books, 1997.

Friedländer, Saul. *When Memory Comes*. Trans. Helen R. Lane. New York: Noonday-Farrar Straus Giroux, 1991.

———. *Probing the Limits of Representation: Nazism and the "Final Solution."* Cambridge, MA: Harvard University Press, 1992.

Hartman, Geoffrey H. "The Book of the Destruction." In *The Longest Shadow: In the Aftermath of the Holocaust*. Bloomington: Indiana University Press, 1996.

Lifton, Robert Jay. *Death in Life: Survivors of Hiroshima*. New York: Vintage Books, 1969.

Lyotard, Jean-François. *The Differend: Phrases in Dispute*. Trans. George Van Den Abbeele. Minneapolis: University Minnesota Press, 1988.

Wiesel, Elie. *Legends of Our Time*. New York: Schocken Books, 1968.

3

Jerzy Kosinski: Did He or Didn't He?

Harry James Cargas

In the June 22, 1982, issue of New York's *Village Voice*, an article was published by Geoffrey Stokes with Eliot Fremont-Smith under the humorless, ambiguous title "Jerzy Kosinski's Tainted Words"—clearly an ugly play on the novelist's first work of fiction, *The Painted Bird*. The thesis of the newspaper piece was that Kosinski, an emigrant from Europe, a Jewish Holocaust survivor (having escaped the fate of millions of Polish Jews during World War II, for, it was implied, very mysterious reasons) was not really the author of his books.

Stokes and Fremont-Smith claim that Kosinski employed massive aid for his fictional writings and that he refused to acknowledge that he did so, even denying such assistance. They insist that Kosinski's English, as a language, was so rudimentary that he could not have produced *The Painted Bird*, *Cockpit*, *Pinball*, *Being There*, *Blind Date*, and so on, without huge amounts of collaboration. Some of these alleged coauthors are quoted in this attack and much of what was said there caused an international literary scandal. I would like to address that scandal.

I knew Jerzy Kosinski. I cannot say that we were friends or that I knew him well. In my opinion, I cannot say that anyone knew him well, including himself. We all wear masks, some more self-deluding than others. There is no attempt in this chapter to psychoanalyze Jerzy Kosinski, merely an attempt to deal with the question raised in *The Village Voice* about authorship. Let me make my position very clear. It seems certain to me from reading and knowing Jerzy Kosinski that his language skills, his wit, and his imaginative abilities were such that he was indeed the creator and writer of his fictional works. The charges against him do not hold up and have a boomerang effect of casting doubts on the investigative report of Stokes and Fremont-Smith and on those who accept their attack.

The first time I saw Jerzy Kosinski was on May 27, 1975, at the annual dinner of the American PEN Center. (PEN, by the way, was not intended by its founders to stand for Poets, Essayists, Novelists—it's just PEN, the international writers' organization.) At the hotel meal were prominent PEN members like Arthur Miller, Muriel Rukeyser, Kurt Vonnegut, Alvin Toffler, and several hundred others. The speaker and honoree was President Léopold Sédar Senghor, of Senegal, cofounder with Leon Damas and Aimé Césaire of the movement of négritude (roughly equivalent to "black is beautiful") and one of the world's most influential poets. Kosinski, the head of American PEN, presided. President Senghor had written an Easter poem for a Catholic magazine that I edited in St. Louis. He was a writer and statesman whom I had admired for some time. I had gotten financial assistance for my trip to New York, and the occasion was clearly not a disappointment.

Kosinski made a few humorous remarks before introducing the guest of honor. I recall one story in particular. He told how, when walking into the Plaza Hotel with the president and the entourage that he, Kosinski, had been mistaken for a bellboy with his light blue suit and was asked to carry in some luggage. He pretended to fill that role, he told the audience, "and I got a pretty good tip." We were all amused. Sometime afterward, Kurt Vonnegut told me not to take any story of Kosinski's at face value. It might or might not be true. It was my first encounter with statements that Kosinski was to make to me over the years that proved to have been false. I know other writers who have told me fictional things about themselves, but often those people had come to believe their imaginations and so in some sense were perhaps not actually lying. I believe that much of what Kosinski told me in our conversations had little—even no—root in reality. I think he knew the untruth to be untrue. Why did he do it? *I do not know.* I can speculate on how much his misadventures caused by the Nazi invasion of Poland impacted him mentally. But these thoughts would merely be speculations and, in a real sense, who cares about my judgment? But Jerzy Kosinski has shared a great deal of truth in his fiction—it being in a different order of truth than fact—and charges that he was not his own writer, I find, are themselves fictional without basis in truth.

At the PEN dinner, I made arrangements with Kosinski to meet with him the following day to discuss the plight of writers around the world who were being imprisoned and/or tortured by governments for their ideas. I knew that Kosinski was very active on their behalf. Here is part of an article I published in *Christian Century* magazine:

> In the past several years the U.S. chapter of PEN has probably been the international organization's most active center in assisting imprisoned authors. The single figure most responsible for

this may be the man who has just retired from serving two consecutive terms as non paid president: Jerzy Kosinski, author of *The Devil Tree, Being There, Cockpit,* the National Book Award-winning *Steps,* and *The Painted Bird,* which garnered France's Best Foreign Book Award the year it was published there.

Kosinski is an enormously compassionate man. When I spoke with him in his Manhattan apartment about his work with prisoners, he was eager to put aside all other tasks to discuss the topic. Kosinski stated, "We concentrate on those who are out of the spotlight." He mentioned that he has been particularly concerned with those arrested in totalitarian states for opposing their governments. These include writers who "displease a bureaucrat, priest, party secretary, etc."

Kosinski has had some remarkable successes in this work through mobilizing diplomats, bankers and other public figures, along with well-known authors, to intercede on behalf of the people he is trying to help. He is attempting to organize further support as well. On June 4 he advocated at a U.S. publishers' meeting the formation of a Committee on International Freedom to Publish which would be run primarily by the publishers themselves. "I'd like to organize their community power," Kosinski commented.[1]

When the PEN talk was over, I wanted to speak with Kosinski because I wanted to tell him that on a much smaller scale, as a Catholic writer and lecturer on the Holocaust, I received similar almost hostile responses from some Christians in my audience because I seemed too critical of the roles Christians played or failed to play during the Holocaust period. But it appeared that nearly all five hundred of the other attendees also wanted to talk to Kosinski, so I simply left a note for him with his companion (later to become his wife) Kiki (Katherina von Fraunhofer) briefly relating my sympathy for his position. Within three or four days he called me in St. Louis and set up a meeting for the next time I came to New York City.

There were several reasons why I wanted to see Kosinski again, in particular to see if I could find out why he had denied being Jewish. Elie Wiesel, with whom I had coauthored a book, once told me that Kosinski had absolutely denied being a Jew to him. When I asked the Polish exile if he had denied his Jewishness, he denied his denials. Our conversation on that topic was closed.

It was only a short time later that the *Village Voice* article attacking Kosinski appeared. It is not a well-written or well-researched piece. If a student had handed such a paper in to me I would have found it unacceptable. An exposé using terms like "probably," "perhaps," "as if," or "apparently" is hardly an exposé. These are indications of speculation, not of proof.

Permit me to give a brief synopsis of the article.[2] It begins by claiming that he treats "his art as though it were just another commodity" put together by "anonymous hired hands" (41) and that he personally manufactures fables about himself in a "frantic" way "as if to cloak his hollowness." I suspected that nobody who really knew Kosinski could accuse him of being hollow. The writers of the article then go after Kosinski's personal life. Did he really escape from Poland? Did he lie, "creating fictional professors in Poland" to write letters of recommendation for him to emigrate? Why did *Time* incorrectly say he had a doctorate? (Is that Kosinski's fault?)

Critic Martin Tucker supported Kosinski's enormous efforts on behalf of writers' freedom after the *Village Voice* article:

When Jerry Kosinski became president of P.E.N. American Center in 1973, he phoned me and asked me to write the P.E.N. Newsletter. During my two-year association with him (I continued writing the Newsletter till 1978, but Mr. Kosinski left the presidency in 1975) he worked tirelessly to promote the goals of this important writers' organization. Equally important, he was generous with his time and critical aid. He often read others' work and wrote painstaking letters of recommendation. He has never asked for credit (or for payment, as he paid his "editors"), but in view of the current slander campaign against him, I believe that his generosity to writers should be brought to public attention."[3]

This came at the same time that Marla Press wrote the following:

Personally, I do not care whether Jerzy Kosinski had the assistance of one or one thousand people in the editing or writing of his novels. It is the creation of art that is at question here, not the accuracy with which such stories as *The Painted Bird* are told. Even Shakespeare begged, borrowed and stole material only to give us the gift of some of the richest literature ever written. It seems that whomever [sic] produces great art, whether it be Shakespeare or Kosinski, must suffer the slings and the arrows hurled by those who can only criticize art and not create it.[4]

But regarding the books themselves, who authored them? One person cited is Barbara Mackey, who had been a graduate student at Yale in 1971 when Kosinski was on the faculty there. We read that "she began to help

Kosinski on [his novel] *The Devil Tree*."[5] Several paragraphs attribute quotations to Mackey:

> As she describes their work situation, "We were in [his] apartment on 57th Street. He would give me a sentence, talk philosophy, then come out with an idea that he wanted crystallized in a paragraph, a page, a chapter. Sometimes it was a little like taking dictation, at others, I was more like an instant editor. I prepared a first, handwritten draft that was then typed out by Kiki.
>
> "The ideas were all his—I think he is a brilliant thinker, central in the world and in American culture—but the words were often mine. The term 'collaborator' isn't right—I shouldn't say that, anyway—it was more organizational. A collaborator would have a roughly equal input, but the intellectual notions are *all* his. If I had been a collaborator," she added wryly, "the book would have been very different—especially about women." (42, italics original)

But then comes a parenthetical statement by the article's authors which reads, "(I had agreed to get back to her to verify those quotes, but Mackey, now assistant director of the Denver Arts Center, suddenly stopped returning phone calls)" (42). First of all, you do not "suddenly stop" whatever you were not doing, but much more important are Mackey's claims that the quotes are not statements that she has made. In an article in *The Denver Post* titled "Former Aid to Kosinski Denies Story" Mackey uses the term "outrageous" regarding the words attributed to her.[6] She not only said the quotes were incorrect but said that she has a tape of her conversation with Stokes to prove it. She says she "made it clear to him [Stokes] that what I was doing when I worked for Kosinski was editing, not collaborating." Then the *Post* story goes on to say that Mackey (her name is misspelled consistently, by the way, in the *Voice* article) saw herself as an "amanuensis" which, she insisted, "means secretary in my dictionary."

Here are two paragraphs from the *Post* write-up:

> Ms. Mackey said she told the *Village Voice* writer that in general "I consider what I did to be editing because I was always working with Kosinski's ideas and his language. That to me is editing, not composing or collaborating . . . Kosinski is precisely attuned to the English language. He has definite ideas of exactly what words he wants. I was simply editing his ideas, his language, his voice or the voice of his narrators."

For the *Village Voice*, she added, "to quote me as saying I
put it into English is outrageous. (DoA)

It is very hard to build a case on alleged statements that are denied. It
was almost seven years before I encountered Kosinski again personally. The
occasion was a conference on March 21, 1982, at New York's Waldorf-
Astoria Hotel, sponsored by The Holocaust Survivors Memorial Foundation
headed by Holocaust survivor Jack Eisner. A distinguished international panel
was assembled, including Dr. Leo Eitinger from Oslo—perhaps the world's
leading authority on the psychiatric impact of the Holocaust on people who,
like himself, were survivors—Dr. Yisrael Gutman, another survivor, director
of the Research Center at Yad Vashem, the Holocaust remembrance center
in Jerusalem, Dr. Yaffa Eliach, a child survivor, founder and director of the
Center for Holocaust Studies located in Brooklyn, and several others. As a
member of the board of directors of The Holocaust Survivors Memorial
Foundation, I was invited to the event. The major speaker scheduled for the
luncheon portion of the meeting was Jerzy Kosinski. About five hundred
persons attended the meal. Kosinski's remarks and interaction at the noon
event were so provocative, the talk and dialogue lasted from 12:30 to 4:15!
Here is part of a newspaper article I wrote on the conference:

> But it was Jerzy Kosinski, author of *The Painted Bird* and other
> novels and supporting actor in the film *Reds* who created the
> most response at a standing room luncheon address which was
> so provocative that it ended at 4:15! In the speech proper, Kosinski
> emphasized the need to confront one's past in order to transcend
> it. "All of my novels," he indicated, "are attempts at self-definition."
>   However questions from the audience were frequently
> hostile in tone. "Why are you not more Jewish?" "Why don't you
> write more about the Holocaust?" "Why haven't you spoken
> directly to the Jewish community?" These implied criticisms were
> greeted with applause by about half of the assemblage. Kosinski's
> polite and firm responses received about equal support.
>   "My past experience is sufficient to define me as a Jew," he
> replied at one point. Later he said that while he someday expects
> to make an initial visit to Israel, he has no need to make a
> pilgrimage because "Israel is part of my spiritual residence." He
> added, "Israel has visited me."
>   The next audience contribution was this challenge: "If we
> all followed your philosophy, we wouldn't be here as a commu-
> nity." To this Kosinski replied that it was not easy for him to
> appear before this particular group. But he continued to insist

that he struggled to find his own identity rather than have one thrust upon him. "The community I carry within me does not require an endorsement from without." It was here that he made his remark that no one could make him a Jew or un-make him one.

Kosinski concluded the proceedings by answering a final challenge: "Why are you here, with Jews?" by observing that he didn't think that there is only one kind of Jew, that Judaism allows for individuality, for uniqueness, for independence. The audience responded with an ovation.

Was Kosinski outing himself as a Jew? Some thought so.[7]

Some time after the *Village Voice* article appeared, Jerzy Kosinski telephoned me at about 1:30 in the morning. I was giving a series of lectures on the Holocaust in Madison, Wisconsin, so he had to awaken my wife in St. Louis, convince her that he had to talk to me immediately, woke my sister-in-law and brother-in-law in Madison and, frankly, scared me. To make an utterly unscientific judgment, Kosinski was bouncing off the walls. He seemed to me to be completely out of control. He said in effect (I cannot recall the exact words) that the *Voice* was persecuting him. They were trying to destroy him as a writer.

I listened, of course. Here was someone in trouble. How could I help? After about ten minutes I gave a naive suggestion. "You must write to the paper and tell them the truth" is what I said. Kosinski reacted very strongly. He could not, he insisted. He had always proclaimed freedom for the press. But, I remonstrated, they lied. This was not to the point, he almost screamed. Didn't I understand, freedom of the press is absolute? I do not agree with that position, but this was no time to argue. I tried to soothe, not arouse. I was not very successful. The conversation ended with both of us agitated, though not with each other.

In February 1979, over three years before the infamous *Village Voice* article, Kosinski appeared two nights in a row on Dick Cavett's nationally syndicated television talk show. Cavett was somewhat typically unable or unwilling to stick to a single line of questioning, but as I recently listened to the audio tape I made of those telecasts I could not help but think that some of Kosinski's remarks answered some questions raised in the newspaper piece three years later.

Kosinski tried very hard on that show to separate his life from his fiction. He did say that his experiences as a youth helped him to be a master at avoiding being cornered. He also noted that his many years of silence as a child were not to be seen as a disadvantage; it was during this period that he learned to listen and to observe—abilities we all know many writers lack.

He told how the inability to speak came upon him through a physical accident and disappeared one day when he was in a hospital; a phone rang and he merely picked it up and began speaking. He did not elaborate any details.

When he spoke about the situation of writing in a foreign language, Kosinski said that in English he could be much more articulate or much less so than if he worked in Polish or Russian, his two other major languages. He went on to say that in either case, "I am either much more myself or not myself at all." In an adopted tongue, he concluded, "I am much closer to what I really am."

Then Kosinski was asked by his host a question raised many times, not always in the friendly manner in which Cavett put it. Is he the main character in *The Painted Bird*? The answer was that of one who understood fiction: "It is an inclusion effort that happened, that might have happened, that could have happened, that happened to a great number of people that I know. In any case, it is a novel. It is not an autobiography." Were Stokes and Fremont-Smith listening?

Cavett followed this up with a naive bit of searching. He wanted to hear if everything Kosinski wrote in his fiction was true. The response was quick. "It's true to the reader—that's the whole point," Kosinski stated.

An article in *Publishers Weekly* referred to what were seen as "less serious charges" that Kosinski gave "conflicting accounts of pivotal events in his life such as how and when he became mute."[8] Of course these are less serious attacks—they are ad hominem thrusts that have nothing to do with Kosinski's fiction. That Kosinski was obsessed with the notion of hiding identity is clear from his earliest writings. Let us briefly walk through some of his novels to clarify my point (I deliberately ignore here Kosinski's first two volumes, which are nonfiction, *The Future Is Ours, Comrade* and *No Third Path*, written under the name of Joseph Novak, although the use of a pseudonym only serves to bolster my argument).

In *The Painted Bird*, published seventeen years before the *Village Voice* smear, the narrator of the story agrees with another character and concludes that "people themselves determined the course of their lives and were the only masters of their destinies."[9] Later we read that "every one of us stood alone, and the sooner a man realized that all . . . were expendable, the better for him" (233). In *Steps*, which the great literary critic Hugh Kenner said echoes Celine and Kafka, we meet a character who spends most of his time alone. In *Being There*, we are introduced to a character appropriately named Chance who has no identity.[10] (Parenthetically, Kosinski told me that Peter Sellers begged for the lead role in the film, was rejected at first, and after two years was finally accepted. The role really reflected Sellers' own lack of identity and thus in a curious manner fulfilled a lack in his personality, after which and because of which, Sellers died.) We read of the main character that "he came to believe that it was he, Chance, and no one else, who made himself be" (6).

Early in *The Devil Tree* the narrator says, "My past is the only firmament worth knowing, and I am its sole star." This "star" person is blamed in a letter from a woman friend who charges that "you live in an exile of your own making, excusing almost everyone, venturing out only in the name of exploration and expansion" (p. 10). He later asks the revealing questions which we can imagine Kosinski asking himself: "Am I, perhaps, my own archetype, a man who at any time can transform himself into his opposite?" (p. 36). And later in this same book, the same character thinks that he is aware "that as soon as people claim to know who I am, I can no longer act freely" (ibid). Surely this is a theme for Kosinski in fiction, as in life.[11] In *Cockpit*, the narrator mentions Theodora: "She had helped me find a shield for the self I wanted to hide."[12] About halfway through the novel, the narrator tells the reader that "I needed to change my identity so often in recent years, I've come to look upon disguise as more than a means of personal liberation: it's a necessity. My life depends on my being able to instantly create a new persona and slip out of the past" (29). Did Stokes and Fremont-Smith miss these passages? If they had wanted to identify the novelist's life with his fiction, how could they have ignored such lines?

If the critical pair wished to insist on more scenes from Kosinski's fiction to equate with his life, why did they ignore certain parts, not others? What were their principles of selectivity? In *Blind Date*, for instance, there are some hints of similarity between George Levanter and Jerzy Kosinski. Which are real clues, which false? What about "Levanter and his mother remained lovers for years, although she continued to find women for him?"[13] How is it that some sentences are suggested as being true of Kosinski and others are not? In *Blind Date*, the son and mother, she now bald and dying, meet after twenty years of separation, something impossible in Kosinski's life.

Kosinski's major characters wanted to be control figures. Fabian, in the next novel of the Polish emigre to appear, *Passion Play*, was described as having "acted always in the conviction that to master his life, to assert dominion over that indifferent span, what he must do was to shape it into drama, each scene so charged, so unrepeatable, that no interval could be permitted to divert him from the spectacle of which he was both protagonist and solitary witness."[14]

In *Pinball* there is Patrick Domostroy, who "had gradually succeeded in turning his private universe into a well-guarded fortress, and up to now he had kept out anyone who might disturb the peace he found there."[15] There is a particular episode in this book which I found quite amusing and I told Kosinski so. It is near the end when Domostroy seduces a naked Donna, who all the while continues to play Chopin on the piano, without interruption. I mentioned that I saw the situation as funny partly because it was impossible. Kosinski reacted quickly, assuring me that it was possible, that he had done it. How could I argue? I was out of my field of expertise.

Kosinski's final novel, published six years after the *Village Voice* assault, is the terribly disappointing *The Hermit of 69th Street*. It is a failed attempt at combining the techniques of James Joyce (puns) and Jorge Luis Borges (false footnotes) and is an attempt by the author to crudely defend himself as an author. He probably hurts his own case, which I feel he never had to make in the first place. His attempt at humor over things like the sexual implications of "69" might be said to be obsessively obsessive. It certainly is not jocular.

What do I think of Kosinski's fiction? I have taught *The Painted Bird* several times and I very much recommend *Being There*. The rest of the novels, I think, are forgettable, with *The Hermit of 69th Street* being on my list of the ten worst novels ever by a major writer. His books have major themes such as the attempt to hide identity and aging. Some others have an obsession with sexuality, which clearly gets in the way of much of his writing. His books include scenes of murder, torture, suicide, drugs, incest, rape, homosexuality, prostitution, adultery, casual sex, bestiality, masturbation.

In *Passing By*, a book of Kosinski's published after his death by his widow, we again read pieces that seem to try to justify what does not need justification—the way a writer approaches writing. He does, here, find time to praise Pope John Paul II, criticize Alexander (Kosinski's spelling) Solzhenitsyn, write of Jews and Jewishness, but never strays far from the topic of authorship. These short pieces are interesting, though not profound.

It is not as if Kosinski made no response denying the charges in the *Voice* article. In talking to John Mutter of *Publisher's Weekly*, the novelist asked why neither Stokes nor Fremont-Smith had spoken to any of Kosinski's editors at the publishing houses. "The best thing was to talk to my editors. They would know best. Why didn't anyone talk to them?"[16] He then cited his work on behalf of freedom of the press as guaranteed by the First Amendment when he served as president of PEN and his many years as a member of the American Civil Liberties Union. He insisted that Stokes and Fremont-Smith "should be free to write what they want to write" (11). But he did see the article as "a classic case of pure malice and reckless disregard for truth" (17).

The *Publisher's Weekly* commentary quoted editor Les Pockell, director of the trade department at St. Martin's Press (and who was Kosinski's editor for *Passion Play*), as calling the *Voice* charges "totally ludicrous" (18). Pockell spoke of Kosinski's being "obsessive" regarding changes in his texts. The galleys for *Passion Play* had to be completely reset because the author made so many emendations.

Austin Olney, an editor-in-chief at Houghton Mifflin, wrote to *Publisher's Weekly* that

> I have been marginally involved with the three Kosinski novels published by Houghton Mifflin and can attest to the fact that he is a difficult and demanding author who makes endless (and to my way of thinking, often niggling) corrections in proof. I have been sometimes overwhelmed by his flamboyant conceits and his artful manipulations, but I have never had any reason to believe that he has ever needed or used any but the most routine editorial assistance. The remarkable consistency of tone in all of his novels seems to me sufficient evidence that they all come from his hands alone. (18)

In 1996, James Park Sloan published a biography simply titled *Jerzy Kosinski.*[17] It pretty much agreed with the *Village Voice* article in substance and even in style. Using much speculation (13), conclusions based on "more likely" and "it must have been" (14), "must have been," "must have" (17), "must have" and "seem" (19), "Apparently" (31) on through the end: "may well have" and "He may have" (449). This work, like the article in *The Village Voice*, would not have been acceptable in my college course!

I am left with one critic who knew Kosinski much better than I did, Byron Sherwin, now a vice president at Spertus College of Judaica in Chicago. In *Jerzy Kosinski: Literary Alarm Clock*, Sherwin tells that Kosinski occasionally "wears a disguise to avoid recognition and to retain the privacy of anonymity."[18] Sherwin says this is consistent with Kosinski's chosen motto, "*Larvatus prodeo*—I go forth disguised" (4). In 1981, before the *Voice* challenge, Sherwin wrote this in discussing Kosinski's work:

> To cede the imagination is to render to others—family, society, the state—the option of imposing their vision upon our lives, their plot upon our existence, their destiny upon our experience. To permit others to edit the experiences of our lives, to create us in their image—from their imagination—is to authorize the indoctrination of our own imaginations. To surrender our individual vision is to commission others to compose the novel which is our lives. Applying his aesthetic position to his political stance, Kosinski reminds us that the essence of totalitarianism is the attempt of the state to inflict its vision, its plot, upon the lives of its citizens. (11)

Later Sherwin observes that "a feature of one's unique nature is one's memory. No two individuals have identical memories. According to Kosinski, one's memories of the past are not a duplication of the past; rather, they are random impressions of past experiences. Thus, one is the product not so much of one's past as of one's memories of past moments. As one critic of Kosinski's work put it, for Kosinski, 'I' is the one who remembers. I remember, therefore I am" (24).

On October 7, 1997, I telephoned Byron Sherwin, whom I had met many years before and whose work in a number of areas I respect. He told me that he was certain that Kosinski wrote his own books. He added that Sloan, the biographer, "missed the boat totally" on the "Polish situation" and on the "Jewish situation." Sherwin called Sloan's attempt at biography "a novel."

Sherwin told me, "The most famous scene in *The Painted Bird* that everyone remembers is the eye-gouging scene. He told me he never saw this in Europe but he showed me an article from the old *New York Daily News* where somebody did this in this country. A lot of scenes in *Steps* he took right out of the daily newspapers in order to show all of these things are not in the realm of the fantastic but are in the realm of the daily news. And this I think is the most important message of the whole thing."

Sherwin added, "It was not coincidental that he chose to commit suicide on May 3, 1991, because that was the 200th anniversary of the Polish Constitution which guaranteed freedom of expression for the first time. It was a statement in itself because he felt himself denied the freedom of expression, particularly in a free country; he had nothing more to say so he had no more reason to live."

Sherwin told me of seeing a number of Kosinski manuscripts in Kosinski's apartment with all of their corrections and revisions, and it was all Kosinski's work.

Perhaps Kosinski's "flaw" was that he was too good a storyteller. Novelist Cynthia Ozick once told Sherwin that Kosinski was the greatest conversationalist she'd ever met. Sherwin quoted Ozick as saying that Kosinski would "be in a group of the top literary people, political people, business people in New York at a cocktail party and he would sit there and just talk for hours and people wouldn't move."

Clearly, not everyone believed his stories to be true. But in the realm of literature, Kosinski tried to write truth, alone.[19]

Notes

1. Harry James Cargas, "Imprisoned Authors: Comrades of Solzhenitsyn and St. Paul." *Christian Century* (December 10, 1975): 1137–1138.

2. Geoffrey Stokes with Eliot Fremont-Smith, "Jerzy Kosinski's Tainted Words." *Village Voice* (June 22, 1982).

3. Martin Tucker, letter to the editor in "Kosinski Is Worthy of Our Support." *New York Times*, November 28, 1982, H23.

4. Marla Press, letter to the editor in "Kosinski Is Worthy of Our Support." *New York Times*, November 28, 1982, H23.

5. Stokes with Fremont-Smith, "Tainted Words."

6. Arlynn Nellhaus, "Former Aid to Kosinski Denies Story." *Denver Post*, June 18, 1982.

7. Harry James Cargas, "Jerzy Kosinski Electrifies Holocaust Survivors Conference." *St. Louis Jewish Light* 35, (March 31, 1982): 2.

8. John Mutter, "Kosinski Denies *Village Voice* Charges of Extensive Writing Help." *Publishers Weekly*, July 9, 1982, 18.

9. Jerzy Kosinski, *The Painted Bird* (Boston: Houghton Mifflin, 1976), 187.

10. Jerzy Kosinski, *Being There* (New York: Harcourt Brace Jovanovich, 1970.)

11. Jerzy Kosinski, *The Devil Tree* (New York: Bantam Books, 1974), 10 and 36.

12. Jerzy Kosinski, *Cockpit* (Boston: Houghton Mifflin, 1975), 64.

13. Jerzy Kosinski, *Blind Date* (Boston: Houghton Mifflin, 1977), 8.

14. Jerzy Kosinski, *Passion Play* (New York: St. Martin's Press, 1979), 17.

15. Jerzy Kosinski, *Pinball* (New York: Grove Press, 1982), 10.

16. Mutter, "Kosinski Denies," 11.

17. James Park Sloan, *Jerzy Kosinski: A Biography* (New York: Dutton, 1996).

18. Byron Sherwin, *Jerzy Kosinski: A Literary Alarm Clock* (Chicago: Cabala Press, 1981), 4.

19. Within half an hour after I completed this manuscript, I received a telephone call from Leopold Page (Leopold Pfefferberg, to whom Thomas Keneally's book *Schindler's List* is dedicated) to say good things about an interview with Page that I had just published in *Martyrdom and Resistance*. I did not mention Kosinski's name; Page brought it up. He said that about two weeks before Kosinski's suicide the two men had spoken on the phone. During the conversation, Page told me, Kosinski denied that he (Kosinski) was Jewish. In Page's words to me, "Kosinski was a very complex man." It seems to me that I have to "report" this information. It does not invalidate my chapter, but if Page's words are accurate, they do shed some light on Kosinski's state of mind.

Works Cited

Cargas, Henry James. "Imprisoned Authors: Comrades of Solzhenitsyn and St. Paul." *Christian Century* (December 10, 1975): 1137–1138.

——. "Jerzy Kosinski Electrifies Holocaust Survivors Conference." *St. Louis Jewish Light* 35 (March 31, 1982) 2.

Kosinski, Jerzy. *Being There*. New York: Harcourt Brace Jovanovich, 1970.

——. *Blind Date*. Boston: Houghton Mifflin, 1977.

——. *Cockpit*. Boston: Houghton Mifflin, 1975.

——. *The Hermit of 69th Street: The Working Papers of Norbert Kosky*. New York: Seaver Books, 1988.

——. *Passing By: Selected Painted Bird Essays, 1962–1991*. New York: Random House, 1992.

——. *Passion Play*. New York: St. Martin's Press, 1979.

——. *Pinball*. New York: Grove Press, 1982.

——. *Steps*. New York: Random House, 1968.

——. *The Painted Bird*. Boston: Houghton Mifflin, 1976.

——. Address at Annual Dinner of PEN. May 27, 1975.

——. Address to Holocaust Survivors Memorial Foundation. New York: March 21, 1982.

——. Appearance on Dick Cavett, PBS, 1979.

Mutter, John. "Kosinski Denies *Village Voice* Charges of Extensive Writing Help." *Publishers Weekly*, July 9, 1982.

Nellhaus, Arlynn. "Former Aid to Kosinski Denies Story." *Denver Post*, June 18, 1982, DoA.

Sherwin, Byron. *Jerzy Kosinski: Literary Alarm Clock*. Chicago: Cabala Press, 1981.

Sloan, James Park. *Jerzy Kosinski: A Biography*. New York: Dutton, 1996.

Stokes, Geoffrey with Eliot Fremont-Smith. "Jerzy Kosinski's Tainted Words." *Village Voice*, June 22, 1982, 1, 41–43.

4

By the Light of Darkness:
Six Major European Writers Who
Experienced the Holocaust

HUGH NISSENSON

I write
In the barracks At night,
By the light
Of darkness.

Etty Hillesum (1914–1943)

My subject is the work in translation of six major twentieth-century European writers who experienced the Holocaust: Anne Frank, Etty Hillesum, Jacob Presser, Emmanuel Ringelblum, Tadeusz Borowski, and Primo Levi. I've chosen the writers whom I consider to be the best stylists on that subject. The five adults among them share a common theme—a vision of the Holocaust as a new historical reality.

Borowski, Levi, Frank, Hillesum, Presser, and Ringelblum were acutely sensitive to their respective spoken and written languages. Levi translated fragments of Dante's *The Canto of Ulysses* into French and repeated his verse as a gift to a fellow prisoner in Auschwitz. Anne Frank was particularly proud of her Dutch:[1]

September 2, 1942 . . . the two ladies speak abominable Dutch . . .
Whenever I quote Mother or Mrs. van Daan, I'll write proper Dutch instead of trying to duplicate their speech.[1]

Even in translation, the work of all six writers shares two stylistic characteristics: clarity and concision. Their unadorned, vernacular prose often has the impact of poetry. Listen to the letter Etty Hillesum wrote to a friend in Amsterdam while on a train to Auschwitz from the Westerbork concentration camp. Her words were scribbled across an addressed postcard, which was thrown from the train and found by Dutch farmers on September 7, 1943, outside Westerbork.

> Christine:
>
> Opening the Bible at random I find this: "The Lord is my high tower." I am sitting on a rucksack in the middle of a full freight car. Father, Mother and Mischa are a few cars away. In the end, the departure came without warning. On sudden special orders from the Hague. We left the camp singing, Father and Mother firmly and calmly, Mischa too. We shall be traveling for three days. Thank you for all your kindness and care. Friends left behind will still be writing to Amsterdam; perhaps you will hear something from them. Or from my last letter from camp.
>
> Good-bye for now from the four of us.
>
> Etty.[2]

The simple, soaring sentence, "We left the camp singing," was written by an artist at the height of her powers.

Three months earlier, while still in Amsterdam, the twenty-eight-year-old Hillesum wrote in her journal,

> Looked at Japanese prints . . . this afternoon. That's how I want to write. With that much space round a few words. They should simply emphasize the silence.[3]

On April 5, 1944, in another part of the same city, fourteen-year-old Anne Frank embraced her vocation as a writer:

> I know I can write . . . I want to go on living even after my death! And that's why I'm so grateful to God for having given me this gift, which I can use to develop myself and express all that's inside me! (250–251)

Anne Frank was an awakening artist; she linked the development of her gift for words to her inner life and her hope for literary immortality— and said so clearly, in colloquial speech. Shortly after the twenty-three-year-old Polish writer Tadeusz Borowski was liberated from Auschwitz, he wrote:

> I take out fresh paper, arrange it neatly on the desk . . . and with a tremendous intellectual effort I attempt to grasp the true

significance of the events, things and people I have seen. For I intend to write a great, immortal epic, worthy of this unchanging, difficult world chiselled out of stone.[4]

Each of these authors is an intensely self-conscious stylist. On Sunday night, September 20, 1942, Etty Hillesum, awaiting deportation from a Westerbork barrack, gave herself in her diary the best three words of advice about being a writer that I know:

Verbalise, vocalise, visualise. (175)

Later she wrote:

(September 30, 1943) . . . How much I want to write. Somewhere deep inside me is a workshop in which Titans are forging a new world. (186)

Emmanuel Ringelblum, the epic historian of the Warsaw Ghetto, who wrote in Yiddish, used a cinematographic technique to dramatize the typhus epidemic raging around him on March 10, 1941:

A scene: An auto with [Germans] riding in it comes along. A Jewish hand wagon blocks the way at Karmelicka Street. The car can't move. One of the [Germans] gets out and begins beating the Jew. A shudder runs down the Jew's back. A man in the car calls out: "Let him alone. He's contagious." The attacker reconsiders and lets the Jew be.[5]

Ringelblum wrote in the third person, from the point of view of an omniscient narrator. The anonymous narrator's insertion of one visualized detail—"A shudder runs down the Jew's back"—brings his whole scene to life.

Some of the writers kept their sense of humor and jotted down jokes being cracked around them. Anne Frank, on Thursday, October 1, 1942:

. . . told by Mr. van Daan:
What goes click ninety-nine times and clack once?
A centipede with a club foot. (50)

Emmanuel Ringelblum, on October 23, 1940:

A Jew alternately laughs and yells in his sleep. His wife wakes him up. He is mad at her. "I was dreaming someone had scribbled on a wall, 'Beat the Jews! Down with ritual slaughter!' " "So what were you so happy about?" "Don't you understand? That means

the good old days have come back! The Poles are running things
again!" (179)

Borowski had an ironist's eye:

> Trucks leave and return, without interruption, as on a monstrous
> conveyor belt. A Red Cross van drives back and forth, inces-
> santly: it transports the gas that will kill these people. The enor-
> mous cross on the hood, red as blood, seems to dissolve in the
> sun. (38)

Borowski was arrested in Warsaw by the Gestapo and sent to Auschwitz
in 1943. As a non-Jew not subject to selection for the gas chamber, he
viewed himself with the same mordant irony:

> I smiled spitefully at my own wit and walked away humming a
> popular camp tango called, "Cremo". . . (55)

"Cremo" is short for "crematorium" in "crematorium Esperanto." Crematorium Esperanto is a phrase invented by Borowski for the international jargon
that evolved in the camps.

Borowski keeps his readers off guard by constantly modulating his tone
of voice. He suddenly drops his irony:

> And every one of the people who, because of eczema, phlegmon
> or typhoid fever, or simply because they were too emaciated,
> were taken to the gas chamber, begged the orderlies to remem-
> ber what they saw. And to tell the truth about mankind to those
> who do not know it. (175)

Surely, for all six authors, writing was an act of bearing witness. But it
also must have been done for its own sake, out of a love for language and
the specific form being worked.

The form being worked was often the literary diary, or journal, meant
for eventual publication. Anne Frank carefully rewrote parts of her Diary
with that in mind. Her Diary, in fact, personified as "Kitty," "dearest Kitty,"
even "My dearest darling," is an important, silent character in the Diary—
a combination secret friend, confidant, and schoolgirl crush.

Etty Hillesum and Emmanuel Ringelblum also wrote masterpieces in
the form of the literary journal, which they intended for eventual publication. Jacob Presser, who was a historian, turned the journal form into a great
Holocaust novel, *The Night of the Girondists*. It purports to be written by a
Jew in Westerbork during the week before his deportation to Sobibor.

Anne Frank's precocious talent and intellect ripen in her Diary. The world is shrinking; her mind expands. She re-creates the claustrophobic atmosphere of the crowded Secret Annex with an accretion of vividly observed selected details—stale air, damp laundry, blackout screens, melting butter, soured milk. She captured the essential in a few words:

> (undated 1944) Talk, whispers, fear, stench, farting and people continually going to the bathroom; try sleeping through that! (256)

On May 10,1944, Mouschi, her beloved cat, peed:

> The puddle immediately trickled down to the attic and, as luck would have it, landed in and next to the potato barrel. The ceiling was dripping, and since the attic floor has also got its share of cracks, little yellow drops were leaking through the ceiling and onto the dining table, between a pile of stockings and books. I was doubled up with laughter, it was such a funny sight. There was Mouschi crouched under a chair, Peter armed with water, powdered bleach and a cloth, and Mr. van Daan trying to calm everyone down. (292–293)

Frank wrote action well. Her verbs make her scene move: the pee trickles, drips, and leaks, Anne laughs, Peter wipes, Mr. van Daan soothes. The ardent specificity of Frank's prose and her ability to create vibrant images are expressions of her budding genius. Before our very eyes, a marvelously intelligent and gifted girl becomes a young woman—a liberated modern young woman, at that.

Two months before her arrest, Anne Frank wrote:

> Men presumably dominated women from the very beginning because of their greater physical strength. . . . Until recently, women silently went along with this, which was stupid, since the longer it's kept up, the more deeply entrenched it becomes. Fortunately, education, work and progress have opened women's eyes . . . Modern women want the right to be completely independent! (319)

Etty Hillesum also seems a contemporary of ours. She was a Dutch Jew in her midtwenties, who recorded in her 1941 Amsterdam diary her simultaneous affairs with two older men, "S." and "Han."[3]

> [H]ow can I explain that, whenever I have had physical contact with S. in the evening, I spend the night with Han? Feelings of guilt? In the past, perhaps, but no longer. (104)

Celebrating her sensuality, aroused in the face of death, Hillesum wrote,

> [I]t only lasts a few days at a time, this rising wave. And that little
> bit of sensuality is what I then try to project on to the whole of
> life, until it overshadows all the rest.

Etty Hillesum was a mystic. Her religious sensibility was influenced by
Christianity, but not Christological. Her diary entry for May 18, 1942:

> The threat grows ever greater, and terror increases from day to
> day. I draw prayer round me like a dark protective wall, withdraw
> inside it as one might into a convent cell and then step outside
> again, calmer and stronger and more collected. (113)

Hillesum's erotized mysticism—her love for the God she felt within
her—enriched her perception of the world and quickened her prose:

> (September 22, 1943) . . . At night the barracks sometimes lay in
> the moonlight, made out of silver and eternity—like a plaything
> that had slipped from God's preoccupied hand. (180)

Her mysticism intensified her empathy for her fellow Jews. In her diary,
Hillesum wrote:

> (September 17, 1943) I am suddenly reminded of that woman
> with the snow white hair and the fine oval face. She carried
> a packet of toast in her knapsack, all she had for the long
> journey to Poland, for she was on a strict diet. She was so
> incredibly lovely and so serene with her tall girlish figure.
> One afternoon I was sitting out in the sun with her just in
> front of the transit barracks . . . She said . . . to some girls who
> came over to join us, "Remember, when we leave early tomor-
> row morning each of us may cry just three times." And one of
> the girls replied, "I haven't been issued a ration book for that."
> (174–175)

Above all, Etty Hillesum's diary bore witness to historic truth:

> (July 28, 1942) Nothing can ever atone for the fact, of course,
> that one section of the Jewish population is helping to transport
> the majority out of the country. History will pass judgement in
> due course. (166)

Anne Frank's isolation in the Secret Annex paradoxically protected her from that reality for a while. She was in many ways an ordinary middle-class adolescent—a bit of a snob:

> (Sunday, December 13, 1942) ... The people in this neighbor-hood aren't particularly attractive to look at. The children espe-cially are so dirty you wouldn't want to touch them with a ten-foot pole. Real slum kids with runny noses. I can hardly under-stand a word they say. (76)

Anne Frank was ambivalent about being Jewish. Her diary entry after the "end of Part One":

> One day this terrible war will be over. The time will come when we'll be people again and not just Jews ... [but] We can never be just Dutch, or just English, or whatever, we will always be Jews as well ... but then we'll want to be. (262)

With all Dutch Jews, Anne Frank and her family eventually suf-fered in Westerbork at the hands of Jews doing the Germans' dirty work. The other writers being considered were obsessed by the active complic-ity of Nazism's Jewish—and Polish—victims in their own physical and spiritual annihilation. That's the second reason I've chosen to write of them. From our vantage point, it's the major theme they share.

In 1941, aged forty-two, Jacob Presser was recruited by the Germans to teach in the Jewish school they had set up in Holland. Two years later, Presser's wife was arrested, sent to Westerbork, and deported to her death in Sobibor. Presser was hidden by Christian friends until the Occupation ended. The recipient of a chair in modern history at the University of Amsterdam, he wrote this about Westerbork in his definitive historical study, *The Destruc-tion of the Dutch Jews:*

> Here, the awful truth about collaboration—an ever decreasing number of Jews helping to deport an ever decreasing number of their fellows—stood out still more starkly, not least because at Westerbork this task was carried out with such exemplary efficiency.[6]

As an artist, Presser turned his research about Westerbork into imagina-tive fiction. His novel *The Night of the Girondists* (1957) was awarded the Van Hoogt Prize for Creative Literature. Read now, it turns out to be an early postmodernist work of art—one that fuses fact and fiction, illusion and reality.

The Night of the Girondists is a historian's riff on the literary journal. The novel is narrated in the first person by a Dutch Jewish intellectual, an assimilated anti-Semite named Jacques Suasso. Presser makes Suasso a self-conscious writer like Frank and Hillesum, who writes with an eye for eventual publication. Presser's artistry persuades his readers that they are reading the real thing—a historical document, written by a gifted writer, that was smuggled out of Westerbork. In the very first words of the novel, Suasso plunges into his own story with a mastery of narrative technique that dramatizes his situation in three simple, vernacular sentences:

> I'll try just once more. Perhaps it won't work, either, and the figures won't add up, any more than they would a fortnight ago, any more than last week. Twice now I have torn up the precious scrap of paper, but this is my last chance; delaying, putting off is impossible now that I am myself in the punitive barracks, with full assurance of "rolling off eastward."[7]

Suasso tells his story in fits and starts, till he suddenly gets going like a train. He witnesses the Monday night selections for the Tuesday morning train:

> I have seen a woman bite the jugular vein of her sister, whose name was not called, and who had thus escaped; and a man who had put out his eyes right in front of me because another, three steps away, was sitting, sobbing with joy. I have seen it, seen it myself, many nights of perdition. I HAVE SEEN IT. (65)

Suasso rummages through European literature, trying to connect his experience with the European past. He mockingly evokes the devil, hell, Dante, Faust, Goethe, Rimbaud, Weininger, Lamartine, Carlyle, Dickens; he thinks of Boswell, quotes Aldous Huxley; he has them all at his fingertips—but comes up empty-handed.

Presser's novel covers the last week of Suasso's life. Come dawn, next Tuesday, he's on the train to Sobibor. The transports always leave on time. He should know. He packed plenty of his fellow Jews on them.

Suasso relieves his soul—and assures his own literary immortality—by telling his story and making sure it's smuggled out of Westerbork. He explains how and why he voluntarily went to the camp in order to join its Jewish OD (Ordnungspolizei, the Order Police):

> A scant hundred men, popularly known as the Jewish SS. This was a telling thrust, since we were both Jews and SS, completely in-

fected by our enemies, whom we imitated in gait, in posture, even in our manner of speech: "zackig," "schneidig," "real soldiers," "with plenty of zip". (27–28, quotation marks as in original.)

The Westerbork Jewish SS packed one hundred thousand fellow Jews into sealed boxcars on ninety-three consecutive Tuesdays between July 1941 and February 1944.

Suasso loads his own mother, also an anti-Semite; he packs off Ninon de Vries, the girl he loves, and an ex-student of his named Mona Something—her last name escapes him—whom he taught in class 5b of the Jewish school.

The SS commandant of Westerbork orders the deportation to Auschwitz of all inmates from the Jewish Institution for the Insane at Deventer. Suasso, along with the other Jewish slaves, obeys:

And so, through the pitch-black night, we carried stark naked, yelling lunatics, their arms tied, to the cars; when I paused for an instant to vomit, (SS Man) Adelphi himself gave me a kick "Faster Jew!" (37)

Primo Levi wrote in his foreword to the 1992 British edition of Presser's novel:

It is naive, absurd and historically inaccurate to maintain that an evil system like Nazism sanctifies its victims; quite the reverse, it leaves them soiled and degraded, it assimilates them, and all the more so to the degree that the victims are at their disposal, virginally innocent of any political or moral constructs. (ix)

Soiled, degraded, assimilated—above all, assimilated—Jacques Suasso the assimilated anti-Semitic Jew experiences—what? Not a religious conversion, exactly, but a change of heart. He's moved by the quiet courage of a crippled young rabbi named Jeremiah Hirsch, who quotes to him a few words from the Book of Joshua: "For the Lord thy God is with thee withersoever thou goest."

Condemned to the same ghastly death, the fictitious Jacques Suasso and the real Etty Hillesum grope for hope in the Bible.

Rabbi Hirsch limps through the pages of *The Night of the Girondists* like the lamed patriarch, Jacob, who wrestled all night with God to earn the name Israel. Because of Rabbi Hirsch, Jacques gets his old name back, and for a while before his death literally and symbolically becomes Jacob—the committed, compassionate Jew.

Jacob Presser pulls all this off in seventy-nine pages.

On first reading *The Night of the Girondists*, we don't notice Presser's technical virtuosity, his artfully artless complexity.

We're swept along by his story—Jacques Suasso's story, which Suasso narrates in his unique voice. Suasso constantly juxtaposes the idiomatic and the literary for comic effect. He and his creator, Jacob Presser, wrote *Galgen Humor*—like Tadeusz Borowski and—God help us!—Louis-Ferdinand Celine: three masters of a peculiarly mid-twentieth-century European sardonic tone, which resonates even in translation.

Suasso says:

> I ran into Sam Wolfson, the only other Jew in my student debat- ing club, and, having time to spare . . . went with him as he wanted to show me something special . . . two pounds of poison in five hundred two gram doses . . . little airtight tubes, of which he immediately offered me half a dozen for my own use.

Then he added a potted lecture:

> "Mind what I say, Jacques, because you're only an ignorant arts man—excuse the tautology. This stuff is called potassium cyanide. Don't nod your head—what do you know about it, you should live so long? It's a nerve stuff . . . any handbook will tell you about it—it attaches itself to the hemoglobin of the red cor- puscles, and then they won't absorb any more oxygen. Get it?"

> "Certainly," I replied.

> "Certainly," he mocked . . . "Anyhow, take warning: eat these goodies and you're finished. Two grammes seems to me . . . plenty, but never mind. And here are a couple more. For all the *goyim* to butter their bread with after the war." Because Sam was pretty fierce, and hated Protestants and Catholics alike. (71–72)

The artist Etty Hillesum prayed to become "the thinking *heart* of the barracks." (191) The social historian Emmanuel Ringelblum was the Warsaw Ghetto's unblinking eye:

> (from the summer of 1941) Beggar children stand near the hos- pital on Ogrodowa Street, near the telephone building, and wait for someone to have pity and throw them a piece of bread . . . They walk out right into the middle of the street, begging for bread. Most of them are children. In the surrounding silence of night, the cries of the hungry beggar children are terribly insistent, and, however hard your heart, eventually you have to throw a piece of

bread down to them—or else leave the house. It's a common thing for beggar children like these to die on the sidewalk at night . . . One such horrible scene took place in front of 24 Muranowska Street where a six-year-old beggar boy lay gasping all night, too weak to roll over to the piece of bread that had been thrown down to him from the balcony. (204–205)

Ringelblum's sentences progressively compact and become more and more telegraphic as his condition—the condition of all Jews in the Ghetto—worsens. The final style in which Ringelblum describes the breakup of the Ghetto perfectly objectifies his community's disintegration:

(Yom Kippur, September 22, 1942) The day there was a selection in the shops—the slaughter of women, children, illegals. (313)

The practice of torturing Jews in the cities on Yom Kippur . . . (314)

The slaughter at Schultz's [shop]—the slaughter on Nowolopie Street . . . (315)

Shameful document cited by the Jewish Council about the rumours that there would be a resettlement (of Jews from the Warsaw Ghetto) to the East. (316)

Born in 1900, Emmanuel Ringelblum had "established himself as one of the most promising of the Young Historians group in Warsaw when World War II broke out. He had written four books and innumerable monographs" (x).

Ringelblum immediately assumed the task of recording the collective experience of Warsaw's Jews under German occupation. To help him with the enormous job, he secretly organized what he called a "free society of slaves" (xix)—"The Oneg Shabbat" (Sabbath celebrants) or "O.S." (xvi). The underground O.S. gathered, checked, and collated information from all over Warsaw and its suburbs, which Ringelblum wrote down at night in an inimitable style. He was first and foremost a social historian—but a new kind, one who makes history by—and while—recording it. Historical time intermittently coalesced for him and his community.

(November 8, 1940) . . . There's been the growth of a strong sense of historical consciousness recently. We tie in fact after fact from our daily experience with the events of history. We are returning to the Middle Ages. (82)

Then European history collapsed on them. In June 1942, Ringelblum found himself and his people back in ancient Egypt:

> [Jewish children] are the first to be exterminated. Except for Pharaoh, who ordered the newborn Hebrew thrown into the river Nile, this is unprecedented in Jewish history. On the contrary. In the past, whatever was done with the grownups, children were always permitted to live—so that they might be converted to the Christian faith. (293)

Preserved in rubberized milk cans, Ringelblum's archives document the systematic destruction within five years of Warsaw Jewry's thousand-year-old civilization. Ringelblum is among the great European historians—a Thucydides of his city's tragedy.

Ringelblum was a left-wing Labor Zionist—a Marxist. Marxism sharpened his vision:

> (January, 1942) . . . During these days of hunger, the inhumanity of the Jewish upper class has clearly shown itself. The entire work of the Jewish Council is an evil perpetrated against the poor that cries to the very heaven. (245)

Ringelblum soon understood that the Nazis deliberately and systematically incriminated their Jewish victims in their crimes:

> (November 1–10, 1941) . . . And now there are eight Jews, six women among them, who have been handed over to the Jewish police for execution. Auerswald, the [German] Ghetto commissar, insists that the Jewish police constitute their own execution squad to carry out the sentence in the Jewish prison on Zamenhofa Street—corner of Gesia Street. The chief of the Jewish police, Szcrynski, a convert who goes to church every Sunday and is known to be a grafter of the first water, has agreed to it under threat of being shot himself if he refused. It will be a terrible thing if Jews have to be their own hangmen! (229–230)

Szcrynski the convert: like Presser, Ringelblum excoriated Jews who abjured their Jewishness and assimilated themselves into the gentile culture that spawned the evil devouring them.

> (May 11, 1942) The demoralization of the Jews of Warsaw is frightful. It has reached the point where, when two Jews meet,

one says to the other, "One of us must be serving the Gestapo!" (175)

Emmanuel Ringelblum was a social historian far in advance of his time. He was among the first to describe the phenomenon of victims who identified with their oppressors:

(December 10, 1940) Heard an interesting interpretation of the new mode in high shoes [among Jews]. The power and bearing of the [Germans] is impressive. People are trying to rise above the general mass of mankind [by wearing] the same high shoes as the [Germans]. (109)

(At another date) In a refugee center, [a starving] eight year old child went mad. Screamed, "I want to steal, I want to rob, I want to eat, I want to be a German!"

Ringelblum, the secular Zionist, also celebrated the remarkable efflorescence of traditional Jewish culture in the Ghetto:

(May 30, 1942) The children's Lag b'Omer celebrations were very impressive this year. A large children's program was presented in the big Femina Theater Hall. (287)

Again and again, he chronicled Jewish spiritual and physical resistance:

(February 19, 1941) In the prayer house of the [Hasidim] from Braclaw on Nowolipie Street there is a large sign: Jews, Never Despair! The [Hasidim] dance there with the same religious fervor as they did before the war. After prayers one day, a Jew danced there whose daughter had died the day before. (125)

And ever, and always, throughout his epic, Emmanuel Ringelblum celebrated the inner life of human beings faced with imminent, horrible death:

(June 26, 1942) What are people reading? This is a subject of general interest; after the war, it will intrigue the world. What, the world will ask, did people think of on Musa Dagh or in the Warsaw ghetto . . . Let it be said that though we have been sentenced to death and know it, we have not lost our human features; our minds are as active as they were before the war. (298–299)

Musa Dagh! Ringelblum, the modern historian, recalls a Turkish mass murder of besieged Armenians on a mountain named Musa Dagh in the summer of 1915.

During the summer of 1942, the Germans began breaking up the Warsaw Ghetto and deporting its remaining inmates to their deaths—all with the help of the Jewish police.

> (June 25) It's the devil's own plan, this attempt to use the Jews themselves to starve the Ghetto to death . . . this isn't the first time that the Occupying Power has compelled the Jewish populace to dig its own grave. They do it at every step. It is very painful to admit that [the Germans] always find people to do their dirty work with relish, sometimes even with exaggerated zeal. (302)

"The devil's own plan"—Ringelblum's idiom rings true. Looking back on European civilization from 1939 to 1945, we contemplate, as Primo Levi says in *The Drowned and the Saved*, "a world which was shaking on its foundations . . . completely impregnated with crime."

Tadeusz Borowski writes:

> Observe in what an original world we are living: how many men can you find in Europe who have never killed; or whom somebody does not wish to kill? (122)

The mind boggles—and mythologizes European historical reality, as Suasso did, when he called Westerbork hell. Jacob Presser, in *The Destruction of the Dutch Jews*, quotes a survivor's memories of Auschwitz. She sees the camp in the dark as a writhing, painted image—the actualization of a Christian myth:

> Every night . . . down to the least detail, I keep reliving [everything]. Often, it is as if I were moving through a painting by Hieronymus Bosch, a canvas peopled with fearsome monsters. I behold men and women caught in the jaws of winged horrors. The horizon is invariably hidden behind a red veil of smoke and flame. (494)

Primo Levi thought of Dante in Auschwitz. How was his Inferno divided up? What are its punishments? To Hillesum, Westerbork is "that hell." The secular Jews—Levi, Presser, Hillesum—and the secular Pole, Borowski, associate infernal images, borrowed from Christianity, with Nazism.

Borowski describes an execution in Auschwitz:

He took her by the hand and led her on, his other hand covering her eyes. The sizzling and the stench of the burning fat and the heat gushing out of the pit terrified her. She jerked back. But he gently bent her head forward, uncovering her back. At that moment the Oberscharführer fired, almost without aiming. The man pushed the woman into the flaming pit, and as she fell he heard her terrible, broken scream. (96)

Nazis make everybody think of the devil—another figment of the European religious, artistic, and literary imagination. A militant atheist, the European philosopher Jean Améry, who was tortured by the Gestapo, wrote to Simon Wiesenthal about an SS man the latter had encountered during the war: "Your SS man was a devil . . ."[8]

What seems diabolical about Nazis is that their cruelty was catching. Ringelblum obsessed about the Jewish police:

(December 12, 1942) . . . Another incident, that took place on 24 Lezno Street: A sixteen year old baker's boy beat up a [Jewish] policeman who was trying to take away the boy's mother. The boy tore the policeman's short coat. He was taken to the court-yard of the police headquarters and there given twenty-five [lashes], as a result of which he died. (334)

Tadeusz Borowski was stupefied by the institutionalized cruelty he and his fellow prisoners experienced in Auschwitz:

[Y]ou do miles of somersaults; spend hours simply rolling on the ground; you do hundreds of squat-jumps; you stand motionless for endless days and nights; you sit for a full month inside a cement coffin—the bunker; you hang from a post or a wooden pole extended between two chairs; you jump like a frog and crawl like a snake; drink bucketfuls of water until you suffocate; you are beaten with a thousand different whips and clubs, by a thousand different men. I listen avidly to tales about prisons— unknown provincial prisons like Malkini, Suwalki, Radom, Pulawy, Lublin—about the monstrously perfected techniques for torturing man, and I find it impossible to believe that all this just sprang suddenly out of somebody's head, like Minerva out of Jove's. I find it impossible to comprehend this sudden frenzy of murder, this mounting tide of unleashed atavism. (118–119)

Borowski's job was unloading trainloads of Jews to their death in gas chambers. He did that to survive the summer of 1943.

> Several other men are carrying a small girl with only one leg. They hold her by the arm and one leg. Tears are running down her face and she whispers faintly: "Sir, it hurts, it hurts . . ." They throw her on the truck on top of the corpses. She will burn alive along with them. (47)

Shortly after the war, Tadeusz Borowski turned his whole experience of Auschwitz-Birkenau and liberated Europe into a collection of short stories, *This Way for the Gas Ladies and Gentlemen.* Borowski's implicit theme is the passivity of ordinary people—like himself—faced by Nazi evil:

> Not long ago, the labor Kommandos used to march in formation when returning to camp. The band played and the passing columns kept step with its beat. One day, the [Scrap and Demolition] Kommando and many of the others—some ten thousand men—were ordered to stop and stood waiting at the gate. At that moment several trucks full of naked women rolled in . . . The women stretched out their arms and pleaded: "Save us! We are going to the gas chambers! Save us!"
> And they rolled slowly past us—the ten thousand silent men—and then disappeared from sight. Not one of us made a move, not one of us lifted a hand. (116)

In *Survival in Auschwitz*, Primo Levi writes:

> To destroy a man is difficult, almost as difficult as to create one: it has not been easy, nor quick, but you Germans have succeeded. Here we are, docile under your gaze; from our side you have nothing more to fear; no acts of violence, nor words of defiance, not even a look of judgement.[9]

He reports that prisoners in Auschwitz felt:

> an atavistic anguish whose echo one hears in the second verse of Genesis: the anguish inscribed in every one of the "tohu-bohu" of a deserted and empty universe crushed under the spirit of God but from which the spirit of man is absent, not yet born or already extinguished (*The Drowned and the Saved*, p. 85).

Right after Levi's liberation, and intermittently for the rest of his life, he suffered a recurrent dream:

I am sitting at a table with my family, or with friends, or at work, or in a green countryside . . . yet I feel a deep and subtle anguish, the definite sensation of an impending threat. And in fact, as the dream proceeds, . . . the anguish becomes more intense and more precise . . . I am alone in the center of a grey and turbid nothing, and now, I *know* what this thing means, and I also know that I have always known it; I am in the Lager once more, and nothing is true outside the Lager. All the rest was brief pause, a deception of the senses, a dream; my family, nature in flower, my home. Now this inner dream, this dream of peace, is over, and in the outer dream, which continues . . . a well-known voice resounds: a single word, not imperious, but brief and subdued. It is the dawn command of Auschwitz, a foreign word, feared and expected: get up, "Wstawàch."[10]

Primo Levi eventually jumped to his death down a stairwell. Tadeusz Borowski gassed himself in his Warsaw apartment. Emmanuel Ringelblum was shot to death by the Gestapo among the ruins of the Warsaw Ghetto. Etty Hillesum was gassed in Auschwitz; Anne Frank died of typhus in Bergen-Belsen. Of the six writers whose work I discuss, only Jacob Presser died of natural causes.

The prose each wrote endures because it was beautifully written. The collected works of these six writers constitute a major contribution to twentieth-century European literature. They rank among the best of a new multilingual, European literary genre—Holocaust literature—with its unprecedented subject matter, modern Europe's volitional descent back through its own Dark Ages and the chaos preceding its creation—into the pit.

Hillesum, Presser, Ringelblum, Borowski, and Levi each grasped that civilized Germans were committing what Levi termed, in *The Drowned and the Saved*, "the greatest crime in the history of humanity."[11]

And it slowly dawned on each that the criminals were systematically incriminating their victims: along with physical genocide, the Germans had invented a wholly new kind of crime.

Why?

Seeking some answer, Primo Levi quotes from an interview by Gitta Sereny with Franz Stangl, the imprisoned ex-commandant of Treblinka:

(Sereny) "Considering that you were going to kill them all . . . what was the point of the humiliations, the cruelties?"

(Stangl) "To condition those who were to be the material executors of the operations. To make it possible for them to do what they were doing." (125–126)

Levi: "In other words, before dying the victim must be degraded, so that the murderer will be less burdened by guilt" (126).

The mid-twentieth-century European writers Anne Frank, Etty Hillesum, Jacob Presser, Tadeusz Borowski, and Primo Levi dealt in their work with a unique historical calamity. The Holocaust was entirely mind-made: it realized crackpot anti-Semitic fantasies, rooted in Christianity. Adolph Hitler wrote in *Mein Kampf*:

> [B]y defending myself against the Jew, I am fighting for the work of the Lord.[12]

To Hitler, the whole existence of Jews embodied a protest against the aesthetics of the Lord's image. An artistic, crazed former Catholic and his fellow Germans literally made Europe a hell on earth for millions of Jews. The writers were only six among many civilized Europeans—gentile and Jew—in the power of armed and disciplined hordes of homicidal fanatics, whose murderous frenzy was contagious. The six responded with measured sanity by writing clearly and concisely about their encounter with an unimaginable reality. Frank wrote in an attic, Hillesum a barracks, Ringelblum a bunker.

Ringelblum, ever the objective historian, mentioned himself once or twice in the third person. The others relentlessly explored their inner lives. Jacob Presser, also a historian, turned to fiction to plumb the psychology of a Jewish SS man. All six writers were artists who had the mysterious ability to make images out of words. The clarity and concision of their sentences which convey those images will re-create their experience of the Holocaust in the minds of readers for generations to come. How they wrote such beautiful prose while contemplating such evil, I can't say.

Notes

1. Anne Frank, *Anne Frank, the Diary of a Young Girl*, trans. Susan Massotty (New York: Doubleday, 1995), 34.

2. Etty Hillesum, *Letters from Westerbork* (New York: Pantheon Books, 1986), 146.

3. Etty Hillesum, *An Interrrupted Life, the Diaries of Etty Hillesum* (New York: Pantheon Books, 1981), 116.

4. Tadeusz Borowski, *This Way for the Gas Ladies and Gentlemen* (New York: Penguin Books, 1976), 180.

5. Emmanuel Ringelblum, *Notes from the Warsaw Ghetto: The Journal of Emmanuel Ringelblum*, ed. and trans. Jacob Sloan (New York: Schocken Books, 1958), 5; he always refers to the Germans as "The Others" or "They"—a subject in itself.

6. Jacob Presser, *The Destruction of the Dutch Jews*, trans. by Arnold Pomerans (New York: E. P. Dutton, 1969), 418–419.

7. Jacob [Jacques] Presser, *The Night of the Girondists* (London: Harvill, 1992), 3.

8. Simon Wiesenthal, *The Sunflower* (New York: Schocken Books, 1998), 109.

9. Primo Levi, *Survival in Auschwitz* (New York: Collier Books, 1993), 150.

10. Primo Levi, *Survival in Auschwitz and The Reawakening: Two Memoirs* (New York: Summit, 1985), 373. Italics in original.

11. Primo Levi, *The Drowned and the Saved* (New York: Summit Books, 1986), 14.

12. Adolph Hitler, *Mein Kampf*, trans. Ralph Manheim (Boston: Houghton Mifflin, 1971), 65. Italics in original.

Works Cited

Borowski, Tadeusz. *This Way for the Gas Ladies and Gentlemen*. New York: Penguin Books, 1976.

Frank, Anne. *Anne Frank, the Diary of a Young Girl*. Trans. Susan Massotty. New York: Doubleday, 1996.

Hillesum, Etty. *An Interrupted Life, the Diaries of Etty Hillesum*. New York: Washington Square Press, 1981.

———. *Letters from Westerbork*. New York: Pantheon Books, 1986.

Hitler, Adolph. *Mein Kampf*. Trans. Ralph Manheim. Boston: Houghton Mifflin, 1971.

Levi, Primo. *The Drowned and the Saved*. New York: Summit Books, 1986.

———. *Survival in Auschwitz*. New York: Collier Books, 1993.

———. *Survival in Auschwitz and the Reawakening: Two Memoirs*. New York: Summit Books, 1985.

Presser, Jacob. *The Destruction of the Dutch Jews*. Trans. Arnold Pomerans. New York: E.P. Dutton, 1969.

Presser, Jacob [Jacques]. *The Night of the Girondists*. London: Harvill, 1992.

Ringelblum, Emmanuel. *Notes from the Warsaw Ghetto: The Journal of Emmanuel Ringelblum*. Ed. and trans. Jacob Sloan. New York: Schocken Books, 1958.

Wiesenthal, Simon. *The Sunflower*. New York: Schocken Books, 1998.

5

⚬❈⚬

Memory and Collective Identity: Narrative Strategies Against Forgetting in Contemporary Literary Responses to the Holocaust

GERHARD BACH

A story provides a structure for our perceptions; only through stories do facts assume any meaning whatsoever.[1]

At the outset of *The Bellarosa Connection* (1989), Saul Bellow's treatment of Holocaust survival in the context of memory and forgetting, the narrator, looking back on his professional life as a kind of historian of twentieth-century consciousness, pronounces that "if you have worked in memory, which is life itself, there is no retirement except in death."[2] Bellow here expresses what Alvin Rosenfeld, in a very different context and with a different agenda in mind, had said some ten years earlier in his treatise on Holocaust literature, *A Double Dying* (1980), where he demands that post-Holocaust generations develop a phenomenology of reading Holocaust literature. In generating mind maps, Rosenfeld suggests, such a phenomenology would help readers—particularly of the younger generation—"to comprehend the writings of the victims, the survivors, the survivors-who-became-victims, and the kinds-of-survivors, those who were never there but know more than the outlines of the place."[3]

This essay deals with four fictions by writers who were never "there" but reveal that they do know more about "the place" than its outlines. Thus, in terms of objectives, my one purpose is to illustrate how literary texts may induce readers to generate the kind of mental maps or models Rosenfeld suggests. A cursory reading of these texts will reveal the obvious—namely that such models will vary greatly from one text to the next, and more markedly from one generation of Holocaust writers to the next. Such insight raises more questions than it answers: What possibilities are there to add further detail to the individual mental maps we create? More important, where can we identify "boundaries" between specific groups or generations of Holocaust writers and how do we deal with these boundaries—as markers of separation or of connection? Answering questions such as these takes us from Rosenfeld's phenomenology to Alan L. Berger's taxonomy of universalist and particularist literary approaches to the Holocaust, an approach by which Berger classifies second-generation American Jewish writers, revealing how particularist and universalist patterns function in *current* Holocaust fictional texts. Addressing these issues demands structural focalization, and here three parameters or dimensions are important: the aesthetic, the material, and the methodological.

The first parameter relates to the aesthetic dimension invoked by Adorno's dictum that to write poetry after Auschwitz is barbaric, and the forceful insistence of post-Holocaust literature and art on dislodging Adorno's position. In the wake of Adorno's thesis, the debate over the possibility or impossibility of rendering the atavistic in artistic terms basically has always been conducted as a moral debate. However, the second generation of Holocaust writers, in dealing with what is best summarized as the "aesthetics of disfigurement" (Gila Safran Naveh), have expanded this notion in a twofold way, in connecting the moral issue of Holocaust remembrance (and its artistic modes of expression) with a postmodern discourse that now includes, besides the victims and survivors of the Holocaust, its perpetrators and collaborators as well. In other words, in generating mental maps of Holocaust literature we are now also faced with the question of how to deal, in aesthetic terms, with the "nature of the offense" (Primo Levi). As Martin Amis reminds us in the afterword to *Time's Arrow* (1991), a novel revolving around the issue Levi raises, "The offense was unique, not in its cruelty, nor in its cowardice, but in its style— in its combination of the atavistic and the modern."[4]

The second parameter is defined by the literature selected for this study: Cynthia Ozick's *The Shawl* (1990), Saul Bellow's *The Bellarosa Connection* (1989), Irene Dische's *Pious Secrets* (1991), and Martin Amis's *Time's Arrow* (1991). The reasons for this selection are external and internal. The obvious fact is that these are four fictional texts about the Holocaust all published at about the same time, between 1989 and 1991.[5] In this sense, these works form a coherent group of late-twentieth-century responses to the Holocaust. This external coherence is counterbalanced by some complex internal dissimilarities. First, while Ozick and Bellow belong to the older generation of Jewish American writers, those that are usually grouped as contemporaneous witnesses of the Holocaust who tend to foreground the victims' position, Dische and Amis are representative of second-generation voices projecting perpetrator positions. Second, while Ozick's and Bellow's religious roots in the Jewish tradition are distinct (notwithstanding Bellow's repeated cautionary self-distancing), Dische's and Amis's are not.

The third parameter contextualizes a question that has gained prominence with the increasing diversity of artistic modes of representation, namely how to study the Holocaust as narrative. Which approaches do we espouse in connecting to its geographical, historical, and theological dimensions on the one hand and its creative literary dimensions on the other? Here the current critical focus is directed at the apparent shift in narrative objectives (and techniques) reflecting a shift in the writers' self-positioning in relationship to the Holocaust as an artistic domain.

Since these three parameters constitute major concerns of literary and critical responses to the Holocaust at large, my purpose here is not to reinvestigate territory that has been more than amply covered. Instead, I intend to show that after half a century the Holocaust as a literary topos has begun to generate a new focus. Traditionally, Holocaust writers have been concerned with portraying strategies against forgetting as a moral imperative for their own and future generations. This desire to bear witness has not, as might be expected, slackened with the younger generation of writers, those whose own lives have been shaped by the Holocaust as narrative, that is, by indirect—but no less impressive—means of testimony or witness. Second-generation Holocaust writers and artists thus clearly illustrate Neil Postman's notion that a cultural or religious identity remains unstructured, fuzzy, as long as there is an absence of story. Postman explains that human existence is made meaningful not through facts and the ability to "apply" them but through stories: stories not in the epic sense, but rather "the more profound stories that people, nations, religions, and disciplines unfold in order to make sense out of the world." He concludes, "Without stories as organizing frameworks we are swamped by the volume of our own experience, adrift in a sea of facts."[6]

The validity of Postman's observation in our context is made clear as we witness the widening range of fiction defining, for our age, the patterns of identity formation through acts of remembering. Alan Berger makes this situation the center of his conclusive study of second-generation literary responses to the Holocaust, *Children of Job* (1997). Berger's division of second-generation Holocaust literature into *particularist* and *universalist* branches, while not unusual as such, is an especially helpful distinguishing feature in structuring a literary and cultural spectrum expanding by leaps and bounds.[7] Embracing the theological distinction of the two types of *tikkun* (repair, improvement, perfection), Berger finds ample evidence of the distinct and yet interdependent views individual writers of the second generation have projected.

Those who travel the particularist path put God on trial (din Torah), abandon the Sinai Covenant while seeking to find an adequate alternative, deal with theodicy within a specifically Jewish context, and raise the issue of Jewish-Christian relations. The particularists seek a tikkun atzmi (mending or repair) of the self. . . . Those who travel the second path, that of Jewish universalism, seek to articulate universal lessons emerging from the Holocaust. The universalists do not abandon Jewish specificity, but strive for tikkun olam, the moral improvement or repair of the world, and struggle against all forms of prejudice and racism, ranging from antisemitism to homophobia. This tikkun consists of a mission to build a moral society.[8]

While Berger concentrates his study on the theological dimension of witnessing (and its impact on identity formation of the post-Holocaust second generation), the direction this essay takes is different in that it concentrates on comparing narrative strategies employed by older *and* younger writers in order to distinguish how strategies against forgetting are being changed under the influence of modernist and postmodernist perspectives. The four fictions discussed below make apparent that the universalist position espoused by the "traditionalists" (here Ozick and Bellow) is counterbalanced by the particularist view of the Shoah prevalent among the "revisionists" (here Dische and Amis). The objection that might be raised against my reading of Berger's approach is that his frame of reference is distinctly within the boundaries of second-generation American writers of Jewish descent, while my study also includes writers on the religious and cultural periphery of this spectrum. The issues connected with delimiting or expanding our horizons to exclude or include certain writers must remain open here; it is worthwhile, however, to investigate the possibilities inherent in including among one's critical observations writers who, for want of a better term, are "ethnically outside" but "ethically inside" this spectrum.[9]

When Adorno said, "Nach Auschwitz ein Gedicht zu schreiben ist barbarisch," he expressed an existentialist doubt pervasive among German postwar intellectuals, namely that after Auschwitz art could no longer be considered to have any redemptive quality. Adorno's concern is that the "aesthetic" value of art is dependent on its impulse to generate pleasure in those who "consume" it. Once the Holocaust is made the object of aesthetic pleasure it is perverted, the materiality of its horrifying singularity being elevated to an aesthetic experience. Thus the barbarity of the crimes committed against the Jews continue to be legitimized. Individual suffering is transfigured into an aesthetic universal event. Ezrahi reminds us that Adorno's assertion was made "in the context of a discussion of 'engaged' versus 'autonomous' literature," a debate giving rise to a further concern of "whether the cultural and social degeneration that culminated in Auschwitz commands a literature that is commensurately degenerate."[10]

In Adorno's view, art after Auschwitz cannot but betray the victims. The argument, however, also implies that our generation cannot permit itself to let things rest: the "abundance of suffering permits no forgetting."[11] In fairness to both, Adorno and the issue at hand, this adamant rejection of the redemptive quality and function of art is later modified by Adorno himself as he progressively accepts Camus's resolve that "to talk of despair is to conquer it." It is necessary to bear in mind that the general dispute over Adorno has remained an open issue, and that it will continue to focus our attention on positioning the Holocaust artist in two distinct ways: either as submitting to the cruel facts of history or as conquering them. Ezrahi's comment of the early 1980s still is a valid focus in an ongoing discourse:

> The writer's very effort to "communicate," even within a system
> of altered perceptions, to account for the violence that had been
> committed on the notions of personal and collective survival, on
> moral and ethical values, and on aesthetic traditions which serve
> a continuity of cultural perspectives, is one mark of his trust in
> certain linkages between the past and the future.[12]

The four books briefly discussed below illustrate four different ways of communicating the Holocaust. Cynthia Ozick's *The Shawl* (1989) is a stringent example of Irving Howe's demand that Holocaust fiction communicate to the reader both the external Auschwitz (factual events and experiences) and the internal Auschwitz (individual suffering, coping with memories). Irving Howe's comment, as much a response to as an extension of Adorno, that the distinguishing feature of Holocaust writing is the presentation of facts that have either been recorded or are remembered by witnesses, applies here. What Howe praises in Elie Wiesel's narratives—the writer's unindulgent approach to his or her subject—basically can be claimed for *The Shawl* as well. The combination of two individual narratives set apart by thirty years into one combined narrative seals event to memory, whereby remembering becomes an experience excruciatingly parallel to the witnessing of the actual events themselves. In the first story, "Rosa," Rosa Lubin is forced to witness her daughter's slaughter by a concentration camp guard. In "The Shawl," the same woman is shown thirty years later, living in a rundown Miami boardinghouse for the "retired." She has moved there after destroying her antique store in New York, a store specializing in mirrors—"obsessive" mirrors in a transliteral sense that *reflect* and *refract* memories in traumatizing ways. The act of destruction, however, does not have the desired effect. Haunted by the trauma of memory, Rosa escapes into an illusionary world where she and her daughter may live a life without the harrowing memories of Auschwitz and the continuing harassment of a Floridian Auschwitz-on-the-beach. The controlling metaphor of both narratives is the shawl. In the first, it gives sustenance to the small child but also inadvertently contributes to her destruction. In the second, it returns the magic to Rosa's life in joining mother and daughter in a dreamworld of happy memories, but also contributes to Rosa's estrangement from the world around her. In a final act of despair, where Auschwitz memories mingle with dreams of escape and a general hatred of the world, Rosa buries her telephone in the shawl, wishing to cut herself off from the encroaching present. Yet in this situation, as in the ones before, the shawl's power of sustenance wins over Rosa's self-destructive despair.

The context of *The Shawl* is established by way of juxtaposition: the first part is a chilling testimony of individual life forces struggling against the stupefying dominance of evil. The narrative itself is chilling also, an unrelenting "icy" demonstration and documentation of events in the concentrationary universe. In contrast to the emotional despair culminating in a frozen scream of horror, the second part, set in the scorching heat of Miami, is highly charged by emotive responses of aggression. Here Rosa finds a voice to express frustration, anger, and disbelief. The central scene is set in a beach resort—fenced with barbed wire, gates that allow you in but won't let you out—an alien and lawless world with all the signatures of an Auschwitz revived. Locked behind barbed wire once more, Rosa's trauma of despair comes full circle. In a scene of bearing witness that is charged with terrible ironies, Rosa confronts the hotel manager and testifies to him her disgust and utter revolt at the world's uncaring attitude about those that suffered. It is a testimony forced out of her in circumstances that reveal a gruesome pattern: having escaped the physical imprisonment of the concentration camp has brought Rosa to psychic self-imprisonment, first in New York and now in Florida.

Ozick's tale moves within the sphere of Holocaust survivors' narratives whose psychological scars are deep and likely to be torn apart again at any given moment. While Ozick offers a strain of hope at the end of her narrative, it is a hope scarred by uncertainty. Ozick's tale is representational of survivors' tales in Howe's sense. It works with the psychology of survival through memory and forgetting as agents of representation. In choosing such an approach, Ozick particularizes events and experiences and expresses their continuous destructive impact on the individual's psyche. Narratives of this type concentrate on the *particular* importance of Holocaust literary testimonies, and in doing so they are bound to the evidence they provide. Their stress is on the *story as event*. While this is one direction a major segment of modernist fiction has moved in, there is another direction whose impulse is to shift from *story* (as event) to storyteller. Even in *The Shawl* itself, a shift in this direction is noticeable as Ozick moves from its first part ("Rosa") to its second ("The Shawl"). This is a move from brute external forces, a realm where there is no "Why?," to the realm of fragile and delicate internal motives, where "Why?" becomes the force generating the suffering subject's fear and anger. If we are to follow Ozick in her choice of a positive ending of her narrative, this indicates that the author is implicitly initiating a move from matter (the story as event) to voice (the storyteller).

Bellow's *The Bellarosa Connection* (1989) exemplifies such a move rather dramatically. The novella exemplifies that the shift from story to storyteller implies a shift from objectifying testimony to subjectified witness. At the outset of Bellow's novella, the position of the narrator is projected as that of an observer and a witness, a position he would like to retire from after having made it a successful business. "Now that I am retired, with the Institute in the capable hands of my son, I would like to *forget* about remembering"—which, Bellow is quick to assure us, is "an Alice-in-Wonderland proposition" (Bellow, *Bellarosa*, 1-2).

The events of the narrative revolve around the rescue of Harry Fonstein from Nazi Germany, an operation masterminded by Billy Rose, the legendary 1930s Broadway producer. After his arrival in New York, Fonstein wishes to express his gratitude to his liberator and—just once—shake his hand. Rose refuses. In refusing to acknowledge Fonstein as an individual Holocaust victim, Rose denies him an existence after what would have been certain death in the Shoah: "[Harry Fonstein] . . . the man you saved in Rome—one of them. He wrote so many letters. I can't believe you don't remember," Fonstein's wife pleads with Billy Rose, whose brazenly direct answer comes with deadly force: "Remember, forget—what's the difference to me? . . . Lady, this is one of a trillion incidents in a life like mine. Why should I recollect it?" (53). Eventually, Fonstein dies without having gained the recognition of his "benefactor" whose refusal to remember perpetuates Fonstein's death-in-life situation, a situation not even the rescue from certain death in the concentration camp can remedy.

In this sense, Ozick's and Bellow's survivors find themselves in one and the same situation: they are refused recognition for who they are and what their personal history signifies. They are refused an existential need—to be acknowledged in their plea to bear their testimony. Thus both once more become one of the nameless. The difference in Bellow's novella is that protagonist and narrator are no longer one and the same person. Bellow separates event, memory, witness, and narrative voice. The narrator in *The Bellarosa Connection*, while not second generation himself (he is of about the same age as the Fonsteins, and the events are situated in the year 1959), nevertheless is positioned by Bellow to assume a second-generation narrative stance. Psychically and emotionally removed from the events experienced by the Fonsteins, the observer merely recounts what he sees and remembers, and thus functions as a historical link between the event recounted and our "reading" of the event. The distance thus created results in a shift of the reader's response in no uncertain moral terms: as readers we are called upon to respond not just to the facts laid bare before our eyes but to the underlying human qualities and sensibilities without which such facts would remain meaningless.

What Bellow does here is to create, as a strategy against forgetting, a *double witnessing* situation. The narrator witnesses the act of de-individuation, by way of denial, of a human being whose existence depends on the permission to bear witness. In establishing this complex basis of a double bind, Bellow not only projects the universal in individual victimization, he also projects as universal the impossibility of individual or collective salvation. This is representative of the response to the universalist position that Terrence De Pres speaks of when he points to the impossibility of innocence after Auschwitz: "To be in the world but not of it, to recover innocence after Auschwitz, plainly, will not work."[13] In presenting a narrator who initially is quite naive about this situation and only gradually, by way of repeated "exposure" to the subjective nature of "facts," begins to realize the essence of memory, Bellow impersonates in his narrator (who remains nameless) the premises of a universalist response to the Holocaust.

Irene Dische and Martin Amis take a distinctly different approach to writing about the Holocaust in deconstructing its historicity. As Spiegelman or Lanzman have done in their work, Dische and Amis also blur the lines of history as fact and artifact. Their point in writing Holocaust fiction is to remove actual or perceived barriers between the (fictional) witnesses of the factual Holocaust and the contemporary readers' mimetic conception of it. In Ozick's and Bellow's fictions the past remains "safely" in the past, whereas in Dische's and Amis's novels the barriers are removed. Functionally, these narratives make an appeal to the reader to serve as implicit—and to a certain extent even complicit—*collaborateurs* in the mental reconstruction of Holocaust realities.

Irene Dische is an American writer living in Germany. Her Jewish background, little of which has been disclosed, appears to be ephemeral. After doing fieldwork in anthropology and obtaining a degree from Harvard University, she settles in Berlin in the early 1980s. *Pious Secrets* (1991) is her first novel. Ironically, it was first issued in German translation (*Fromme Lügen*, 1989), and only two years later, in 1991, the original English version was published. The novel is set in the New York of the 1980s. The main locale is a morgue where a group of doctors go about their business of dissecting and patching up bodies. Dr. Ronald Hake's personal interest in his female colleague Dr. Connie Bauer takes (a) the usual turn of an everyday affair and (b) an unusual turn in an unexpected discovery. After a diligent and lengthy "scientific" medical examination of the physical features of Carl Bauer, Dr. Bauer's aging father, supplemented by a "historical" investigation into the family background of the Bauers, Dr. Hake discovers ample "evidence" to conclude that old Bauer actually is Hitler hiding away in retirement in the unsuspecting outskirts of New York. He then leaks his "information" to the *National Enquirer*, which laps up the story. The Bauer home is beleaguered by reporters, and old Bauer suffers a heart attack and dies. A simple narrative of little surprise value were it not for the fact that in the end Connie Bauer, in Hake's presence, reveals to her children a long-hidden truth: it turns out that the Bauers had escaped the German concentration camps by "discarding" their identities and their religion as European Jews to become "devout" American Catholics.

At the end of the novel, the reader is forced to witness his or her own process of deception in the reading process, since it is Dr. Hake who tells the story. Hake's "discoveries" gradually lead the reader to discover truths that undercut actual events. We begin to see in the morgue a station for medical experimentation, the doctors (all their names are German or German-sounding) turn into modern day Mengeles, probings into science turn out to be thinly veiled ideologies of supremacy, and we witness how unsuspecting individuals are made into the scapegoats of national paranoia and xenophobia. In a further twist of Nazi logic, the victim of the Holocaust is forced to become his own victimizer, and Dische shows how the process can be made to appear quite "reasonable," and how easily it can be facilitated in the United States today. The Holocaust is happening here and now, and we all carry it along, hidden somewhere in our subconscious as a "pious secret."

By repositioning the Holocaust in the New World and placing it squarely within the American psyche, Dische presents yet another complex reversal relating to the novel's narrative structure. What appears to the reader as a disturbingly "logical" revivification of Hitler reveals the author's rejection of any remaining universalist notions of *tikkun olam*, or the moral improvement or repair of the world. Dr. Hake, the pedantic moralist of perfection, forces on Bauer—the Jew turned Catholic—a further identity, this time a particular, identifiable, and representational identity—that of his own destroyer. Carl Bauer's example reveals a loss to which, Dische suggests, no alternative exists for the post-Holocaust generation.

Here, too, albeit in reversed form, the Holocaust continues its destructive course. There is a striking parallel here to the concept of memory making, by which a presence is created where otherwise there would be an absence. Dische reverses this process; not the children of the Holocaust but their oppressors are the ones to apply this strategy. The wheel of persecution continues to turn. In this context, De Pres's observation about the impossibility of innocence after the Shoah gains added meaning. Former German chancellor Helmut Kohl, in defending the postwar generation's innocence—"the blessings of a late birth" as he would have it—expressed a naiveté which borders on silent complicity in much the same way as Dische's educated Americans' innocence does. The blessedness of simple daily being, as De Pres would call it, is denied to post-Holocaust generations.

Such innocence of simple daily being is the vantage point from which Martin Amis's novel *Time's Arrow* (1991) takes its cue. The principle of reversed or misapplied notions of history and reality applies here, too. The novel begins with the death of Tod Friendly, a medical doctor, recently retired. The narrator of the person's history, about to unfold, is Tod's "observer soul," an alternate self incarnated into Tod's body at his moment of death. This second self now experiences Tod's life in backward motion, in time reversed. The narrative thus traces Tod's life back to his birth, revealing a most sinister personal and yet representative history. The observer soul himself is capable of sensory impressions and certain emotional responses, including aesthetic judgment, but what he lacks is Tod's consciousness and Tod's memory. Thus he observes and relates all events in forward narration as they reel backward in the life of Tod Friendly. Biophysical processes, for example, are thus experienced by the observer soul in the following manner: "[Y]ou select a soiled dish, collect some scraps from the garbage, and settle down for a short wait. Various items get gulped up into my mouth, and after skillful massage with tongue and teeth I transfer them to the plate for additional sculpture with knife and fork and spoon" (Amis, *Time's Arrow*, 11). The food items, neatly shaped, are then packaged and taken to the supermarket in exchange for money. To the observer soul, the world thus appears to be always (re)constructing itself from individual parts to the whole.

The reader follows the observer soul into Tod Friendly's past, moves with him through several name changes and localities from New York to Portugal, Italy, and Austria, and finally arrives as Odilo Unverdorben at Auschwitz where Tod ("Death") Unverdorben ("Unspoiled," "Innocent") works as one of the doctors in charge of medical experiments. As readers on this journey in reverse we are reconstructing into a forward chronology events the observer soul relates in reversed narrative. We are thus constantly on our guard, checking the observer soul's innocence against our own better knowledge. We witness how Tod's soul progresses into the doctor's disremembered past and thus allows us to gradually reconstitute memory. In other words, Tod's past is the soul's future, into which, however, the soul cannot look. The soul judges on the basis of its own past, which is the doctor's future.

This reversal has stunning consequences as we approach, along with the unsuspecting observer soul, the death camps of Auschwitz. The observer soul experiences the death camps as places where life is created from waste. The brutal murder and obscene experiments in which Tod/Odilo are involved are witnessed and described by the narrator in the same undisturbed, often cheerful manner—a manner unburdened by memory—as other everyday incidents in Tod's previous (the soul's later) life. What the observer soul witnesses at Auschwitz is the creation of a people: "Our preternatural purpose? To dream a race. To make a people from the weather. From thunder and from lightning. With gas, with electricity, with shit, with fire" (120). Bodies are brought to the operating table from heaps outside, Tod extracts poison from them with a syringe, and they spring into life. To the reader, who "knows," the narrative becomes increasingly objectionable to witness, while Amis continues to reveal how the observer soul learns about what he thinks is the blessed realm of the concentrationary universe. "I saw the old Jew struggle to the surface of the deep latrine, how he splashed and struggled into life, and was hoisted out by the jubilant guards, his clothes cleansed by the mire." The observer soul is jubilant as he thus witnesses hundreds of Jews coming to life everyday: "The Jews are my children and I love them . . . and only wish them to exist, and flourish, and to have their right to life and love" (152). This is the innocent message the ignorant observer soul sends out to the knowing reader, who cannot but witness time's arrow following its predetermined course.

The soul's growth is presented by Amis with painful clarity. Since the entire book is written "backward," the reader keeps reconstructing the narrated events into their "rightful" order. The conscious mind and memory enforce a constant shifting of reversed time into forward time. The reader also witnesses the soul's growth with painful reproach. The major reason is that, in its innocence, the soul describes in lighthearted and often humorous ways the events observed, events which we *know* or *remember* as horrible, degrading, beyond the human. But this is precisely what Amis intends with the reversal of time in *Time's Arrow*: to disallow us to review the Holocaust once more with sensitivities schooled by previous exposure to Holocaust facts or texts. The logocentric universe—abysmally perfected at Auschwitz— is dislodged because its historical chronology has been dislodged. In establishing a double directionality of time, Amis creates temporal duplicity, the backward timeline taking us to the utter particularities and minute details of the death camps, while the forward teaches us its universalist message.

We are part of the forward/backward timeline as we accompany Observer Soul/Tod in approaching/returning to the minuscule world of perfected construction/destruction. However, we only see detail and not the master plan behind it as long as we "trust" the observer's narrative. The master plan unravels only in our constant reconstruction of the forward timeline. To do this, *our* memory needs to be consciously employed. In terms of narrative strategy, forgetting and innocence (the backward timeline of events narrated) are counteracted by memory and knowledge (the forward timeline of the reader's conscious constructionist efforts).

How then, do we compensate for what we *know* to be the novel's terrible revelations to the observer soul—the notion suggested that what we witness is the creation of the Jews amid a coprocentric universe? Sara Horowitz suggests a recourse to Walter Benjamin. The desire of the observer soul to create appears to be the same as the redemptive desire of Walter Benjamin's "angel of death," who also has his powers of observation directed to the past. Both Amis's observer soul and Benjamin's angel of death share the aspiration "to reverse temporal movement, to undo history, and to reconstitute the wreckage into its original wholeness."[14] For Horowitz, this is where the comparison ends: while the observer soul is permitted to move about freely in his pastward course, Benjamin's angel of death is irresistibly propelled toward the future. He can only witness destruction; he cannot intervene. He is denied the possibility to undo the course of history. Horowitz's observation, while valid, is not quite conclusive. As suggested above, the observer soul is bound in his course of reversed actions, too, which—unbeknownst to him—has been predetermined by Tod's previous actions. He, too, thus is forced to witness, bound to follow. The two are one in the sense that past and future cannot exist outside the time continuum. The observer soul is unable to look into his own future as long as Tod/Odilo is unable/unwilling to remember his past. Here Amis projects the notion that the possibility of a future for humankind hinges upon our capability and readiness to remember. In this respect, the observer soul suffers as much (and pays as dearly) as Benjamin's angel of death.

Reading Dische and Amis against Ozick and Bellow implies redefining the criteria that constitute contemporary second- or third-generation literary testimony of the Holocaust. The traditional approach seems no longer appropriate for the study of such novels since the moral imperative expected from them is lacking. Nelly Sachs's statement that the literature of the Holocaust can be written only "with one eye ripped out" (25) gains new momentum when applied to second-generation Holocaust narratives since, as we have seen, these narratives demand from their readers definitive constructionist efforts. Unless reality is created from the text, the world remains what Amis, in quoting from Bellow's *The Dean's December* (1982), has called the "moronic inferno." If we engage in the reading process as a cocreative effort, then Sachs's metaphor expands to include the reader as well: "If . . . one *writes* Holocaust texts with only one eye, one also *reads* them with one eye, the other trained, as it were, on the events itself" (Horowitz, 26).

Contemporary criticism thus shifts its focus, now to include also "the uses and abuses of memory, the ideologically differing underpinnings of all representations of the Shoah" (Horowitz, 26). Memory is no longer just an agent, either transporting us back to the Holocaust or transporting the Holocaust into our present, nor is it any longer an individual strategy against forgetting to preserve history. Memory has become agent and object in one. As object it can be abused, as Dische demonstrates with Dr. Hake in *Pious Secrets*. As agent, it can be deconstructed and then reconstructed, as Amis does in the observer soul's narrative in *Time's Arrow*. Implying the individual reader in such constructions of reality, second-generation writers demand of us that we no longer observe and empathize but that we activate our own strategies against forgetting and construct meaning out of memory. To do just that would be a first step in generating a phenomenology of reading Holocaust literature in the context Alvin Rosenfeld demands. It would also assist us in resolving, for our own time, the dichotomy of particularist and universalist conceptualizations of the Holocaust.

The post-Holocaust, end-of-the-twentieth-century generation's relationship to the event itself has become tangential, a fact that has been emphasized more forcefully in the recent criticism on the tradition of Holocaust literature. The second- or third-generation writer touches the sphere of the historical Holocaust but rarely tends to invade it. Examples of such a tangential relationship abound at the end of the twentieth century. Thane Rosenbaum's *Elijah Visible* (1996), for instance, is a touching, often comedic psychological revaluation of his generation's idea of being Jewish in a post-Holocaust world. It is, like many other works of this generation, a self-referential portrait suggestive of where the post-Holocaust generation of American Jews wishes to be situated. Anne Michael's stunningly poetic memory, *Fugitive Pieces* (1996), while paying tribute to child survivors and their saviors and benefactors, portrays memory as a burden haunting those who should best be able to keep it alive—if not historians and archaeologists, then storytellers, poets, and artists. A further variation of this paradigm is Melvin Bukiet's *After* (1996), which forces us back into the concentrationary universe of Auschwitz and at the same time makes that world the apocalyptic here-and-now of our age. Contemporary narrative strategies against forgetting thus are stringently forceful antidotes to an otherwise rampant culture of obliviousness.

Notes

1. Neil Postman, "Learning by Story," *Atlantic Monthly* (December 1989): 121–124.

2. Saul Bellow, *The Bellarosa Connection* (Harmondsworth: Penguin, 1989), 2.

3. Alvin H. Rosenfeld, *A Double Dying: Reflections on Holocaust Literature* (Bloomington: Indiana University Press, 1980), 19.

4. Martin Amis, *Time's Arrow* (New York: Viking, 1991), 168.

5. *The Shawl* consists of two stories individually published, "Rosa" in 1980, and "The Shawl" in 1983. Critical opinions vary as to why Ozick decided to bind them together into a single work. I support Marianne Friedrich's position as put forward in her essay included in this volume, that the two stories are not only thematically tied to each other but that the linkage serves a narrative purpose as well. In combining the two, Ozick achieves a move from external (narrative as event) to internal (narrative as memory) storytelling, or, in Berger's terms, from universalism to particularism.

6. Postman, "Learning by Story," 123.

7. See the special section "The Jewish Literary Revival," *Tikkun* 12, no. 6 (1997), ed. Thane Rosenbaum. The articles by Morris Dickstein, pp. 33–36, and Mark Shechner, pp. 39–41, are particularly useful for this context.

8. Alan L. Berger, *Children of Job: American Second-Generation Witnesses to the Holocaust* (Albany: State University of New York Press, 1997), 4.

9. In an interview with Will Self, Amis comments on his "ethical Jewishness," stressing two factors in particular: "I'm a very definite philo-semite. My first love was Jewish. That's as formative as things get. I do like this kind of heightened intelligence, this tendency towards transcendentalism, which one associates with Jews. . . . The other thing I like is the promiscuity of verbal and social registers. So that the high and the low mix easily together. That's very attractive to me." Will Self, "An Interview with Martin Amis," *The Mississippi Review* 21 (October 1993): 3, 160.

10. Sidra Dekoven Ezrahi, *By Words Alone: The Holocaust in Literature* (Chicago: University of Chicago Press, 1980), 6–7.

11. Adorno, quoted in Ezrahi, *By Words Alone*, 7.

12. Ezrahi, *By Words Alone*, 7.

13. De Pres, quoted in Berger, *Children of Job*, 7. Terrence De Pres, "The Dreaming Back," *Centerpoint* 4.13 (1980): 13.

14. Sara R. Horowitz, *Voicing the Void: Muteness and Memory in Holocaust Fiction*, SUNY Series in Modern Jewish Literature and Culture (Albany: State University of New York Press, 1997), 194.

Works Cited

Amis, Martin. *Time's Arrow*. New York: Viking, 1991.

Bellow, Saul. *The Bellarosa Connection*. Harmondsworth: Penguin, 1989.

Berger, Alan L. *Children of Job: American Second-Generation Witnesses to the Holocaust*. Albany: State University of New York Press, 1997.

De Pres, Terrence. "The Dreaming Back." *Centerpoint* 4, no. 13 (1980): 13.

Dische, Irene. *Pious Secrets*. London: Bloomsbury, 1991.

Ezrahi, Sidra Dekoven. *By Words Alone: The Holocaust in Literature*. Chicago: University of Chicago Press, 1980.

Horowitz, Sara R. *Voicing the Void: Muteness and Memory in Holocaust Fiction*. SUNY Series in Modern Jewish Literature and Culture. Albany: State University of New York Press, 1997.

Ozick, Cynthia. *The Shawl*. New York: Vintage, 1990.

Postman, Neil. "Learning by Story." *Atlantic Monthly* (December 1989): 121–124.

Rosenfeld, Alvin H. *A Double Dying: Reflections on Holocaust Literature*. Bloomington: Indiana University Press, 1980.

Self, Will. "An Interview with Martin Amis." *The Mississippi Review* 21 (October 1993): 3, 143–169.

6

The Rendition of Memory
in Cynthia Ozick's "The Shawl"

Marianne M. Friedrich

As a fiction writer, the commitment to remembering the past is fundamentally important to Cynthia Ozick. "To Holocaust Literature *The Shawl* is undeniably of huge importance."[1] In addition, it represents a landmark within Cynthia Ozick's career because it is her only work so far that deals directly with a Holocaust survivor. It is undoubtedly a brilliant and unique fictional rendition of a brief historical account, taken from Shirer's book *The Rise and Fall of the Third Reich.* A young Jewish mother must witness her starving baby being hurled by a Nazi guard onto the electrified fence of a concentration camp. The unsurpassed universal appeal of Ozick's excruciatingly moving rendition of this event and of its subsequent traumatic effect on the mother stems in part from the uncanny virtuosity of its artistic representation.

At first sight, the complex artistry of this text may appear to be surprising for an author who developed her own artistic credo by ardently rejecting Jamesian "idolatrous" aestheticism. In addition, in the past Ozick has repeatedly voiced her opinion that—parallel to Theodor Adorno's famous statement—the Holocaust should not enter fiction but rather be rendered in a strictly documentary style. However, she admits, the theme keeps coming back to her. In an interview, Cynthia Ozick describes her great abiding fear of "making art out of the Holocaust . . . I worry very much that this subject is corrupted by fiction and that fiction in general corrupts history."[2]

Ozick's abiding deep concern about the incompatibility of fiction and the Holocaust, coupled with her basic artistic credo derived from *Teshuvah* ("return"), which focuses on "process" rather than the finality of a perfected "product,"[3] has led to an extraordinary phenomenon regarding the genesis of *The Shawl.* As Joseph Lowin observed in 1988, the author keeps writing and rewriting her *Holocaust Madonna.* In the meantime she did so five times (her play included), more often than any other of her fictional characters.

Each time she developed a different narrative perspective within a time span of about twenty years. Accordingly, I will first call to mind, in a brief chronological overview, the great variety of narrative approaches that Ozick developed in her persistent commitment to explore the excruciatingly difficult task of dealing with a female Holocaust survivor. Second, I will concentrate on the book-length rendition of *The Shawl* (1989). In focusing on its intertextuality, which has not yet been addressed by criticism so far, I will try to show how Cynthia Ozick, in taking "Bialik's Hint" to heart, materializes her vision of a "new alternative" in fiction, "the explosive hope of [a] fresh form."[4] By establishing in *The Shawl* a midrashic intertextuality in particular, which is based on an ancient oral tradition, Ozick simultaneously addresses a very avant-garde, international trend in fiction, pointing toward an increased emphasis on "secondary orality" in an Ongian sense.[5]

The first precursory story, less focused than any of the later representations of a female Holocaust survivor, appeared in *The New York Times Magazine* in 1971: "24 Years in the Life of Lyuba Bershadskaya."[6] In a strictly *documentary* rendition, supplemented by the integration of photography and drawings, it records Lyuba's survival during ten years in Stalinist labor camps in Siberia and her subsequent desperate fight for an exit visa to Israel. As the interviewer, Ozick serves mainly as a sounding board who sparingly interrupts Lyuba's long, detailed, and gripping account. A number of motives contained in this seminal text reappear in the later versions, *Rosa* in particular. The most dominant motive, the driving and transforming force that appears to have kept Lyuba alive throughout the most atrocious, subhuman experiences, is her fierce commitment to remembering the past, to keeping her memory alive until she can finally give it permanency by writing her own book-length autobiography.

In 1977 Ozick writes the superb short story "The Shawl." In the most general terms, the shawl here is a symbol of life, a tallith[7] or a magic shield that protects Rosa and her baby Magda against the powers of death. In a vigorous strategic move from the long and emotionally more neutral documentary reportage to a highly focused, close-up rendition of concentration camp reality, the author now opts for the distancing objectivity of an *auctorial voice*. This momentous move in terms of narrative perspective, which relentlessly targets and provokes the reader's emotional response, enables her simultaneously to achieve an unsurpassed brevity through a rich and contrapuntal employment of metaphors. Ozick's understanding of metaphor as a major instrument to preserve the memory of Jewish history, as a "universalizing force" (Ozick, *Metaphor*, 279), "a serious moral instrument" (278), is powerfully and convincingly realized in this brief text.

During the same year, Cynthia Ozick rewrites a midrash on "The Shawl" in her prize-winning novella *Rosa*. This time, Rosa Lublin appears thirty years later, as a "mad woman," a scavenger in Miami. Rosa's obsessive, idolatrous worship of her shawl, which finally loses its magic, stands for the gradual healing process in Rosa from her idolatrous worship of the dead Magda. Rosa's post-Holocaust trauma necessitates a predominantly *introspective* mode of representation. Introspection is supported and beautifully maintained by an intricate and complex web of free indirect style, fragmented inner monologue, and dialogue mixed in between Rosa's compulsive letters to her deceased daughter Magda. Significantly, the synecdochical *closure* of "The Shawl" is complemented by the textual *openness* of *Rosa*. Ozick achieves this openness, which allows for a variety of different readings, by firmly anchoring the text in the concrete fictional reality of the world of Miami. It is only due to this mimetic foundation that the text may be read symbolically and at different levels simultaneously. It makes possible, for example, the extraordinary mythic widening and deepening of the text which Elaine Kauvar, in her congenial and unsurpassed interpretation, has laid bare convincingly. Ozick parallels Rosa's symbolic journey into her past, into "hell," by invoking Aeneas's descent into the underworld as a "guide into the subterranean world of a [Holocaust] survivor" (Kauvar, *Ozick's Fiction*, 201). By the added integration of the myth of Demeter, the Greek goddess of fertility and renewal, and her daughter, Persephone, the story's basic tension of Memory as Moloch versus *L'chaim!*[8] takes on a new universal dimension in supporting its final cathartic resolution. At the story's end, as Sarah Cohen points out, "Rosa, . . . leads herself out of the bondage of worshipping the magical shawl with its resurrection of the dead Magda."[9]

After Ozick had written both stories, "The Shawl" and *Rosa* in 1977, she waited three and six years before publishing them separately in *The New Yorker*. Reflecting the author's abiding reluctance to publish a precarious subject matter, it took her another nine years before she decided in 1989 to surprise us with her fourth rendition by publishing both the short story and the novella together in book form under the overarching title *The Shawl* (1989). Interestingly, Cynthia Ozick's fifth venture is a play, an adaptation of *The Shawl*.

I now turn to the book-length rendition of *The Shawl*. To begin with, compared to their previous publications in *The New Yorker*, the short story and the novella, each a complete and independent work of art, were reprinted together in the book without any textual changes. Thus *Rosa* may be read as a sequel to "The Shawl." However, by yoking the two tales together an essentially new text has been created. As Joseph Lowin pointed out already, once the reader knows both stories, neither story can be approached without reference to the other. Thus the reader is compellingly drawn into a midrashic mode. One story always contains the other and comments on it in a synchronous relationship.[10] In this context, Lowin's assessment of Jewish writing in general as an ongoing process may be called to mind. In Jewish writing, he states, "[s]tory begets commentary, which in its turn begets judgment, which in its turn begets further story and so on." As a result, Jews "comment on their history and, more importantly, they comment on their texts" (Lowin, "Novel Tradition," 19–20).

I argue that it is precisely this kind of intertextuality that determines the new and dominant narrative principle in *The Shawl*. Significantly, the newly created closure of the synchronous intertexuality of two tales, which in themselves already carry several layers of meaning, becomes opened up again, modified by the introduction of yet another text. In keeping with the epigram as a common form of haggadic fiction, Ozick selects the concluding epigram of Paul Celan's *Todesfuge* as an epigraph to her new text.[11] The concluding two lines of *Todesfuge* read:

> *dein goldenes Haar Margarethe*
> *dein aschenes Haar Sulamith.*

The eminent relevancy of this epigraph for Ozick's text has so far not yet been addressed by criticism. Conspicuously, Ozick refrains from offering the epigraph bilingually, as she has done in the past. Apparently, in this case she found a translation uncalled-for in dealing with one of the most famous poems of postwar Germany, the reputation of which, since Paul Celan's death in 1970, has grown exponentially. (Only Rilke, among this century's German poets, can match Paul Celan's impact on German and world poetry.) The flow of essays and books on Celan has recently grown to flood-tide proportions—more than three thousand items by now.[12] In addition, more than a hundred musical compositions exist that deal with *Todesfuge*. The same number of paintings have *Todesfuge* as their theme. Among them is Anselm Kiefer's well-known exhibition of his series *Sulamith* and *Margarethe*, which focuses exclusively on the concluding epigram, and which was well received in major museums in the United States between 1987 and 1989. Also, of particular interest with regard to Ozick's text is the fact that Celan's authentic oral rendition of *Todesfuge* has been preserved on records during his lifetime. (It was also recorded repeatedly in 1990 in a six-hour German television program on Celan.)

These recent developments of a hermeneutic explosion stem from a dominant understanding of the word *Fuge* (fugue) as "combining" or montage of many different texts, as opposed to the equally valid understanding of *Fuge* as a musical structure. This reminds me vividly of the heated debates which the first publication of *Todesfuge* generated in Germany forty-five years ago, when I was a student in Heidelberg of Hans-Georg Gadamer, a prominent Celan scholar. "It will take us a century of research," Gadamer predicted, "before we can fully understand the uncanny and complex intertextuality of this groundbreaking work." At the time, the famous controversy over the contradiction between the poem's fascinating musicality on one hand and its most shocking contents on the other culminated in Theodor Adorno's statement that it was "barbaric" to write any poetry at all after Auschwitz.

The many points of contact of *Todesfuge* with Ozick's text are most striking, indeed. I can only touch upon a few aspects here to show how Ozick's new introduction of only two lines further modifies and expands the intertextuality of *The Shawl*.

Todesfuge appeared in the series of poems called *Mohn und Gedüchtnis* (Poppy and Memory). The tremendous emotional power the poem conveys in rendering the memory of the essence of Auschwitz can be appreciated best in an oral rendition. As the title indicates and in keeping with the complicated musical structure of a fugue, *Todesfuge* simulates a musical score. This is achieved by polyphonic sequences of verbal sound patterns, soundscapes, which are subdivided into single voices carrying clusters of meaning. By the employment of counterpoint throughout, pairs of opposites define the text's basic structure. Significantly, the opposition of the first person plural "we" versus "he" also defines the poem's perspective. "We" represents the polyphonic chorus of the victims as the speakers who describe "him," the perpetrator of their death, "the master from Germany." Thus the poet serves only as a mouthpiece, the choreographer of an oral representation. The traditional first person singular perspective of lyrical poetry has been radically abandoned in favor of a choral speaking, a communal voice of the dying. By way of repetition, the contrapuntal pattern develops in a growing crescendo: "We" versus "he," "black-eyed" versus "blue-eyed," "ashen hair" versus "golden hair"; "[w]e shovel a grave in the breezes" versus "a man lives in the house," "we drink" versus "he whistles, commands, strikes." The polyphonic chorus concludes by finally merging into the hymnal salutation of the epigram:

> *dein goldenes Haar Margarethe*
> *dein aschenes Haar Sulamith.*

Similar to Ozick's rendition in the short story, the contrasts in *Todesfuge* between up and down, light and dark are particularly effective. They are shocked into incisive paradoxical metaphors. The poem's "grave in the breezes," for example, reminds us of Rosa's "walking in the air," or "slowly turning into air."[13] The pervading central metaphor of "black milk" in *Todesfuge* is paralleled by Ozick's opposition of "milk" versus "dead volcano" (4). The German word for daybreak, *Frühe*, in the first line "Black milk at daybreak we drink it" simultaneously signals "early in history" and the poem's pervading, "never-ending draught of the Black Milk becomes a metaphor for the suffering of the entire Jewish people from the days of the Babylonian captivity to the Nazi death camps."[14]

The name Shulamith is biblical, referring to the beautiful woman in the Song of Solomon. Interestingly, Celan wrote twenty-five love poems all dedicated to Shulamith. They were written in Bucharest around the same time that *Todesfuge* was first published in Rumanian in 1948.[15] The amount of biblical allusions in *Todesfuge* is overwhelming, and it has been demonstrated that they predominantly suggest *Widerruf* (recall), that God's promises to Israel have not been kept (Glenn, *Paul Celan*, 71). However, the *Deus Absconditus* in *Todesfuge* can be evaluated appropriately only within the context of the series of poems, in which Celan intentionally placed *Todesfuge* at its center. The series as a whole intimates an overarching movement toward *Gegenlicht* (glare, backlight). And it is in *Gegenlicht*, according to the critical consensus, that by invoking the Mothers of the Old Testament a renewed presence of God is intimated, recovered.[16] Celan understood the suffering of the Jewish people as charisma. Thus Celan's text embraces, reiterates in a new light "the unanswered [individual] question at the heart of *Rosa*" (Kauvar, *Ozick's Fiction*, 198).

Breaking away from the traditional paradigm of connecting Shulamith and the Mothers of the Old Testament with Maria, who represents the New Testament, Celan replaces the name Maria with Margarethe (Buck, "Lyrik nach Auschwitz," 25). He also changes the original purple color of Shulamith's hair into "ashen." This significant paradigmatic change in the use of *"dein goldenes Haar Margarethe"* is quite complex. It cuts into the maudlin aspect of the German romantic ideal by alluding to the "golden hair" in Heinrich Heine's "Loreley."[17] Simultaneously, it refers ironically to Gretchen in Goethe's *Faust*, the quintessence of the Enlightenment. Gretchen was at first condemned to death for killing her own child. Thus by extension, in Ozick's text the equation Shulamith-Rosa-Demeter is juxtaposed against the Medea myth contained in the figure of Faust's Gretchen. In addition, the typical German name Margareta derived from the Greek for "the pearl" also implies Christian symbolism (Glenn, *Paul Celan*, 72). Accordingly, the name implies German/Christian as opposed to the Jewish Shulamith.

The most conspicuous and central connection between Ozick's story and the poem is given, of course, in the repeated hint at Magda's blue eyes and fair hair. Thus Ozick parallels the problem of Jewish identity that haunts Rosa's memory of her dead daughter, fathered by a Nazi, with an alternate identity crisis that haunts Celan's memory of his dead mother. This connecting motif of a deeply troubled mother/child relationship, overshadowed by the problem of Jewish identity, becomes more apparent in a poem preceding *Todesfuge*; it is called "Aspen tree":

My yellow-haired mother did not come home. (Hamburger, *Paul Celan*, 33)

Moreover, in a striking analogy to Rosa's imagining her shawl as a "shroud," one poem in Celan's cycle is titled "Shroud." Another poem is dedicated to Celan's mother, who had been deported from her Bukovinian home in Czernowitz and later was shot to death. The poem carries the title "Black Flakes" in analogy to "black milk." Its central and repeated metaphor of a shawl, evoked by the mother's voice, suggests the same meaning of a protective shield that Ozick's short story conveys:

> Oh for a cloth child, to wrap myself when it's flashing with
>   helmets . . .
> A shawl, just a thin little shawl, so I have by my side.

And the poem concludes in the son's voice:

> I wove the shawl.[18]

Interestingly, parallel to Ozick's switch from the positive understanding of "shawl" in the first story to an ironical undercutting of "shroud" in the novella, *Todesfuge*, too, alludes to "shroud" ironically. This is achieved by a metrical citation (Felstiner, *Paul Celan*, 37). The repetitious cadence alone, "we drink and we drink," summons a protest ballad by Heinrich Heine:

> Old Germany, we weave your shroud . . .
> we weave and we weave it. (37)

As in this case, several literary allusions in *Todesfuge* point at Celan's painful disillusionment with a once revered and rich German cultural heritage. Ironically, Celan's highly educated mother, whom he had loved dearly, had always wanted to instill and nurture in him her own enthusiasm for German classical literature and the high German language.

To a degree, *Todesfuge* grew out of this most painful and deep-seated paradox in Celan's life following the Holocaust. A conflict, which in certain ways reminds us of that of Rosa Lublin who writes her letters to her dead Magda in a sophisticated literary Polish. Celan, too, who could express his suffering adequately only in his mother tongue, addresses his dead mother in "Aspen Tree":

> *And can you bear, mother, as once 'on a time,*
> *the gentle, the German, the pain-laden rhyme?* (49)

In the light of this aspect alone, it appears to me unjustified to read the epigram of *Todesfuge* as an unequivocal reconciliation; many have done so. However, most appropriately, Shulamith and Margarethe are connected in the concluding lines by the epigrammatic form, which simultaneously allows for an emphasis on their contrapuntal opposition.

In conclusion, *Todesfuge* is intricately woven into the fabric of *The Shawl*. As we are drawn into a midrashic mode, it modifies Ozick's text by interpreting it, commenting on it. As we are reading *The Shawl* through the perspective of *Todesfuge*, the memory of the individual voice of Rosa merges with the memory of the communal chorus in Celan's poem. Moreover, the short story explicitly connects with the poem by repeatedly invoking the liturgical community of the dead.[19] In terms of its artistic rendition, *Todesfuge*, as an integral part of *The Shawl*, coincides precisely with Ozick's vision of haggadic fiction as "liturgical literature." As the author explains, "Literature is also a poem. But it is meant not to have only a private voice. Liturgy has a choral voice, a communal voice; the echo of the voice of the Lord of History."[20]

As Ozick's combined tales in their closure are, so to speak, plugged into the orally oriented, open-ended intertextuality of *Todesfuge*, the newly created intertext as a continued (and to-be-continued) process becomes substantially widened and deepened by a new dimension. As Ozick comments: "A liturgical literature has the configuration of a ram's horn, you give your strength to the inch-hole and the splendor spreads wide. A Jewish liturgical literature gives strength to its peoplehood and the whole human note is heard everywhere, enlarged" (Ozick, *Art and Ardor*, 174–175).

In taking "Bialik's Hint" to heart, Cynthia Ozick no longer believes that the rendition of memory should be confined to New Yiddish. She is now convinced that "all languages have [the] . . . capacity" to accomplish this important task (Ozick, *Metaphor*, 239).

In *The Shawl*, Ozick has achieved the desired fusion of the narrative strategies of both, the literary tradition of the Enlightenment and the Jewish tradition (237).

Notes

1. Elaine M. Kauvar, *Cynthia Ozick's Fiction: Tradition and Invention* (Bloomington: Indiana University Press, 1993), 179.

2. Francine Prose, Interview with Cynthia Ozick, New York Times Book Review (Sept. 10, 1989): 1.

3. Bonnie Lyons, "Cynthia Ozick as a Jewish Writer," Studies in American Jewish Fiction 6 (Fall 1997): 17.

4. Cynthia Ozick, *Metaphor and Memory* (New York: Vintage International, 1991), 237.

5. Walter J. Ong, *Orality and Literacy* (New York: Routledge, 1982).

6. Trudi Vocse "24 Years in the Life of Lyuba Bershadskaya," *The New York Times Magazine*. March 14, 1971, pp. 27–29, 81–84.

7. Alan L. Berger, *Crisis and Covenant: The Holocaust in American Jewish Fiction* (Albany: State University of New York Press, 1985), 53.

8. Victor Strandberg, *Greek Mind/Jewish Soul: The Conflicted Art of Cynthia Ozick* (Madison: University of Wisconsin Press, 1994), 150.

9. Sarah Cohen, *Cynthia Ozick's Comic Art: From Levity to Liturgy* (Bloomington: Indiana University Press, 1994), 164.

10. Joseph Lowin, *Cynthia Ozick* (Boston: Twayne Publishers, 1988), 121.

11. Michael Hamburger, ed. and trans. *Paul Celan: Poems: A Bilingual Edition* (New York: Persea Books, 1980), 50–53.

12. Pierre Joris, ed. and trans. *Paul Celan: Breathturn* (Los Angeles: Sun and Moon Press, 1995), 13.

13. Cynthia Ozick, *The Shawl* (New York: Vintage International, 1989), 4, 6.

14. Jerry Glenn, *Paul Celan* (New York: Twayne Publishers, 1973), 73–74.

15. Theo Buck, "Lyrik nach Auschwitz. Zu Paul Celans 'Todesfuge,'" in *Datum und Zitat bei Paul Celan, Akten des Internationalen Celan Colloquiums, Haifa 1986*, ed. Chaim Shoham and Bernd Witte (Bern: Peter Lang, 1987), 39.

16. Irene Zivsa, "Paul Celan," in *Hauptwerke der deutschen Literatur* (Munich: Kindler, 1974), 450.

17. John Felstiner, *Paul Celan: Poet, Survivor, Jew* (New Haven: Yale University Press, 1995), 36.

18. Quoted in Felstiner, *Paul Celan*, 19.

19. Amy Gottfried, "Fragmented Art and the Liturgical Community of the Dead in Cynthia Ozick's *The Shawl*," *Studies in American Jewish Literature* 13 (1994): 39–51.

20. Cynthia Ozick, *Art and Ardor* (New York: Knopf, 1983), 169.

Works Cited

Berger, Alan L. *Crisis and Covenant: The Holocaust in American Jewish Fiction.* Albany: State University of New York Press, 1985.

Buck, Theo. "Lyrik nach Auschwitz. Zu Paul Celans 'Todesfuge.'" In *Datum und Zitat bei Paul Celan. Akten des Internationalen Celan Colloquiums, Haifa 1986.* Ed. Chaim Shoham and Bernd Witte. Bern: Peter Lang, 1987.

Cohen, Sarah Blacher. *Cynthia Ozick's Comic Art: From Levity to Liturgy*. Bloomington: Indiana University Press, 1994.

Felstiner, John. *Paul Celan: Poet, Survivor, Jew*. New Haven: Yale University Press, 1995.

Glenn, Jerry. *Paul Celan*. New York: Twayne Publishers, 1973.

Gottfried, Amy. "Fragmented Art and the Liturgical Community of the Dead in Cynthia Ozick's *The Shawl*." *Studies in American Jewish Literature* 13 (1994): 39–51.

Hamburger, Michael, ed. and trans. *Paul Celan: Poems: A Bilingual Edition*. New York: Persea Books, 1980.

Joris, Pierre. ed. and trans. *Paul Celan: Breathturn*. Los Angeles: Sun and Moon Press, 1995.

Kauvar, Elaine M. *Cynthia Ozick's Fiction: Tradition and Invention*. Bloomington: Indiana University Press, 1993.

Lowin, Joseph. *Cynthia Ozick*. Boston: Twayne Publishers, 1988.

———. "A Novel Tradition." *Hadassah Magazine* (March 1987): 19–21.

Lyons, Bonnie. "Cynthia Ozick as a Jewish Writer." *Studies in American Jewish Fiction* 6 (Fall 1997): 13–23.

Ong, Walter J. *Orality and Literacy*. New York: Routledge, 1982.

Ozick, Cynthia. *Art and Ardor*. New York: Knopf, 1983.

———. *Metaphor and Memory*. New York: Vintage International, 1991.

———. *The Shawl*. New York: Vintage International, 1989.

Prose, Francine. Interview with Cynthia Ozick. *New York Times Book Review*, Sept. 10, 1989.

Strandberg, Victor. *Greek Mind/Jewish Soul: The Conflicted Art of Cynthia Ozick*. Madison: University of Wisconsin Press, 1994.

Zivsa, Irene. "Paul Celan." In *Hauptwerke der deutschen Literatur*. Munich: Kindler, 1974.

7

A Speck of Dust Blown by the Wind Across Land and Desert: Images of the Holocaust in Lanzmann, Singer, and Appelfeld

GILA SAFRAN NAVEH

On the issue of preoccupation with historical memory, Ralph Waldo Emerson, the nineteenth-century American essayist, critic, and transcendental thinker, once pointedly remarked with a metaphor only too chilling in our context, "Why drag about this monstrous corpse of your memory?"

Now Emerson was witty and at times quite penetrating; here, however, he betrays uncommon shallowness. This attitude with respect to remembering the past fails to understand what the French Jewish writer Marcel Proust perceived so accurately: "reality takes form only in memory." To find significance and meaning in our present life necessitates at some level relating to our historic past. We need to confront it honestly, to reflect upon it, to learn from it, and to build upon it in some constructive way.

When confronting the Holocaust to keep it alive in humanity's memory, as writers, we are facing a serious dilemma. We proceed invariably to represent it artistically, which is tantamount to partaking in the process of its mythification. This in turn means that, in essence, when confronting the Holocaust we are dealing inevitably with issues of narrative strategy, rhetoric, and tropes and are moving away from the historical reality of this catastrophic event. In other words, in attempting to reflect about the Holocaust, however honestly, as writers, we come face-to-face with the drama of writing and of representation.

To that extent, when trying to re-create the recent past by re-presenting it, namely, by making it present in film or in fiction to the millions who never experienced it, we must ask ourselves a different set of questions. For example, we might want to ask ourselves what kind of writing or cinematic images are capable of revealing with most vigor the particular, as well as the universal aspects of the Holocaust, and relate most effectively the deeds of history? In other words, we need to ask ourselves questions about the kind of artistic techniques which can make the Holocaust "real" to us, despite the lack of its presence (or, as Derrida would put it, despite "the absence of its presence").

A great deal has been said and written lately about representational "acting out," the rhetorico-narrational tactics by which one is compelled "to regress" and experience the event "as if s/he were part of that tragic event, during the Holocaust."[1] In essence, this injunction is not unlike the one in the Passover Haggadah, which comments that "every man [and woman] ought to feel as if he himself came out of slavery in Egypt."

To ask whether indeed the strategy of "acting out" and "working through" is a more potent narrative approach, capable of eliciting a more appropriate reader/viewer response and remembering, I submit below works by two writers and a writer/filmmaker who utilize this "new" technique. Specifically, I explore whether writing and film do in fact acquire more power by identifying with and forcing the readers/spectators to relive the painful experiences of the victims. On the other end of the continuum, I question whether we can provide a reading of these authors' work that answers the question in the affirmative and whether these answers can be supplied by an admittedly liturgical or ritual reading, or reception, of the authors investigated below. My contention is that a positive answer could prove helpful to those of us having to choose among a plethora of narrative strategies of transmission, and find ourselves in dire need of a reliable model.

Admittedly, much has already been written about the Holocaust, but if we inquire how much of what has been written is actually literature, we will find that it is quite a small part. "Literature with a true voice and a face one can trust is very scarce," claims Appelfeld. I tend to agree with Appelfeld, who also states that, "while the literature of testimony remains the authentic literature of the Holocaust and part of Jewish chronology, testimonial literature embodies too many inner constraints—not only psychological—to become literature as that concept has taken shape over the generations."[2]

We notice that in survivors' remembrance, there is an inherent double bind. The dilemma expressed by Elie Wiesel, Primo Levi, and innumerable other survivors, less talented and less known, comes immediately to mind. The survivor reveals but at the same time conceals. Clearly, the testimony of the survivor is first and foremost a search for relief from the burden of memory and is discarded perhaps too hastily. She or he is torn between two imperatives: the desire to keep silence and the desire to speak. On the one hand, the inability to express his or her experience and the feelings of guilt, and on the other, the desire to articulate what has happened to him or her: an experience that is gigantic, thoroughly unreal, and inconceivable.

Two problems surface here: survivors either attempt to cut the Holocaust off from everyday life and "normalcy" and force it into the distant crannies of madness and pathology, or endow it with mystical, enigmatic qualities, inexpressible in language. In essence, for the generation of Auschwitz, the act of writing—narrating, composing, choosing, interpreting—seems to bestow order on a reality that had none. We recall here Theodor Adorno's claim that after Auschwitz it would be barbaric to write lyric poetry. The repulsion of artistic expression after the Holocaust is further augmented by a clear suspicion of art, which is linked in the mind of the survivors to the very culture that turned them into victims.

"Their question *how to speak* of the unimaginable, becomes for the second generation, *do I have the right to speak*," claims Ellen Fine.[3] Professor Alan L. Berger takes us a step further:

> In the case of second-generation witnesses, it is not a matter of "rescuing" the Holocaust. It is, rather, the *tikkun* of bearing witness to the Shoah's continuing and multidimensional sequelae, of which the second-generation creative works themselves form a significant part.[4]

Yet, despite all challenges, the Holocaust haunts us as a specter. We cannot rid ourselves of those memories which never cease their demands that we bear witness and that we write them into stories. The efforts to find powerful artistic representations of the Holocaust speak of the ardent need to fathom it. Along these lines, Robert Jay Lifton, the noted psychiatrist, explains: "Artistic re-creation of an overwhelming historical experience has much to do with the question of mastery."[5] To achieve "mastery" is in some sense to get respite and also to reach a closure, that is to say, to push the event—in this case, the atrocities of the Holocaust—into some remote region of our psyche, and, as Freud claims, to "fore-close" it.[6] However, the problem with foreclosed material is that it resurfaces and makes its presence felt in various neuroses. Thus, this direction in Holocaust representation and transmission seems slippery, at best. And even if this were the best possible way, the pool of survivors dwindles constantly.

I wish to bring to attention another, quite engaging, model for representing the Holocaust. Claude Lanzmann's book based on his film *Shoah* was cited for offering a most powerful praxis. To be sure, Lanzmann's is a work of continual lamentation or grieving that is tensely suspended between the acting out of a traumatic past and the difficult effort to work through it.[7] In it, acting out or reliving the past tends to outweigh attempts to work through it. Interestingly, Lanzmann relies on "antimemory" or on the silences and indirections of memory to arrive at the object of his quest: the incarnation, actual reliving, or compulsive acting out of the past—particularly its traumatic suffering—in the present.[8] To our mind, this "tragic" identification, akin to Freud's notion of *transferential relation*, provokes a repetition of the trauma in the other and in its desire to relive that suffering in the shattered self. However, this repetition take place, as transference always does, in the safe and empathetic climate of therapeutic circumstances. As for the artist, rather than seeing it as problematic, Lanzmann explains the paradox in the following terms:

> Blindness should be understood here as the purest mode of looking the only way not to turn away from a reality that is literally blinding: clairvoyance itself. To direct a frontal look at horror requires that one renounce distractions and escape-hatches, first the primary among them, the most falsely central, the question why, with the indefinite retinue of academic frivolities and dirty tricks [canailleries] that it ceaselessly induces.[9]

Relying on Primo Levi's brilliant writing, Lanzmann emphasizes in his own interpretative moment that the law Primo Levi learned from the SS guard, "Hier ist kein Warum" or "Here there is no why," is also valid for whoever assumes the charge of transmission of the Holocaust experience. In his opinion, the act of transmission alone is important and no intelligibility, that is, "no true knowledge preexists the transmission." The transmission *is* the knowledge. And transmission in this sense means not only testimony but also embodiment, actual reliving, or, in psychoanalytic terminology, acting out the traumatic event.[10]

> In acting-out we reincarnate or relive the past in an unmediated [transferential] process that subjects us to possession by haunting objects and to compulsively repeated incursions of traumatic residues: hallucinations, flashbacks, nightmares. However, this search for full presence is phantasmatic and entirely uncontrolled.[11]

But the alternative of a fully satisfying representation and understanding has been quite assertively dismissed as invalid by scholars like Jacques Derrida. He has successfully attacked totalizing master narratives and totalizing theories of liberation. For example, in *La mythologie blanche*, Derrida has convincingly rejected totalizing master narratives as the embodiment of the metaphysical idea of representation and as the reproduction or mimetic recreation of a presupposed full presence. In many of his other well-known essays, Derrida has indeed stubbornly come back to remind us that full presence never existed.[12]

What then is the process of "transmission" that Lanzmann contracts with the *Warum* (the *why* question) and equates with knowledge? I suggest that Lanzmann invites us to return to the first step: testimony or witnessing— that of the primary witness, particularly the survivor or victim, and that of the secondary witness emphatically attentive to the voice, silence, and gestures of the primary witness.[13] In essence, in Lanzmann's book as in his film, when we are made to witness the reenactment of the murder of the witness, this second Holocaust spontaneously appears before the camera. To our question, whether in turn we can become *contemporaneous* with the meaning and with the significance of that enactment, Lanzmann responds:

The film is not made with memories; I knew that immediately. Memory [*le souvenir*] horrifies me. Memory is weak. The film is the abolition of all distance between the past and the present; I relive this history in the present [*j'ai revécu cette histoire au présent*].[14]

In her pivotal work, "The Return of the Voice: Claude Lanzmann's Shoah," Shoshana Felman too indicates that Lanzmann's approach in Shoah is of empathy or positive transference unperturbed by critical judgment. In fact, her own style mimes the fragmentation in the film and underscores the notion of impossibility of witnessing in a world in which "trauma is tantamount to History and true writing is necessarily a 'writing of disaster.'" As the boundaries between witnessing and trauma are blurred, when we recognize what escapes cognition and mastery, the world becomes a *univers concentrationnaire*.[15]

Now, while acknowledging Lanzmann's artistic cinematic gesture, we also suggest that, however ingenious Lanzmann's model may seem to literary critics today, it essentially emulates the model already offered by Kafka. Kafka's poetic language and style, "like a mass grave, [it] saves space and time."[16] Some sixty-five years before Lanzmann's *Shoah* and some fifty-five years before Maurice Blanchot's coining the term "écriture du désastre," that is, "writing of disaster,"[17] Franz Kafka suggested that we read "books which come upon us like ill-fortune, and distress us deeply . . . and are an ice-axe to break the sea frozen inside us." Kafka's originality consists precisely in having sacrificed truth for *transmissibility* (my emphasis), claimed Walter Benjamin, another brilliant Jewish thinker who fell prey to the Nazi regime. By privileging transmissibility, Kafka created the literature we have come to know as Kafkaesque.[18] Paul Celan, the poet who witnessed the Holocaust, followed closely the Kafkan model.

Appelfeld and Singer, in their most innovative moments, also inscribe their work on the Holocaust in the Kafkan tradition which, poignantly, Claude

Lanzmann follows in film as well. In their artistic representations, the passionate desire to remember and bear witness to the horrors seen or uncovered does not result in a simple return to mimesis. Their work, like that of Kafka (or Paul Celan, for that matter), "does not seek to reproduce a presupposed reality, but the discovery of a reality, either not yet existing, or not yet perceived. For them, reality is not simply there; it must be searched and won."[19]

The scope of this essay does not allow for a comprehensive analysis of these authors' representational techniques. I refer below only to two representational images which, together with the images in Lanzmann's *Shoah*, inhibit our feeling of closure and interfere with our catharsis. The first passage is from *Badenheim 1939*, by Aharon Appelfeld:

> But their amazement was cut short. An engine, an engine coupled to four filthy freight cars, emerged from the hills and stopped at the station. Its appearance was as sudden as if it had risen from a pit in the ground, "Get in!" Yelled invisible voices. And the people were sucked in. Even those who were standing with a bottle of lemonade in their hands, a bar of chocolate, the head-waiter with his dog—they all were sucked in as easily as grain of wheat poured into a funnel. Nevertheless Dr. Papenheim found time to make the following remark: "If the coaches are so dirty it must mean that we have not far to go."[20]

The second passage comes from *Enemies, A Love Story*, by Isaac Bashevis Singer:

> What happened to me can never be fully told. The truth is, I don't really know myself. So much happened that I sometimes imagine nothing happened. I have completely forgotten many things, even about our life together. I remember lying on a wooden plank in Kazakhstan, trying to recall why, during the summer of 1939. I took the children on a visit to my father, but I simply couldn't find any sense or reason for what I had done.
>
> We sawed logs in the forest—twelve and fourteen hours a day. At night it was so cold I couldn't sleep at all. It stank so, I couldn't breathe. Many of the people suffered from beriberi. One minute a person would talk to you, making plans, and suddenly he would be silent. You spoke to him and he didn't answer. You moved closer and saw that he was dead. . . . My mother fell at their feet and they trampled on her with their boots and spat

at her. They would have raped me, but I was having my period and you know how I bleed. Oh, later it stopped all right. Where does one get blood if one doesn't have bread? You ask what happened to me? A speck of dust blown by the wind across land and desert can't tell where it's been.[21]

The "grain of wheat poured into a funnel" and "the speck of dust blown by the wind across land and desert," semiotically signifying the Jewish people during the Holocaust because they were treated like specks of dust and grains of wheat, are the sort of signs Charles Sanders Peirce calls an "index." In contrast to the arbitrary symbol (or sign proper), the index is a sign in which a causal, or more generally existential, relation connects signifier to signified. The signifiers "speck of dust" and "grain of wheat," being caused by God, signify Him indexically.

The "grain of wheat" and "speck of dust" in Appelfeld and Singer reveal God symbolically as well. If a symbol is an "arbitrary rule for consciousness which connects the sign with what it stands for," there are several traditional rules at work here: new signifying chains are superimposed by Appelfeld and Singer. Jewish literature has a rich tradition of "specks of dust" and "grain" symbolisms their readers remember. The signifiers "grain/seed" and "speck of dust," indicating the Jewish people who were chosen by God (see numerous biblical statements), the Jewish prayers that elaborate on man being but "a speck of dust" or "a grain," the idea of annihilation or "turning into dust" (the Jewish people), together with the allusions to God's promise to Abraham "to make his grain/seed into a great nation," and the notion of *yom hol*, literally, "day of dust," opposed to "the holy/good days," open new semiotic vistas connecting in the mind of the reader God, the Jewish people, and the Holocaust.

But both Appelfeld and Singer use this indexical and symbolic relation even more ambiguously. Small and insignificant, easily sucked into a funnel or blown across land and desert, the grain of wheat and the speck of dust also represent opportunity for rebirth, reshaping, and transforming. Rebirth and reshaping and transforming that the reader has to accomplish out of nothing clearly resonate with Kafka's or Paul Celan's injunction for language to "search and win reality which isn't simply there." In this framework, the nothing, or *niemand*, that is, the speck of dust or the grain of wheat, receive new meaning in the hothouse of language craftily shaped by Singer and Appelfeld.

An interesting picture of the world takes shape in their work. In a world in which "God is hanging on the gallows" and dead,[22] and where people are dying in the gas chambers, artistic language is in charge of recreating being. Language alone, this arbitrary signifying system, can call us and God into being by engendering a new vantage point from within which we can be seen as living.[23] The nothing that is the speck of dust and the grain of wheat come into full being in Singer and Appelfeld because of their linguistic deftness. Mysteriously, these authors artistic language transforms the grain of wheat and the speck of dust and endows them with life.

An arresting reversal becomes visible. Rather than attempting to excise and expunge the Holocaust out of ordinary life and push it into the far recesses of human pathology to be forgotten, the way survivors try to do, Appelfeld and Singer, like Kafka, Paul Celan, or Lanzmann, bring the Holocaust to life. And they contaminate with it the habitual, the everyday occurrence, and the common. These artists successfully create what Cynthia Ozick has called, in reference to Norma Rosen's writing, "a mind engraved with the Holocaust."[24]

If a sign is something that stands for something else to someone at some point in time, then the grain of wheat and the speck of dust become unique signifiers that cause the signified rather than being caused by it. "Grain" and "dust" are language, words which in this particular sense are creating being. That is to say, the grain and the speck of dust are words that will the Holocaust into being. And more. These words bring the Holocaust into being in everyday life. In a strict sense, these writings' language actually "creates" the Holocaust. The Holocaust becomes reality in and because of language, through the reversal of being-language relationship, namely through the structure given to the indexical sign. As Shimon Sandbank accurately asserts, "the strong mimetic impulse as witness of horror—and of overcoming Adorno's saying on the impossibility of poetry after Auschwitz, is to make language recreate reality and create a perspective from which it can be seen as being."[25] In the metaphorical assertion of Appelfeld, Lanzmann, and Singer, we also uncover the "miraculism or supernaturalism" John Crowe Ransom speaks about when he states:

> If we are ready to mean what we say, or believe what we hear . . . [then] the miraculism which produces the humblest conceit is the same miraculism which supplies religion their substantive content. . . . it is poetry and nobody else who gives God a nature, a form, faculties, and a history. The conceit is a metaphor if the metaphor is meant.[26]

Ultimately, in the writing of Appelfeld, Singer, and Lanzmann reality *is meant*. This gives their representation of the Holocaust its being in the world. And in this sense, these creative writers make the transmissibility of the Holocaust not only primordial in the Kafkan sense, they make it indeed possible at this point in time.

Notes

1. Lore Segal, "Memory: The Problem of Imagining the Past," in *Writing and the Holocaust*, ed. Berel Lang, p. 58.

2. Aharon Appelfeld, "After the Holocaust," in *Writing and the Holocaust*, ed. Berel Lang (New York: Holmes and Meier, 1988), 84–85.

3. Ellen Fine, "The Absent Memory," in *Writing and the Holocaust*, ed. by Berel Lang, (New York: Holmes and Meier, 1988), 43.

4. Alan L. Berger, *Children of Job* (Albany: State University of New York Press, 1997), 19.

5. Robert Jay Lifton, *Death-in-Life: Survivors of Hiroshima* (New York: Vintage Books, 1969), 397. And see Saul Friedländer, *Memory, History, and the Extermination of the Jews of Europe* (Bloomington, Indiana University Press, 1993). Friedländer claims that: "Aside from being aware and trying to overcome the defenses already mentioned the major difficulty of historians of the Shoah, when confronted with the echoes of the traumatic past, is to keep some measure of balance between the emotion recurrently breaking through the 'protective shield' and the numbness that protects this very shield" (130).

6. Sigmund Freud, "Foreclosure," in *The Complete Works*, ed. James Strachey, vol. 11 (London: Hogarth Press, 1968). And see "The Dynamic of Transference," *Standard Edition*, vol. 12 (London: Hogarth Press, 1912); "Remembering, Repeating and Working Through," vol. 12 (London: Hogarth Press, 1914); see also "Mourning and Melancholia," in *The Standard Edition of the Complete Psychoanalytic Works of Sigmund Freud*, trans. James Strachey (London, Hogarth Press 1953–1974), 12: 145–156, and 14: 237–260.

7. Claude Lanzmann, "Les Non-lieux de la mémoire," in *Au sujet de* Shoah: *Le Film de Claude Lanzmann*, ed. Michel Deguy (Paris: Gaillimard, 1990) 281–282. See also Lanzmann, "Seminar with Claude Lanzmann, 11 April 1990," *Yale French Studies*, no. 79 (1991), 96–97.

8. See illuminating discussion by Dominick LaCapra, "Lanzmann's Shoah," *Critical Inquiry* 23, no. 2 (1997): 231–270.

9. Claude Lanzmann, "Hier ist kein Warum," in *Au sujet de* Shoah: *Le Film de Claude Lanzmann*, ed. Michel Deguy (Paris, 1990). Primo Levi, "Here There Is No Why," in *Survival in Auschwitz*, trans. Stuart Woolf (New York: Simon and Schuster 1986). Here he explains that the SS guard would say "There is no why."

10. Lanzmann, "Hier ist kein Warum," 112–113.

11. LaCapra, "Lanzmann's Shoah," 240.

12. See Jacques Derrida, *La mythologie blanche* (Paris: Gallimard, 1969). Derrida clearly showed that there is no full presence that may be represented. What

we have is a past which we hope to reconstruct upon traces and traces of traces, left to us in the present.

13. LaCapra, "Lanzmann's Shoah," 237.

14. Claude Lanzmann, "Le lieu de la parole," in *Au sujet de* Shoah: *Le Film de Claude Lanzmann*, ed. Michel Deguy (Paris, 1990): 301.

15. Shoshana Felman, "The Return of the Voice: Claude Lanzmann's Shoah," in *Testimony: Crises of Witnessing in Literature, Psychoanalysis, and History* (New York, 1992), 204–283. Cf. LaCapra, "Lanzmann's Shoah," 231–270.

16. Suzanne Shipley Toliver, "Literature of the Holocaust: From Their Suffering Art?," in *Assessing the Significance of the Holocaust*, ed. Abbey Ingber and Benny Kraut (Cincinnati, 1986), 3. Cf. Richard Exner, "After Auschwitz 1," in *On the Limits of Knowing the Holocaust* (Santa Barbara, 1984), 41.

17. See Maurice Blanchot, *L'écriture du désastre* (Paris, 1980). See also Maurice Blanchot, *The Writing of Disaster*, trans. Ann Smock (Lincoln, 1986).

18. Walter Benjamin, "Some Reflections on Kafka," in *Illuminations*, ed. Hannah Arendt and trans. H. Zohn (New York, 1969).

19. See Paul Celan, *Collected Prose*, trans. Rosmaire Waldrop (Manchester, 1986), and see Shimon Sandbank, "The Sign of the Rose: Vaughan, Rilke, Celan," *Comparative Literature* 49, no. 3 (1997): 195–208.

20. Aharon Appelfeld, *Badenheim 1939* (Boston: Godine, 1980), 147–148.

21. Isaac Bashevis Singer, *Enemies, A Love Story* (New York: Farrar Straus Giroux, 1972), 73–74.

22. Eli Wiesel, *Night* (New York: Hill and Wang, 1960), trans. Stella Rodney, 62

23. Sandbank, "The Sign of the Rose," 204–206.

24. Cynthia Ozick, "Roundtable Discussion," in *Writing and the Holocaust*, ed. Betel Lang, (New York: Holmes and Meier, 1988), 282.

25. Sandbank, "The Sign of the Rose," 206.

26. John Crowe Ransom, *The World's Body* (New York: Scribner's Sons, 1938), 138.

Works Cited

Appelfeld, Aharon. *Badenheim 1939*. Boston: Godine, 1980.

——. "After the Holocaust." In *Writing and the Holocaust*. Ed. Berel Lang. New York: Holmes and Meier, 1988.

Berger, Alan, L. *Children of Job*. Albany: State University of New York Press, 1997.

Benjamin, Walter, "Some Reflections on Kafka." In *Illuminations*. Ed. Hannah Arendt and trans. H. Zohn. New York, 1969.

Blanchot, Maurice. *L'Écriture du désastre*. Paris, 1980.

———. *The Writing of Disaster*. Trans. Ann Smock. Lincoln, Nebraska, 1986.

Celan, Paul. *Collected Prose*. Trans. Rosmaire Waldrop. Manchester: Machester University Press, 1986.

Derrida, Jacques. *La mythologie blanche*. Paris: Gallimard, 1969.

Exner, Richard. "After Auschwitz 1." In *On the Limits of Knowing the Holocaust*. Santa Barbara: University of California Press, 1984.

Felman, Shoshana. "The Return of the Voice: Claude Lanzmann's Shoah." In *Testimony: Crises of Witnessing in Literature, Psychoanalysis, and History*. New York, 1992.

Fine, Ellen S. "The Absent Memory." In *Writing and the Holocaust*. Ed. Berel Lang. New York: Holmes and Meier, 1988.

Freud, Sigmund. "The Dynamic of Transference." In *Standard Edition of the Complete Psychoanalytic Works of Sigmund Freud*, Vol. 12. Trans. James Strachey (London, 1912).

———. "Foreclosure." In *The Complete Works*, Vol. 1.1. Ed. James Strachey. London: Hogarth Press, 1968.

———. "Mourning and Melancholia." *Standard Edition of the Complete Psychoanalytic Works of Sigmund Freud*. Trans. James Strachey (London, 1953–1974), 12: 145–156, and 14: 237–260.

———. "Remembering, Repeating and Working Through," *Standard Edition of the Complete Psychoanalytic Works of Sigmund Freud*, Vol. 12. Trans. James Strachey (London, 1914).

Friedländer, Saul. *Memory, History, and the Extermination of the Jews of Europe*. Bloomington: Indiana University Press, 1993.

LaCapra, Dominick. "Lanzmann's Shoah." *Critical Inquiry* 23, no. 2 (1997): 231–270.

Lang, Berel. Ed. *Writing and the Holocaust*. New York: Holmes and Meier, 1988.

Lanzmann, Claude. "Les Non-lieux de la mémoire." In *Au sujet de* Shoah: *Le Film de Claude Lanzmann*. Ed. Michel Deguy, Paris, 1990.

———. "Hier ist kein Warum." ("Here there is no why") In *Au sujet de* Shoah. Ed. Michel Deguy. Paris, 1990.

———. "Seminar with Claude Lanzmann, 11 April 1990." *Yale French Studies* 79 (1991).

Levi, Primo. *Survival in Auschwitz*. Trans. Stuart Woolf. New York, 1958, 1986.

Lifton, Robert Jay. *Death-in-Life: Survivors of Hiroshima*. New York: Vintage Books, 1969.

Ozick, Cynthia. "Roundtable discussion." In *Writing and the Holocaust*. Ed. Berel Lang. New York: Holmes and Meier, 1988.

Ransom, John Crowe. *The World's Body*. New York: Scribner's Sons, 1938.

Sandbank, Shimon. "The Sign of the Rose: Vaughan, Rilke, Celan." *Comparative Literature* 49, no. 3 (1997): 195–208.

Shipley Toliver, Suzanne. "Literature of the Holocaust: From Their Suffering Art?" In *Assessing the Significance of the Holocaust*. Eds. Abbey Ingber and Benny Kraut. Cincinnati: Cincinnati University Press, 1986.

Singer, Isaac Bashevis. *Enemies, A Love Story*. New York: Farrar Straus Giroux, 1972.

8

Writing to Break the Frozen Seas Within: The Power of Fiction in the Writings of Norma Rosen and Rebecca Goldstein

SUSAN E. NOWAK

In Rebecca Goldstein's masterful work, "The Legacy of Raizel Kaidish: A Story,"[1] we encounter a family indelibly marked by the Shoah. Young Raizel and her survivor-parents know no reprieve from its insistent, haunting presence. Every aspect of their life together is inextricably bound to the legacy of death camps, selections, and the never-ending trauma of guilt and self-hatred. Theirs is a saga in which the dead are more present than the living, evil more certain than good, and despair more perduring than hope. Indeed, for Raizel the Shoah never belongs to a distant past that is clearly separate from her world, her time, her life. Images, stories, and personalities from the camps fill her imagination until they seem more real than anything else in her young life:

> My moral education began at an early age. It consisted at first of tales from the camp . . . my images of the camp were vivid and detailed. The pink rosebuds on my wallpaper were not as real to me as the grey and drab green of the barracks, the brown of the mud. It seemed to me that I knew the feel through decaying shoes of the sharp stones in the main square, the sight, twice daily, of the terrifying roll-call. It seemed I too had quickly glanced up at the open sky and wondered that others outside saw the same sky. (281–282)

The same insistent, haunting presence weaves its way through Norma Rosen's essay, "Notes Toward a Holocaust Fiction."[2] This time we accompany a couple as they walk the streets of Vienna. For the husband, the city is filled with memories that resist the facade of postwar renovation and cleanliness. Memories of a happy childhood and loving parents are linked forever to parents murdered by the Nazis and a harrowing escape on a *kindertransport*. For the wife, Vienna intensifies feelings of guilt, shame, and fear. Born and raised in the United States, the safety of her childhood leaves her feeling like an outsider, even though she senses the Holocaust's presence everywhere they visit. Terrified that she is not capable of resisting the city's post-Holocaust allure, she struggles to identify her relationship to the catastrophe. Indeed, the couple is never alone in Vienna; every step of their journey reverberates with the Shoah's presence. Furthermore, its presence proves to be larger than they are, dwarfing their search for a *tikkun* (healing) with memories of premature and sudden death, orphaned children, and abandoned relatives. At every turn, the Shoah's presence presses against the fiber of their relationship, invading their words, rendering them silent, and thrusting them apart in anger and confusion. But at the same time it binds them one to the other. Battling the seductive beauty of postwar Vienna and the self-willed amnesia of its residents, they slowly begin to grasp that their individual identities are bound to the Shoah's ineluctable presence. Despite the radical dissimilarity of their lives, it is clear that the destruction of the European Jews is and always will be "the shadow that lies beneath, the past within the present" (Rosen, 108).

The Power of Autobiography and Memoir

The writing of Rebecca Goldstein and Norma Rosen is a direct response to the inescapable presence of the Holocaust. Drawing upon the rich resources of memory, imagination, and critical self-reflection, both of these writers confront the difficult task of living in a world that has inherited a painful and traumatizing legacy but not a sure path to healing. Each writer probes the scope of this traumatic legacy as she examines our self-understandings, explores our hopes, scrutinizes our relationships, and observes our behaviors. With metaphor and symbol, each draws a direct line from the Shoah to the moral despair and spiritual malaise gripping our families, social institutions, and religious communities. Through imagery and story, they reveal a world in which every philosophical, ethical, and religious tenet has been assaulted and thrown into question. In this world, commonly held assumptions about decency, integrity, and honor have been shaken to their foundations; indeed, the very fabric of our cultural, social, and theological heritage has been ruptured. The severity of this rupture is compounded by the fact that we continue to live in the midst of this devastation with very little healing. Rosen writes perceptively about its impact upon our psyches:

Worst of sadistic fantasy? Decency once warned us to push it down. Allow it free rein now. What is your most bestial imagining? No, more than that. Worse. Given power by actuality. Caring for a child, reading Wordsworth with students, comforting a sick friend, we are all caught forever, at the bottom of the mind's mud, in mockery of love. These things have been. And quite, quite recently, polluting the human psyche forever. (106)

Through their stories, Goldstein and Rosen bear graphic witness to the rupturing of traditional certainties about the nature of Jewish identity, the relationship of good and evil, and the universal obligation of ethical action. Furthermore, by bearing witness to this rupture, both writers help us identify and articulate questions that have always haunted humanity and yet are all the more pressing in a post-Auschwitz world. In particular, they wrestle with questions of theodicy, the loss of innocence, the sanctity of human life, and the moral dilemmas of the oppressed. Both writers recognize that these questions possess a universal resonance; they reflect the absolute despair that is part and parcel of the Shoah's legacy at the same time that they move us to confront our social, ethical, and theological impoverishment.

Moreover, this recognition fuels their respective commitments to create a genre capable of confronting the complex reality of the Shoah. In a move that reflects one of the primary shifts within post-Holocaust Jewish self-understandings, both authors turn to autobiography and memoir. For many Jews, this cataclysmic event threatened to overthrow the tradition and its classical sources. These sources were not proving adequate to the overwhelming crisis Judaism faced.

Most important, the classical sources no longer provided a coherent worldview within which to construct and maintain a viable sense of Jewish identity. In response, many Jews began to deal with questions of identity, meaning, and purpose through personal experience rather than archetypal norms. Personal experience provided the *context* and *content* through which Jews living in the aftermath of the Shoah could address, in a meaningful and credible manner, issues such as survivor trauma, intergenerational communication, and the development of a post-Holocaust consciousness.

Rebecca Goldstein

The creative works of Goldstein and Rosen reflect this shift at the same time that they explore its implications. None of their main characters are observant in a traditional sense. In fact, there is not even any mention of traditional Jewish sources, that is, TaNaK (Hebrew Bible) and the Talmud, or traditional Jewish practices, such as, Sabbath observance, Passover celebrations, or textual study. For all of the characters, personal experience is the primary avenue through which they remember, transmit, and memorialize the Shoah's legacy. Goldstein's exploration is pursued through the figures of the mother-survivor and her daughter. The mother is engaged in a Herculean effort to resolve a moral dilemma that continues to haunt her after her release from the camp. The intensity of this dilemma never abates; throughout the remainder of her life it determines her every action and thought. Upon her release from the camp and return to medical school in Berlin, she immediately looks to philosophy for a resolution. Without even a passing glance at the rich tradition of Jewish ethical thought and moral guidance, the mother-survivor immerses herself in philosophical inquiry. However, in one of the most powerful moves of this story, Goldstein makes it clear that this highly esteemed source ultimately fails her. Traditional philosophical inquiry, just like traditional Judaism, is unable to help her attain lasting insight, resolution, or peace. Moreover, the mother's ceaseless interrogation of philosophy causes tremendous suffering in her daughter's life. The primary focus of her mother's moral training, the daughter feels secondary to her mother's ethical pursuit. Ceaselessly compared to the phantom camp heroine, Raizel, who was murdered because the mother-survivor informed on her, this second Raizel feels helpless to duplicate her model's courage and moral rectitude. As the mother's obsession grows and the daughter's feelings of abandonment intensify, the distance between them widens. It is only when the mother turns to the "text" of her own life and shares her betrayal of the first Raizel that an understanding between the two becomes even a remote possibility. Although the mother does not share the fact or significance of the betrayal until just before her death, it is the vehicle that allows the daughter to understand her mother for the first time.

Furthermore, Goldstein masterfully employs autobiography (through the figure of the mother-survivor) and memoir (through the daughter's narrative voice) within a fictionalized account to examine the intergenerational nature of the Shoah's legacy.[3] By placing the mother's autobiographical account within the daughter's memoir, Goldstein underscores the intergenerational impact of the mother's moral dilemma. Within the mother's life the moral dilemma is consistently present yet continually irresolvable; indeed, it lies at the core of her person and defines her identity. During her internment in the camp, it forced her to adopt a survival strategy that undermined her former moral standards.[4] Ironically, this strategy, which enhanced her chances of survival, undermines her efforts to rebuild her life after the camp. Until the day of her death, it overshadows her relationship with her husband, thwarts her emotional connections, and threatens her daughter's ability to thrive. But Goldstein's story makes it clear that the moral dilemma envelops the second generation as thoroughly as the first, albeit differently. The mother's never-ending anguish and guilt become the daughter's inheritance. The daughter's entire life is shaped by her mother's obsession with a decision made under circumstances of extremity. Even though the daughter never experiences that extremity in actuality, it is an integral part of her psychological makeup and becomes the standard by which she judges herself. Furthermore, she realizes that, in her mother's eyes, her life is justified *only* as an act of reparation. The entire purpose of her birth had, in reality, nothing to do with her. Its sole rationale was her mother's desperate need to mend the rupturing of her pre-Shoah moral standards. With this realization, as tragic as it is, the daughter's odyssey of self-healing can begin. She assumes responsibility for coming to terms with the Shoah's legacy, understanding that if she is to find meaning in her own existence, she must create it for herself. Rebellion, anger, and compassion guide her efforts. Finally, Goldstein introduces the daughter's indecision about bearing a child to extend the parameters of the dilemma to the third generation. Again, reflection upon personal experience is key. In response to the flawed and diminished sense of self with which she was raised, the daughter embraces a very different understanding of the parent-child relationship. Her experience of emotional deprivation transforms her vision of parenthood; it becomes the opportunity to honor the integrity of a child's autonomous identity. Never disowning her mother or denying her legacy, the daughter nevertheless prepares the way for the third generation to experience that legacy differently.

Norma Rosen

Bringing together imagination and literary analysis, Norma Rosen combines critical reflection upon the nature of Holocaust fiction with creative and powerful storytelling. "Notes Toward a Holocaust Fiction" effectively examines the ethical implications of this genre at the same time that it generates a story especially strong in its grappling with the development of a post-Holocaust consciousness. In the first section of the essay, Rosen lays out her rationale for joining fiction to autobiography and memoir. These three genres allow her to bear witness to the Shoah's complex, multidimensional nature while privileging the experience and memory of those who were caught up in its horror and terror. Out of a deep respect for the victims and an equal concern not to "add to the sum of pain," she consciously delimits the scope and focus of her writing (105). Every statement is overshadowed by the memory of a young child, a distant relative, who she believes was murdered by the Nazis. The power of this memory is intensified by the fact that her family chose not to take him in, despite the pleading of the boy's father. The tragedy of this choice is amplified when Rosen confides in us that the boy in the photo was approximately the same age as her husband. By naming the first section of her essay after her young relative ("The Boy in the Photograph") and directly evoking her husband's experience of escape, Rosen subordinates the entire corpus of her literary analysis to their experience. Highlighting two very different yet intrinsically related experiences, she privileges the experience and memory of the Jews who stood in the grip of the Shoah's murderous intent.

Furthermore, the constant reference to the experience and memory of the victims underscores her awareness that she is forever an outsider to the evil and terror that reigned during the "Kingdom of the Night." To cross the line and attempt to speak in the victims' voices would diminish and trivialize their witness. Her task is to wrestle with the Shoah's impact both within and without the Jewish world and yet not usurp the victims' privileged voice. She must forge a credible and authentic relationship to the Shoah. Within Rosen's literary universe this relationship, like the Shoah itself, is complex and multidimensional. It honors the uniqueness of survivor testimony, recognizes the diverse and distinct voices of their Jewish heirs, and challenges the non-Jewish world at large. As such, it frees her to explore the feelings of insurmountable loss, unending grief, and total abandonment that haunt the survivors and their families at the same time that it allows her to chart a path for those Jews who have inherited the legacy without personally experiencing the horror. Moreover, it heightens the integrity of her voice as she confronts the indifference of the non-Jewish world, its failure to accept responsibility for the scourge of anti-Semitism, and its perpetuation of religious bigotry after Auschwitz.

There is yet another reason that Rosen must forge a credible and authentic relationship to the Shoah. "Notes Toward a Holocaust Fiction" attests to her conviction that the development of a post-Holocaust consciousness after Auschwitz is nothing less than a moral imperative. Deeply aware of humanity's tendency to reject that which cannot be assimilated safely, Rosen employs fiction, autobiography, and memoir to describe her own struggle to accept and assimilate the Shoah's legacy as an integral dimension of her own self-understanding. With candor and sincerity, she reveals the desire to escape the demands of this task imposed on her by history but required by the very depths of her being. Longing for the refuge of an "as if" world that has no connection to the diabolical Kingdom of the Night, she resists a legacy that offers no reprieve from remembrance, memorialization, and witness:

> On and on it goes, this argument with ourselves. When we commit to our pastimes—when we eat, make love, reproduce, create shapes of language on paper—each stroke of joy casts up a dark

echo. That is my story, or rather, it is mine to the degree that it is not mine alone. (110)

Rosen's journey toward a post-Holocaust consciousness is filled with yearning for an identity untouched by the Shoah's omnipresent, death-laden shadow. Poignantly she grieves the loss of a life that has no room for "the ordinary," whether pleasure or heartbreak:

> Ordinary pleasure and, I suppose . . . "ordinary heartbreak," which we try to encompass in our post-Holocaust era in order to create life out of survival, are in some ways forever beyond us. The delicacy of a sweetmeat, a delectable food that completely fills and satisfies, cannot fill and satisfy us because we are already filled with our history. Even if we wish to forget the past, so simple a thing as a fork knocking against a fish bone may remind us. (108–109)

It is important that we read her testimony carefully because it describes the development of a post-Holocaust consciousness as a moral act embraced as an act of witness. Rosen's evocative description of her resistance illuminates, paradoxically, her inextricable connection to the Shoah. Moreover, it models the power of fiction joined to autobiography and memoir. These genres are indispensable for the internal journey required of everyone, Jew and non-Jew, after the Holocaust.

Rosen's Holocaust fiction is premised on the understanding that the Shoah's impact did not end when the camp gates swung open and it will not disappear with the death of the last perpetrator. The travesty of decency that became routinized and commonplace in the camps inflicted humanity with an ontological wound so radical that it may, indeed, be beyond full restoration. As Rosen attests, in the Kingdom of the Night the rule of fantasy and imagination was brought to an end. Reality outstripped both of them as a fertile source for perversity and brutality: "in Holocaust fiction there can be no invention of event. Whatever can be imagined has happened. The Holocaust transformed to reality what should have occurred only in nightmares." (105) Exquisitely combining fiction with autobiography and memoir, Rosen's writing challenges us to wrestle with the Shoah's indelible imprint upon our cultural, psychic, and social makeup in the hope that we, too, will begin to intuit that this imprint, paradoxically, is our path to self-understanding and identity.

Holocaust Fiction (Re)visioned

Together the creative works of Norma Rosen and Rebecca Goldstein model Holocaust fiction as a self-reflexive, dynamic, and transformative genre (Rosen,

105). In their hands this genre does not just "mirror" the remains of a world torn apart by vicious anti-Semitism, religious intolerance, and ethical failure. It engages the insistent, haunting presence of the Shoah in a manner that seeks a *tikkun* (repair, healing) of the rupture pervading our social, ethical, and theological heritage. Herein lies one of the most significant aspects of their respective literary contributions. Within Goldstein's and Rosen's literary universe it is not enough that we acknowledge the rupture. It is a moral obligation to accept responsibility for repairing this rupture on both a personal and transpersonal level.[5] Their fictionalized accounts intend to draw the reader into a transformative process in which the question "How, after the Holocaust, can we live now?" lies at the center.[6] Through the evocative dynamism of memory and imagination, each writer attempts to break through the numbing, debilitating "frozen sea" of post-Holocaust resistance by drawing the reader into stories of ruined lives, damaged relationships, and lost meaning. Every effort is made to locate the reader in the narrative so that he or she will recognize—perhaps for the first time—that this is his or her world. Metaphor, irony, and ambivalence are consciously crafted to draw the reader into a relationship with the story so that it takes root in her or his mind, body, and emotions.

Next, each writer's fictionalized account confronts the question of the revitalization of ethics in a post-Holocaust world. Heirs to a memory in which children are mercilessly thrown alive into pits of flame by learned and "cultured" people, Rosen and Goldstein know that easy answers do not exist. Each turns to the interplay of memory, imagination, and critical self-reflection in the hope of gaining insights that do not betray the victims' cries. They bring traditional understandings of moral conduct, behavior, and practice face-to-face with the Shoah in an effort to find the roots of a credible ethic (105). They push the boundaries of traditional notions of identity, community, and unity, rejecting any formulation that tries to evade the legacy of the Shoah's omnipresent and elusive shadow.[7]

Finally, Holocaust fiction provides the arena in which Rosen and Goldstein begin the work of revisioning identity and ethics as a post-Holocaust act of *tikkun*. Fiction provides each writer with a fragmentary glimpse and a veiled understanding of the world repaired and revitalized. Both share the conviction that to glimpse the world repaired is to bear responsibility for creating it. Neither claims completeness, balance, nor certainty, but each is convinced of her responsibility to engage the task. Such engagement means confronting the "frozen seas" within the writer and the reader. Both writing and reading emerge from a deep hope that the frozen seas may be broken. The ability to engender and sustain hope in the face of the Kingdom of the Night may, indeed, be their greatest literary contribution.[8]

Notes

1. Goldstein's short story appears in *America and I: Short Stories by American Jewish Women Writers*, ed. Joyce Antler (Boston: Beacon Press, 1990), 281–289.

2. Rosen's essay appears in *Accidents of Influence: Writing as a Woman and a Jew in America* (Albany: State University of New York Press, 1992), 105–123.

3. Alan L. Berger's study of second-generation literary works provides important insights into the intergenerational nature of the Shoah's legacy. For Berger's systematic analysis of the intergenerational dimension, see his *Children of Job: American Second-Generation Witnesses to the Holocaust* (Albany: State University of New York Press, 1997).

4. Marlene E. Heinemann explores the impact of the collapse of the survivor's former moral standards upon his or her self-understanding during imprisonment and after in her *Gender and Destiny: Women Writers and the Holocaust* (New York: Greenwood Press, 1986), 40.

5. Claire Satlof provides a provocative discussion of the development of fiction as a feminist enterprise. See Satlof's "History, Fiction, and the Tradition: Creating a Jewish Feminist Poetic," in *On Being a Jewish Feminist: A Reader*, ed. Susannah Heschel (New York: Schocken Books, 1983), 186–206.

6. Alan L. Berger discusses a parallel phenomenon within second-generation literary achievements. In this context, the achievements attempt to effect a *tikkun* that embraces both the personal and transpersonal level. See Berger, *Children of Job*, 188.

7. The writings of Rebecca Goldstein and Norma Rosen directly connect the traditional concepts of *tikkun atzmi* and *tikkun olam* one to the other. After Auschwitz, repair of the self is, ultimately, repair of the world. The reality and memory of six million dead extends the traditional insight that to save or repair one life is to save an entire world. Thus, both writers bring together particularist and universalist understandings of Jewish identity without collapsing their distinction. The intrinsic interconnection between *tikkun atzmi* and *tikkun olam* has important implications for the revitalization of ethics and the development of credible moral guidelines.

8. Goldstein and Rosen stress the experiences and contributions of women in this regard. By placing women at the center of their analyses, they illumine dimensions of the Shoah that heretofore have been neglected or ignored. Focusing on relations between the sexes and between mothers and daughters, both writers highlight aspects of Jewish experience, identity, and community to expand our knowledge and understanding of this catastrophic event. Each writer makes the relation between gender and literary politics explicit and reveals its importance to the development of vital and credible Holocaust literature. Emphasizing the intersection of anti-Semitism, racism, and sexism, they challenge the reader to acknowledge the dialogue between Judaism, modernity, and feminism. Furthermore, they underscore the authority of women's experience, insights, and critical reflection within Holocaust fiction.

Works Cited

Goldstein, Rebecca. "The Legacy of Raizel Kaidish: A Story." In *America and I: Short Stories by American Jewish Women Writers*. Ed. Joyce Antler. Boston: Beacon Press, 1990, 281–289.

Rosen, Norma. "Notes Toward a Holocaust Fiction." In *Accidents of Influence: Writing as a Woman and a Jew in America*. Albany: State University of New York Press, 1992, 105–123.

9

Art and Atrocity in a Post-9/11 World

THANE ROSENBAUM

We now live in a time of terror. It preys on our fears and vulnerability, and provides all the necessary justification for having those fears in the first place—because the threats are real. That's what terrorism does. It puts images that would otherwise live on only as fantasy into our head, with real antecedents, tangible proof that our fears are not wholly imagined. There was the fall of the World Trade Center and the continued suicide bombings in Israel, the revival of anti-Semitic fervor in France, and the sympathetic tilt toward the purveyors of violence and the lack of moral equivalence in the press. One thing is for sure: such movements of extreme vulnerability only deepen and reinforce the dark, historical fears of what it means to be a Jew in the world.

But precisely at times such as these, we must be reminded not to focus so much on our fears, but on our loss, to think about the moral duties of mourning and memory. Despite the gravity of what we are now witnessing, we must resist the impulse to personalize, because the moral imperative is otherwise.

I am a post-Holocaust novelist, which means that I rely on my imagination—my capacity to reinvent worlds and reveal emotional truths—in order to speak to the Holocaust and its aftermath, one generation removed from Auschwitz. I don't write about the years 1939–1945. I see that time period as holy ground, the last millennium's answer to Mount Sinai. Instead, I focus on the looming dark shadow of the Holocaust as a continuing, implacable event, how it is inexorably still with us, flashing its radioactive teeth, keeping us all on our toes, imprinting our memories with symbols of, and metaphors for, mass death.

Yes, there were survivors of the Holocaust; one out of every three Jews of Europe did miraculously survive. Yet when we speak of survival and survivors, what do we mean? What are we talking about? What is the quality of a survivor's life? Are vital signs measured only in terms of pulse rates and heart beats, or is there something even more vital, other signs of life that can't be measured solely by medical criteria? Sometimes a heart can be broken even though it beats just fine. Physical survival, alone, is not a satisfying victory. There were millions of lost lives. But even among the survivors, there was unspeakable spiritual damage—dead souls—which inevitably is more long lasting and far reaching, since it invades the bloodstream and the DNA, infecting new generations, making it nearly impossible to engage fully, faithfully, in everyday life.

That's my fictional landscape, where my characters live, what they face, what they know to be true, the secrets they possess but are afraid to share. There is something patently absurd about reentering the world of the living after so much collective loss. Just think about it: when everything that you once loved was taken away from you—murdered, stolen, gassed, and burned—and you are now left to the world all by yourself, what incentive and reasons do you have to start over again? Unlike Job, most people would not, and should not, accept replacement children for the ones who were taken away and murdered. And yet they did. Holocaust survivors started over. They rebuilt their lives. They persevered and somehow managed to focus entirely on a future improbably before them.

Yet survivors, and even their children, had no reason to assume that the odds were with them this time around, even though, after surviving Auschwitz, you'd expect to receive a general immunity from life's worst tragedies. Survivors knew better. Things don't necessarily work out for the best. You hope and wish for more, but survivors are first and foremost realists, and fatalists. The Nazis robbed them of their faith in a normal, carefree, ordinary life. And yet the post-Holocaust world is invariably forced to live with faith; it depends on faith, almost as fossil fuel for man's continuing march away from the Stone Age. Yet we all know that the very things we have placed our faith in will eventually disappoint us. But we go on with our faith anyway, because we are commanded to do so—not by a god, but by our instincts for moral survival.

And so the post-Holocaust paradox: We have a moral duty to remember, to honor, to ritualize and acknowledge our collective and individual losses and pain, and yet we can't go too far in our obsessions with memory, because to do so presents risks and obstacles to our ability to engage in and enjoy the fullness of life, even as we have been robbed of so much of that richness.

Lately I've been thinking more and more about the ways in which my life as a novelist seems both necessary and yet strange in the gross aftermath of what happened to this nation on September 11. Because everything has now changed. Even our perception of the Holocaust has changed. It had to because atrocity now has a new and a different face and name. The lessons are more animated and pronounced. The moral obligations of remembering and acknowledging loss are something all Americans now share. We have passed into a new century, and with the World Trade Center reduced to rubble and replaced bizarrely by blue light, the Holocaust may no longer be front and center in the cultural consciousness, but yet our imaginations will always be active when it comes to dealing with human tragedy. And I'm not so sure that's such a good thing.

It seems to me that it's much tougher being a novelist nowadays. Why talk about art when the imagination is pathetically artless and inferior when compared to the real, hard horrifying events of the actual outside world? The make-believe, invented worlds that dominate fiction are frankly boring in a modern world that has a far more active imagination than mere artists could ever imagine.

After all, what goes on in my head, the stuff I make up, the lies of my art, the fakery that is fiction, seems kind of pointless when America and Israel are so much consumed with terror, doesn't it? This is not a time to toy around with fantasy. Indeed, quite the opposite is true. This is a time to surrender to, and be humbled by, real life, to recognize that the imagination no longer has anything on the hard news of the day. For the artists of the post-Holocaust world—even the more recent world—we can no longer say that it is our job to allow our imaginations to get away from us.

Because the truth is, or seems to be, that we can't. Artists are always looking to stay one step ahead of reality. But artists are also supposed to be able to dream up what politicians and bureaucrats could never imagine on their own. That's what it means to live inside your head, and not in the real world. But after the Holocaust and September 11, what is more real and terrifying: the imagination of writers or the imagination of terrorists? Whose imagination is more stretched, who forces you to suspend your disbelief more: the suicide bomber strapped with explosives, or the novelist masquerading as moral philosopher?

What artist could have imagined the attack on the World Trade Center? Or for that matter, the Palestinian teenager who walks into a Tel Aviv pizzeria not for a slice, but purely to find a place to detonate himself? It is unimaginable. And most artists wouldn't touch such a story even if they could dream it up, largely because no one would believe it. Even Hollywood, a place devoted entirely to fantasy, would find the fall of the World Trade Center and the fiery hole in the Pentagon too unbelievable to sell to a sophisticated, jaded, seen-it-all mass audience.

It was bad enough that the terrorists had the ambition and courage to sacrifice their lives for their cause, but that they did it so well (in terms of the overall carnage they inflicted) is even more galling and impressive. Say what you want, these are murderers with imagination. They are totally indifferent to human life, even their own. They make no demands, nor issue any threats. They use no words. All they do is make a lot of noise and carnage; the explosions somehow speak for themselves. But no one listens to that kind of language. The terrorist lives to terrify, and he, or she, dies in order to make that terror even more real. We fear the noise and run away from it, but we don't wish to hear or decipher it. We just want to see it disarmed. Sometimes silence is louder than any bomb, but silence doesn't make for good feed on the six o'clock news.

There is a great deal we can learn from the Holocaust, and the art that was created out of those ashes, to help us better understand how to cope in the aftermath of this more recent tragedy. Indeed, is this world that much darker than the one that witnessed eleven million lives—six million of whom were Jews—annihilated in six years? Should we have been smug in thinking that we were that much safer than the Jews of Europe? Sixty years has given rise to so many improvements and domestic conveniences in the world— from high tech to biotech, those fast computers, silent guns, and smart bombs. Surely what it means to be modern is that as technology improves, so too does humanity. But just as our lives have progressed, so too have our grievances. We are far better at saving life, and also more skilled at taking it away. Everything that we do is now mass produced, including our weapons of destruction and killing machines. We are efficient in every regard, most especially in the way we manufacture death.

So while my imagination can't compare to the inventive, murderous minds of terrorists, I can speak to the coping lessons of the post-Holocaust world, courtesy of the Nazis and their own special brand of mass death.

The first lesson is this: don't let anyone fool you—what we are living through now is not a, or the, Holocaust. What we are facing now is not genocide—for Jews or anyone else. How it is that the terrorists invaded our airspace and then punched a hole in the sky by removing the World Trade Center from the horizon of lower Manhattan, I'll never know. It is unfathomable. And it is mass murder. And it is an act of war. But it is not genocide. The terrorists of September 11 wished to leave us a political and religious message. But the Nazis were all about ideology. For them, the crime of existence was reason enough to kill.

The Nazis weren't about grievances, or making cultural or territorial demands, but rather racial cleanliness and elimination. They were neat freaks, racially speaking. They weren't blaming the Jews for anything in particular— or anything that they even believed in—other than that the Jews were alive and living among them. The terrorists thought nothing of the lives that had gone to work early on September 11, those who would die in airplanes, office towers, and government buildings. They didn't even consider their own lives. But the Nazis thought too much about the bodies that burned and the souls that got suffocated in those gas chambers and cremating ovens. The Nazis killed with indifference, but they weren't indifferent as to *whom* they were killing. The terrorists, on the other hand, did not discriminate. They must have realized that there might even be Muslims working inside the World Trade Center, and they went ahead and snuffed the life out of those buildings anyway.

Also, just as a mathematical exercise, I can't help but note the disparity in actual numbers and casualties that distinguish the Holocaust from September 11. What happened on that date may be this country's single greatest tragedy, but a comparison with the Holocaust, and genocide, is ludicrous on any scale. Simply for the purpose of proportion, here's a grotesque mathematical exercise that illustrates the point: if three thousand people were murdered in the World Trade Center, how many World Trade Center terrorist strikes would it take to add up to the eleven million people murdered by the Nazis? The answer is thirty-six hundred strikes. Numbers have a way of becoming numbing. The loss of a child or parent is personal, and it is felt deeply, right to the bone, the most exposed nerves, the rawest of emotions. But when you start talking about round numbers like a hundred strangers, people who are different from you, whom you don't know, the mind can't comprehend, because it's not as personal and the loss is too remote, unfelt and abstract.

You need the intimacy of family, and the prior history of friendship, to feel true loss—the father who won't be able to attend another Little League game, the mother who won't be around to burn dinner—to unboggle the mind, to make the pain more real, to personalize and humanize the loss. Of course, when you're talking about three thousand people, the mind completely shuts down, goes blank, fogs up. And now try six million. Even harder to personalize and make comprehensible. And no matter how many pictures of dead firemen, cops, insurance brokers, and bond traders we see, none of us will be able to appreciate and grasp the magnitude of the loss and ache of this brand of personal suffering, unless we are one of the families or friends of those firemen, cops, insurance brokers, and bond traders.

But these, after all, were New Yorkers, neighbors, people we might very well have known. Now think about six million mostly East European Jews, many of whom were very religious. Unlike the bond trader who may have lived next door, Holocaust victims, in so many ways, were unlike you. Six million Jews, and five million others—gypsies, homosexuals, Freemasons, Polish Catholics. Eleven million people shot, starved, gassed, and burned. The number is staggering. You can't possibly process it in your head. One of my students explained that she went to college where there were three thousand undergraduates, and so for her, she imagined the attack on this country as the equivalent of showing up to school on Monday and realizing that everyone was gone, dead. But what about eleven million people? As a cruel coincidence, Israel today has a population of six million people.

Stack up eleven million pennies. Write your name eleven million times on a blackboard. Walk eleven million miles. When you get right down to it, you can't compare anyone, or anything, to the Nazis when it comes to mass death.

All of it is unthinkable, so we don't think about it. But we must avoid the tricks that our minds play on us. It is so easy to depersonalize loss, to block it out, to pretend that if you don't consider it, then it will simply go away. That it won't exist unless we make it part of our lives. But the whole point of evil and the demonic is that it resists our efforts to understand it. That's why I object to the president's continued message of labeling our attackers as agents of evil, or the axis of evil. First of all, these people don't think they're evil; they think we're evil. That's why they did it. And second, that's exactly what they want us to think—calling someone evil is basically saying that we can't understand you, you're not like us, we'll never be able to figure you out, nor should we even try, because you're evil! But now is exactly the time in our nation's history when we *must* figure these people out, we *must* know them, see what makes them tick before the next bomb goes off. We can't afford to consign them to a category that we can't, and won't, comprehend because that's too easy, and it's exactly what evil expects, and wants us to do.

Yet, throughout all this, we have an even higher burden to contemplate the proper role of memory in the aftermath of atrocity. In this way, there is much we can learn from Holocaust art, and how, if at all, it can be applied to the tragedy that is now known as September 11. Is there a proper role for the artist, and specifically the novelist, at this time in our nation's history? Can we make art in a time of atrocity? Does the imagination have anything to say when it has to compete with the actual horror of collapsing skyscrapers, biologically contaminated air, and pizza shops and cafes that blow up while everyone in them is having a good time trying to get away from the very fear of running into a suicide bomber?

Unlike the fiction writers of other nations around the world, American novelists have not been known for writing serious political novels. The Czechs, the French, and the Russians, among others, have been much more prolific and successful in this regard. What we do best are ironic, domestic satires, and neurotic and unselfconscious, self-referential dramas. Perhaps this has something to do with the fact that prior to September 11, this country was relatively immune to political crises that take place on this soil. It is the privilege of being a superpower surrounded by two oceans, and having decorous Canada to the north and debt-ridden Mexico to the south, that our artists have been free to write about the insular, moral struggles of the domestic private life, rather than dealing with acts of extreme barbarism, inhumanity, and cruelty, or threats from an external world that might wish to see us eliminated.

Those who wrote about the Holocaust, however, did not have the same luxuries in choosing what would influence them artistically. They were not able to write from a safe distance. Holocaust writers were motivated by the darkest of dramas, the most unimaginable of dreams—their own and those that belonged to others. They were all essentially ghost writers. For memorists and fiction writers on the Holocaust, metaphors would take on great significance, because in a world of madness and atrocity, the only language worth speaking is the metaphorical tongue, which provides instant code words and sign language for ready, unobscured speech. When everyday language fails, because ordinary words can't express the enormity of extraordinary events, we are forced to rely on metaphors, which are immediately recognizable for their unambiguous meaning.

For virtually everyone in the post-Holocaust world, some words can never be used again without conjuring an overriding metaphor for something else. Just as train tracks, numbered arms, gas, ovens, and cattle cars have very specific Holocaust imagery, so too now will skyscrapers, terrorism, box cutters, firemen, hijacking, and antibiotics live in ways that transcend their usual meanings. And for Israelis, pizza shops and cafes have a meaning wholly different from just being places where one can go out and get a bite to eat. And of course, ghosts now have a different and yet specific association to us, as well. We are surrounded by New York ghosts—three thousand and counting. They do live among us. That's what happens when life is aborted so callously, maniacally, and maliciously. Spirits have no choice but to stay with us for a while. We should embrace them, because they are here—at least in metaphor. From now on, when it's time for Halloween and there is a knock at the door, it may not be a child, but the ghost of the child's father, wanting to be remembered.

Metaphors. We are now haunted by them. We will never be able to look at a fireman in the same way again. And when a dentist prescribes Cipro for an infected tooth, what we'll be thinking is not root canal, but what happened to this country on September 11, below Canal Street. And as for tall buildings, well, from now on they won't ever be associated again in our minds as only offering clear vistas to the sky. Because we know buildings can come down—even the tallest ones, particularly the tallest ones. September 11 has given us a new vocabulary for word association. Not even an obscure stationery-store item like a box cutter will mean the same thing ever again, especially after our writers go to work marshaling these metaphors into works of art.

But are they allowed to do this? Are artists capable of, or permitted to, recreate or reimagine nightmares? How far should the artistic license extend, or is it limitless, constrained only by the limits of the imagination itself? Is this the time for our artists to act in the only way that they know how—to write forcefully about what has just happened to us all, to provide spiritual and moral relief when all we have right now is misery, fear, and confusion? And then again, perhaps it's all too soon, not just for art, but for everything. Perhaps that's what the ghosts among us expect us to do—nothing. Retaliation is good, but reflection is perhaps even better. Silence might be the loudest sound of all, because silence has a way of being its own language, the kind of words that we need most right now.

But the problem is that Americans aren't particularly well-suited to be mourners. True grief demands silence, the quiet that comes from the soul listening to itself, the modesty and humility of loss. But in so many ways we are a nation compulsively afraid to sit with our sadness. Instead, we generate noise, the acute, reflexive American phenomenon of trash-talking, immoderate speech, and speaking out of turn, all for the purpose of sometimes avoiding the more painful experience of having to think, and feel first, before saying a word.

In the aftermath of the September 11 tragedy, there was undeniably insufficient silence. Everyone had something to say, yet everyone claimed to be in shock. But those who are truly caught in the blown circuitry of shock would ordinarily find themselves too numb to speak or to do much of anything else. The horror of what happened on September 11 should have resonated in a giant expression of collective numbness, a nation awestruck by the awfulness of it all, rendered totally mute.

Yet, alas, we live in a shock-proof society. The fall of the World Trade Center towers might have been the occasion to finally shatter this emotional armor, proving that we are not hopelessly desensitized, that we know an atrocity when we see one. But perhaps not. We act as though we have seen it all before, which in this case we haven't, although perhaps after CNN's recycled imagery of the towers being struck and finally coming down, it must have seemed to everyone as though we had in fact seen this unique tragedy before, too.

Perhaps this failure to feel comes because we are unaccustomed to waiting. This is a nation of quick fixes, instant remedies and gratification, while history, especially tragic history, requires that we sit back and ponder before making historical judgments. Yet it wasn't so much that we were all surrounded by too much talk. Given the gravity of the attack and the Pearl Harbor manner in which it was inflicted, the impulse to spread the word is entirely human and understandable. Conversation carries the survivor forward. Yet the speech of the survivor is his or her prerogative, and his or her burden. This is not true of mere witnesses, or for the incessant chattering of the media. Indeed, what was especially distressing in this moment, and in some cases offensive, was the way in which the media chose to treat the tragedy as if it presented not so much moral challenges as aesthetic opportunities.

Soon after the catastrophe, the *New Yorker* and *The New York Times Magazine,* for instance, along with other newspapers and magazines, including television news shows, assembled an A list of literary writers whom they asked to somehow make sense of the unimaginable, to describe what they had either witnessed or were feeling on that day, and to perhaps illuminate the loss. The immediacy of these nearly simultaneous recollections and essays raises the question of whether they could have ever succeeded as either art or aesthetics. Doesn't art require some measure of physical and emotional distance, a cooling-off period, quiet time to take it all in? But aside from whether these essays amounted to literary achievements, one wonders also whether the attempt to create art itself under these circumstances was a wholly premature, if not morally impious and transgressive, act.

The twentieth-century German philosopher Theodor Adorno warned that it would be barbaric to make poetry in the aftermath of Auschwitz. He meant that beauty did not exist in a concentration camp, and although the impulse to render beautiful what is otherwise grotesque may be a genuine expression of human longing, the quest itself is ultimately an immoral one. When faced with atrocity on such a grand scale, like the attack on the World Trade Center, aesthetic writing can seem smug, overly self-conscious, morally distracting, historically trivializing, and artistically vulgar—all at the same time.

Primo Levi wrote that language has a tendency to fail when words of common usage can't be expected to describe events so out of the ordinary, such as his survival of Auschwitz. But when words must be used because memory requires it, those words should be delicately and judiciously chosen, they should be accurate without being too ornate, and sufficient time must pass so that the artist can gain from the wisdom of humility and the perspective of hindsight. Indeed, it took decades before survivors and other artists were able to set down in some literary form what they had witnessed, or had reimagined, in the Holocaust.

But that's not what happened in the short weeks following September 11. In this instance, everyone had an aesthetic opinion, as if aesthetics had anything to do with the sacrificial slaughter of innocents.

Then again, the world that existed after the Holocaust was a more contemplative and modest one. There was more respect for privacy. Not everything had to be a news flash or a sound bite. People were more modest and took their time to compose their thoughts. Today, everything is on a timer. We must know everything immediately. We believe we can understand everything immediately. And when you tell us once, we walk away smugly assuming that we already got it, figured it all out, until we need to know more. We speak when not spoken to, and answer even when we don't know and have nothing to say. All so that we can interrupt the silence. Because that sound is so painful, so intolerable, that we must fill our ears with noise—mostly our own.

Newsstands and TV ratings have a way of feeding off tragedy, and magazines and newspapers have no economic incentive to make moral statements by keeping their editorial pages blank. Instead of offering their readers a gesture of wordlessness, a reminder of the limits of the printed page, editors went out and deployed their poets to supply answers, to describe evil, to domesticate horror. But why send in a poet to explain and interpret what can't be described? Or even worse, to make beautiful what is ultimately hideous and grotesque?

And as for the writers themselves, while most are inexorably driven by the imperative to write, one wonders whether anyone declined an invitation to produce a literary piece on the grounds of modesty, that it was simply too soon to absorb all the information and emotion necessary to do the tragedy justice and honor.

But could artists even qualify, or function, as suitable journalists in the extreme case of the attack on the World Trade Center? Surely the newspapers and magazines who sought out these artists were making a statement of how they wanted this story presented. Otherwise they would have left the job of pure reportage to their own staff reporters. But they weren't looking for literal truth, which couldn't be captured under these extreme circumstances anyway, no matter how faithful the witnessing. Instead they opted for artful, imagined, emotional truth, which is appealing in some instances to assist in the description of ordinary events, but has no place here, where the event itself is so out of the ordinary, and a much higher burden must be placed on faithful description.

Many artists attempted to convert death into something beautiful. And to do that is not only impious and indecent but confuses morality with aesthetics. We have to judge and punish the terrorists on moral grounds, not aesthetic ones. And as for aesthetics, we're not there yet; we're not even close. Relying on art to understand what happened on September 11 is the same thing as talking too much; it serves to insulate you from reality, and helps you avoid the painful moral issues of experiencing grief and loss through silence. This is not a time for the making of art, because murder is not a work of art, but rather a moral crime.

What is ultimately objectionable is not writing that records and preserves memory, but the making of art out of such a murderous act. There is no beauty in those buildings falling down, no matter how powerfully and eloquently evoked—at least not now. For now, it's probably best to simply show the pictures, and even then, moderately and modestly so, spared from all that exploitation and entertainment. Ground Zero is a collective grave. It is hallowed ground, not an exhibit, not a peep show, but a monument of death. I wish they would turn off those cylinders of blue light that are intended to memorialize the buildings that once stood there. This is no time for a light show. Those blue pillars don't replace anything. You can't work in them, can't travel up in their elevators. They offer no windows of the world.

The media may not realize it, but its most poignant contribution to reportage and memory is those daily obituaries of those who died. Such seemingly endless snapshots of the life that was emptied out of the World Trade Center does more to convey horror and humanize loss than anything else.

At some point the survivors of September 11 may choose to write memoirs, and let us hope that they will take their time in composing them. And others will no doubt be inspired to one day create art, as well. And when that happens, hopefully they too will show the true measure of a grief-stricken nation by having the humility to wait until the silence is over.

As a novelist, I wouldn't touch the World Trade Center, and the looming tragedy around it, as a centerpiece for a new book. I can't even speak about what happened to this country on September 11, other than what I have written here. I'm not ready to write, or talk, about it yet. Maybe what I wish most is to ask everyone else to talk less, and to not expect too much in the way of clarity and closure. Yes, it's too soon for that, too. Clarity and closure are very American aspirations, but they are unrealistic and frankly immoral in the world in which we now live, and the crises that we all now face.

We do this with the Holocaust all the time. That's why we favor movies such as *Life Is Beautiful, Schindler's List,* and even *The Diary of Anne Frank,* which have life-affirming, sugarcoated, feel-good endings. We want to feel better about the world, but the world doesn't deserve it. It is selfish on our part, a wish that makes us feel temporarily better, but ultimately leaves us empty. The victims deserve more than banalities and platitudes, or distortions and trivializations of truth.

We will not find closure, not matter how long we look, no matter how hard we wish. And we will not be better after September 11, or come out stronger in the end. There's a hole in the sky where the World Trade Center once towered, but this new emptiness in the Manhattan skyline doesn't mean that we'll be able to see things from now on more clearly. Shock takes time to settle in before the mind and heart can formulate something meaningful to say.

That's why I object so strongly to—and in fact am sickened by—former Mayor Guiliani's, and now Mayor Bloomberg's universal, prerecorded exhortations for us all to go about our lives, to live our days as if they were normal ones, to not let the terrorists disrupt our daily routines. I understand why they ask this of us. They are trying to prevent a panic, to keep us functioning, and to not show fear. But I don't care what the terrorists think; I care what the ghosts feel. It is frankly disrespectful to all those lost butchered lives to go about our days as if nothing out of the ordinary had happened to us. We should not have been moving forward, simply living our lives, so soon after the tragedy. Our lives are no longer simple, nor were they ever. Not with the FBI warning us each day to be on heightened alert, not with our medicine cabinets brimming with stockpiled Cipro, and most important of all, not with that palpable, irredeemable loss that surrounds us.

And it seemed equally disrespectful for this nation to express and define its patriotism by way of shopping. Yes, I understand that its purpose was to provide an economic stimulus, to invigorate our economy after the financial disruptions that September 11 brought upon us. But forgive me for pointing out this irony: presumably one of the motives of the terrorists in striking America was directly related to our mass consumerism and insatiable materialistic values. And yet as a response to, and as an act of defiance against our attackers, we were encouraged by our elected officials to demonstrate the mettle of what it means to be an American by going out to a restaurant, taking in a Broadway show, and stopping in at Banana Republic for a new shirt. What kind of mourning and grieving process is that? How is that honoring the dead? What does that say about our willingness to reflect on what had just happened, to stand in awe of what was done, and what can never be repaired?

For those who live in New York City, we are all now familiar with the steadily murmuring sound of the wind, which shouldn't be confused with the noises of the shifting seasons. Seasons have nothing to do with it. What we are instead hearing are the voices of ghosts, the silent screeches of spiritual outrage, the restlessness of lives prematurely taken by the most unnatural of causes. These noises won't go away, not for a while, perhaps not ever. In the meantime, we should learn to sit with the sadness, and listen to the silence.

2

Jewish American Literature

10

Africanity and the Collapse of American Culture in the Novels of Saul Bellow

Gloria L. Cronin

Until we can understand the assumptions in which we are drenched we cannot know ourselves. . . . We must take the work first of all as a clue to how we live, how we have been living, how we have been led to imagine ourselves, how our language has trapped as well as liberated us, and how we can begin to see—therefore live—afresh.

—Adrienne Rich[1]

I see my eyes in your eyes through my eyes.

—Indigo Girls[2]

Fundamental to the works of Western modernity and American literature in particular are their enduring fascination with the "primitive" Other. For the most part, this antibourgoise impulse manifests itself in curiosity about the life forms of people who have not been thoroughly industrialized, or even "civilized" in the modern sense.[3] From the turn of the twentieth century to the present, this Africanized primitive helped to structure modernism itself. By the turn of the twentieth century there were a number of public and private collections of African art owned by the avant-garde in Paris and collections in other European capitals. Picasso's revolutionary painting *Les Demoiselles d'Avignon* (1907) with its appropriation of African mask forms transformed and Africanized modern art in the same manner that the Nordic invasion of Harlem nightspots and the widespread influence of jazz in Europe and America following Paul Whiteman's symphonic jazz concert, Experiments in Modern Music (1924), transformed modern music. Likewise, Josephine Baker's parodic *Danse Sauvage* (1925) ultimately transformed twentieth-century dance, while Alain Locke's *The New Negro* (1925) and Nancy Cunard's *Negro* (1934) eventually altered the canon of American literature. At the heart and center of the modernist movement was Gertrude Stein, in whose salon were prominently displayed African figures. Small wonder F. Scott Fitzgerald summed up the entire moment with the general label the Jazz Age, indicative of the general mystique Africanity held for these Euro-American architects of the modernist movement. Yet this white artistic and literary investment in Africanity, which gave birth to the Negritude movement, *vogue negre*, and pan-Africanism, made no attempt to portray accurately or really know the black African social world behind its borrowed African objects.

Likewise, the primitivist colonialist discourse that developed in Europe, Britain, and America was not based on any real knowledge of Africanity or any love for African people or their cultures. It had its origins in the traumatic Elizabethan encounter with Africa during the Age of Discovery, and hardened during the course of eighteenth- and nineteenth-century British, European, and American imperialism. By the early twentieth century, the moment of the Jazz Age, it had become a rather highly charged racist discourse imbued with negative connotations suggesting that Africanity epitomized the antithesis of modern European discipline, order, rationality, cleanliness, godliness, taste, and sexual morality. Against a supposedly primitive benighted black Africa, industrialized, imperial white Europe measured its modernity and advanced status as the reigning world power. Accordingly, it defined people of African descent as irrational, uncivilized, backward, and pagan. Not surprisingly, Freud, the greatest of modern myth makers, associated the primitive with the sexual licentiousness of the id, with neurotics, and with children. Gertrude Stein's famous sympathy for black characters in her novels, and for expatriate black writers such as Richard Wright and Claude McKay, can now be seen as romantic racism, the chief hallmark of modernist patronage of Africanity. For Stein and so many of her "lost generation," admiration for Africans was remote and nostalgic—blacks were useful to the construction of the emergent European modernist movement because they signaled the uninhibited, the libidinous, the dynamic, and, above all, the exotic. For the European and American avant-garde Africanity and blackface cross-racial switching of masks served to overthrow the old conventions of a jaded Eurocentric bourgeoisie, which through Africanity, its diametrically opposed Other, Western culture could rejuvenate and reconfirm its preeminence through its seeming embrace.

Within the literary texts of the modernist period, and on into the post–World War II moment of Saul Bellow and his contemporaries, demeaning colonialist tropes of blackness became that black backing on the white mirror of the twentieth-century literary enterprise. Out of a paradigmatic shift involving romanticism, empiricism, commercialism, a complex modernist interracialism emerged in the service of white self-meditation. It was all the more potent as a means of maintaining white racial architecture because it was a Western fantasy about blackness and whiteness revealing the deeply embedded racial ideologies in the specular operations of its mostly white authors. Interestingly, Saul Bellow, modernism's most noted critic in post–World War II America, has also recirculated these primitivist tropes throughout his career, and with increasing animus. In the early novels, *Dangling Man* and *The Victim*, there are the discernible beginnings of this tendency. By mid-career in novels like *Henderson the Rain King, Mr. Sammler's Planet, The Dean's December,* and *A Theft,* it has become a pronounced reflex. In *The Actual* and *Ravelstein,* it has become less overt. In all but the final two works, Bellow's white protagonists regularly transfer their own internal white conflicts to black darkness, and thence to silenced black bodies as they grow increasingly paranoid about the proximity and power of black presence in their lives. Toward the peak of Bellow's career, Africanity and blackness come to represent the collapse of Western culture, lawlessness, animality, and urban desolation.

Almost nothing is known about Bellow's first attempt at writing a novel, *The Very Dark Tree,* except that it was about a white man who turned into a black man. Bellow reports having tossed it down the garbage vent in a cheap apartment building, after deeming it unfit for publication. It would seem that blackness has fascinated Bellow from the very beginning of his career.[4]

In *Dangling Man* (1944),[5] Joseph expresses his own condition of boredom and ennui in terms of an imprisoning and inadequate whiteness. When he hears by mail that his friend Tad has gone to Algiers, and that Stillman is still traveling in Brazil, he complains, "I grow rooted in my chair. . . . When I do go, I do not go far. My average radius is three blocks" (13–14). Algiers and Brazil suggest exotic primitive Africanized spaces tantalizing in their fantasy of a curative spiritual horizon beyond Joseph's narrow world. However, as yet there is no personified black presence in the novel. The individual embodiment of these cultures is remotely suggested rather than evoked.

By the second novel, *The Victim* (1947),[6] Bellow's depiction of the dreadful, decaying urban landscape of New York during a burning hot summer is troped as a threatening, chaotic, primeval jungle of terrors. There is still no individual black embodiment of Africanity in this novel, but there is the terror-filled landscape of Asa's New York described as a pitiless African lion, "something inhuman that didn't care about anything human and yet was implanted in every human being too, one speck of it, and formed a part of him that responded to heat and glare, exhausting as these things were" (51). By implication, post-Holocaustal, inhuman New York is African and black.

In *Henderson the Rain King* (1959),[7] Bellow invokes both Africanity and individual Africans in the service of his discussion of literary modernism and white self-presence; however, he works through stereotypical tropes of African individuals. Through its deliberate parody of Conrad's *Heart of Darkness*, Hemingway's African novels, and the immensely popular Tarzan stories, *Henderson the Rain King* becomes a comic archive of all the primitivist racial tropes of nineteenth-century colonialist literature. As such it also reinscribes them in the contemporary white master narrative. It reveals Bellow's familiarity with African ethnographies, travel narratives, boys' adventure tales, journalistic accounts, and novels of African adventure. Here we find Africa simultaneously depicted as the heart of darkness and the cradle of civilized enlightenment in parody of both Conrad and Lawrence. Africa is alternately primitive, violent, and filthy, while Africans themselves are noble savages, savage savages, "pet" natives, faithful native bearers, desexualized black mammys, earth mothers, harem goddesses, tricksters, heathens, killers, wicked witch doctors, conspirers, healers, and exotics. African degradation and African backwardness are the principal tropes of Africanity that emerge.

Dahfu, a Western-educated comic rendition of the noble savage, is a black man in whiteface playing a black man. As a latter day transcendental philosopher, blood brother, and friend of beasts, he is a fabulous character out of a white child's storybook. When he is not a parody of Don Quixote and Ernest Hemingway, he is an intellectualized, upscale, blackface version of Tarzan, who improves his nobility by playing with lions. The multiple racial cross-dressings here are complex. Clearly he is a construct through whom Bellow and Henderson parody the formulas of the modernist novel and redress the plight of Western culture in the wake of late romantic modernist despair. Africanity therefore serves as a medium for white self-meditation, but real Africa and Africans remain foreclosed from the novelist's imagination. Dahfu, far from being an African, is Henderson's shadow self. Accordingly, Toni Morrison sees Henderson as deeply indebted to Africanity. For her Henderson is "a new white man in a new found land: leaping, pounding, and tingling, over the pure white lining of the gray Arctic silence . . . whose Whiteness, alone, is mute, meaningless, unfathomable, pointless, frozen, veiled, curtained, dreaded, senseless, implacable."[8] As Bellow carefully crafts our last vision of Henderson dancing on the frozen polar whiteness with an orphaned African child in his arms, and the soul of the Black King packed away in his baggage, we realize that he has had to steal, kidnap, adopt, and transport literal African "blackness" in order to rescue himself from a problematic modern American whiteness.

The white racial architecture of *Mr. Sammler's Planet* (1970),[9] eleven years later, reveals a far more virulent use of primitivist tropes of Africanity. This time Africanity has a real face, though still no name as it emerges in the mythic figure of the legendary, nameless, black pickpocket. Sammler describes him as a dangerous black "animal," but clearly he functions as Sammler's nemesis, alter ego, and antitype. In one of the novel's most famous scenes, Bellow even illustrates the racial dynamics of mutual contempt as the pickpocket boxes Sammler up in a vestibule and threatens him by exposing himself to him. In another pivotal scene, Bellow depicts the complexities of the mutual racial gaze that passes between the two men as they stare at each other from two ends of a crowded bus through twin pairs of dark, masking glasses.

Bellow's contempt for the chaotic, ethnicized 1960s scene in American culture is registered in this novel in a very powerful series of Africanized primitivist tropes of cultural collapse. When Sammler thinks to phone the police he desists, because all the smashed telephones and urinals reflect to him African degradation, the filthy primeval forest come to New York City. He is an elderly European Jew acculturated at the end of the Austro-Hungarian Empire who now finds himself "striding blind" (6) inside the landscape of an Africanized American society, which looks to him like Byzantium, Italy, Greece, Asia, or Africa, a new region where black barbarism has eclipsed the civilized (white and Jewish) world: "New York was getting worse than Naples or Salonika. It was like an Asian, an African town, from this standpoint. The opulent sections of the city were not immune. You opened a jeweled door into degradation, from hypercivilized Byzantine luxury straight into the state of nature, the barbarous world of color erupting from beneath" (6–7). It is the world of Henderson's "African" jungle ruled, in Sammler's mind, by "this handsome, this striking, arrogant pickpocket, this African prince or great black beast [who] was seeking whom he might devour between Columbus Circle and Verdi Square" (14). Sammler later notes, "From the black side, strong currents were sweeping over everyone. Child, black, redskin—the unspoiled Seminole against the horrible Whiteman. Millions of civilized people wanted oceanic, boundless, primitive, neckfree nobility, experienced, a strange release of galloping impulses, and acquired the peculiar aim of sexual niggerhood for everyone" (130).

Nearly all the stereotypical representations of blackness as degeneracy within the white master narrative are evoked in this passage: the black man as sexual degenerate, interloper, barbarian, savage, source of moral corruption, dangerous, offensive, hedonistic, and criminal. Despite the novel's seeming awareness of the dynamics of a mutually constructed American racial gaze, the book fails, as does *Henderson the Rain King*, to convey any particular moral passion about issues of race. Bellow is more interested in the philosophical and literary archaeology of literary modernism, and in denouncing 1960s radicalism, than he is in really engaging the topic of American racial architecture. Sadly, what most readers remember about the book is its racial trope of sexual "niggerhood." By 1964 Bellow's use of primitivist Africanity as metaphor for cultural disorder has become reflexive. In just such ways Morrison accuses that the white modernist imagination "sabotages itself, locks its own gates, and pollutes its vision" on matters of race (*Playing in the Dark*, xi).

Emily Budick has noted that for all its attempt to produce "a highly moral text," this book "may create problems for both its black and Israeli readers, for Bellow's African American character serves as a code and warning in relation to two related phenomena. He represents American ethnicity gone wild. And he stands for that other national identity that proved for many Jews irresistible and might be seen in light of the power and violence unleashed: The State of Israel" (150).[10] Sammler's description of New York being worse than Naples or Salonika is dubiously racial because for all that it is a "general depiction of the human race, especially in the aftermath of the Second World War and its various catastrophes, including (but not exclusively) the extermination of European Jewry" (151), it is a denunciation of blackness. However, her strongest moral objection is that

> in using a black character to represent moral and sexual degeneracy, especially when the major concern is Jewish history, the book cannot escape troubling racist implications. This potential racism is rendered more central and more offensive by the passages comparing New York to Africa, with currents of corruption coming from the "black" side. It is not helped much by the fact that the black character is rendered in Bellow's novel as a figure of power and energy. He is, clearly, a deeply felt, deeply internalized alter ego and fantasy image of Bellow himself. He is potent in a way that the similarly aristocratic Sammler never quite was and certainly, in his old age and half-blindness, never can be again. (151–152)

She further notes that for many Jewish writers this conversation between and about blacks and Jews means "dissolving their specific ethnic identity into a universalist mode, declaring such separateness, strangeness, and ethnicity as they wish to preserve through their identification with blacks. The African American becomes a nostalgic marker of what, as Jews, they feel themselves to have lost in their acceptance into the American mainstream."[11]

Likewise, Joshua L. Charlson argues that Bellow makes use of "a certain conception of the ethnic body as a site over which power struggles take place."[12] He argues that the pickpocket is Sammler's double, not his other, a sort of "postmodern agent" (529) whose presence creates "inconsistencies" (530) within the text. Ultimately he causes a breakdown in Bellow's realist aesthetic because "in the cause of its conservative critique, however it uncannily places before Sammler—and before us—the postmodern ethnic body as a reminder of racial difference that continually rises from the repressed of the American collective unconscious" (536).

In *The Dean's December* (1981),[13] Bellow focuses even more directly on American racial traumas through his direct examination of inner-city crime and the black community. This time there are several black characters and they all have names. Some are evil and some are heroic. However, once again Bellow draws upon a familiar stock of primitivist and contemporary sociological tropes of dreadful blackness as the trope for the collapse of the American inner city as well as Western culture. Part of the plot involves the investigation of the murder of white Rick Lester by two blacks, Lucas Ebry and Riggie Hines. In his attempt to understand the doomed black inner-city population in American society, Bellow once again reveals through Dean Corde and his dubious nephew Mason the distortions and opacities of white American racial perception. The dean's speculation is that a disciplined young white student, Rick Lester, religious and married, has been followed home from a bar by two vicious blacks, Lucas Ebry and Riggie Hines, who proceed to abuse his innocent hospitality, murder, and rob him. Mason's speculation is that the murder was committed by another black man, not his friend Lucas Ebry. Furthermore, he argues, the white, supposedly religious, married and heterosexual Lester was sexually kinky, racially offensive in a black bar, and then stupid enough to take the two blacks home for a sexual orgy that ended with them gagging, binding, and tossing him out the window. As mostly white readers, we are lost between two narratives of interracial violence, both of which reflect more negatively on the black participants than the white Rick Lester. The confused dean muses,

> It was like seeing through a barrier of vapor or gas. Reconstruction was all the more problematic because of the emotional heaviness of all the circumstances, even time and weather. It has been one of those choking, peak-of-summer, urban-nightmare, sexual and obscene, running-bare times, and death panting behind the young man, closing in. Some unconscious choice had been made, some mixture, an emulsion of silliness and doom shaken up and running over. (38–39)

Later, as Corde reviews his notes on the crime, after visits to the courts, hospitals, detoxification centers, and the prison, he realizes "that on his own turf, which was also theirs, he has found a wilderness wilder than the Guiana bush" (158). Supposedly objective journalistic and sociological research, even "in-country," has not dissipated the barrier or vapor of gas that obstructs his seeing. His habit of racial dichotomizing into "us" and "them" precludes this. He notes that the lawyers and clients in the courtrooms he visits "wore dashikis, ponchos, cloaks, African amulets, rings and beads—symbolic ornaments symbolizing nothing. There were brash strong women, subtle black small women who had little to say. Their skulls sometimes were terraced, very curious; or else their hair was teased out, dyed worked into small viper-tangle braids; put up in blue, pink, yellow plastic rollers" (159). The legal system seems to him as an Africanized wilderness of mostly black plaintiffs and black parolees stylin' African.

Central to Bellow's account of this primitive disruptive blackness at the heart of American urban culture is his almost allegorical depiction of Winthrop and Smithers struggling to survive together as heroic and violent, doomed black men who are clear-headed about their own fate in late twentieth-century American culture. Winthrop has lost count of how many people he has previously murdered and has nearly killed himself with a drug overdose. When he sees that he is going to die "in a hotel room near Sixty-third and Stony Island, the end of the el tracks, the tip of rat-shit Woodlawn" (190), he has to threaten violence to get himself admitted for methadone treatment. It is here he sees the dying Smithers and helps the hospital staff to save his life. From there Winthrop and Smithers open a detoxification center and try to help other black men in the deepening wilderness of the inner-city drug culture. Violence, chaos, and the collapse of culture are all depicted in dread-filled black tropes. Dean Corde's black underclass is "a damned monstrous wilderness of people doomed and stripped utterly bare, a group representative of the last phase of the proletariat which is entirely naked, without illusions because there was nothing to support illusions and suffering" (206). In his view it cannot be redeemed, and the race war will be to the death:

> Of course, they aren't proletarians. They're just a lumpen population. We do not know how to approach this population. We haven't even conceived that reaching it may be a problem. So there's nothing but death before it. Maybe we've already made our decision. Those that can be advanced into the middle class, let them be advanced. The rest? Well, we do our best by them. We don't have to do any more. They kill some of us. Mostly they kill themselves. (206–207)

Perhaps to counterbalance the black characters associated with underclass life and criminality in *The Dean's December*, Bellow draws the almost equally sinister portrait of an elegant but nameless black American ambassador. Corde describes him as a "discreet, soft-spoken, almost gentle, mysteriously earnest, handsome black man" (59) of "breeding" and "delicacy" (60). With him, thinks the desperately lonely and isolated Corde, "conversation was definitely possible" (61). However, it is not long before Corde realizes that for all that "he was sympathetic, exquisitely decorous, . . . he didn't need to hear it all" (65). At this point the portrait falls apart. This man who has no name is an exquisite diplomatic functionary, an actor who styles the part of intelligent listener/conversationalist so well even Corde almost falls for it, so hungry is he for intellectual companionship. Like the exquisitely dressed black pickpocket of Sammler fame, this unnamed black diplomat is the outward sign of an elegant black impostorship. He is a black man posturing as civilized European with his exquisite clothing and French wife.

From *Mr. Sammler's Planet* on to *A Theft* (1989), Bellow's principal vision of blackness in America is that of the eclipse of white culture by the violence-ridden Africanized primeval forest, of which the Ugandan situation in *The Dean's December* functions as both analogy and prophecy:

> Children born outside the law and abandoned by parents can be eaten by dogs. It must be happening in places like Uganda now. The army of liberators who chased out Idi made plenty of babies. Eaten by dogs. Or brought up without humanity. Nobody teaching the young language, human usages or religion, they will go back to the great ancient forest and be like the wild beasts of Orpheus. None of the great compacts of the human race respected. Bestial venery, feral wanderings, incest, and the dead left unburied. Not that we have any great forests to go back to. There was Jonestown in the Guyana jungle, where they put on public displays of racially mixed cunnilingus as a declaration of equality, and where some cannibalism seems to have occurred, and finally the tub of Kool-Aid poison. But that wasn't the ancient forest, it was the city. (251)

This horrific updated version of the Africanized ancient forest, which is now the face of the American inner city, suggests that Conrad's heart of darkness trope now lies even more firmly embedded within Bellow's contemporary American master narrative of Western culture. Dean Corde, like his creator, for all his genuine humanitarian concern, is blind to the discursive operations of blackness: "I see more than a white mask facing a black one. I see two pictures of the soul and spirit—if you will have it straight. In our flesh and blood existence I think we are pictures of something. So I see a picture, and a picture. Race has no bearing on it" (204). But he is self-deceived. And whether Bellow admits this or not, race always "has a bearing on it" in American cultural history. In *The Dean's December* his account of blackness is ultimately buried inside a global account of other doomed populations. The racial issues he started to explore get subsumed under global and class issues and finally disappear in the universal chaos. Despite the similarities Bellow draws between the respective barbarities of American democracy, Eastern European totalitarianism, and Ugandan collapse, American and global racial issues will not neatly disappear into this generalized political paradigm. Nor can they be made to disappear into the gorgeous universalist visions of the giant Mount Palomar telescope inside of whose grand optical arrangements the observer might be tricked into believing that the Africanized wilderness has literally or metaphysically disappeared under galaxies and galaxies of brilliant shining stars.

As recently as *A Theft* (1989),[14] Bellow sharpened his use of the trope of Africanized wilderness as white cultural decay in his depiction of the morally outraged Clara Velde. Clara, upon finding her well-bred German au pair girl has slept with an underclass black man on her beautiful silk couch, reveals the relationship between the hellfire and old-time religion and the racial ideologies she has brought from the white Bible Belt back country of Indiana and Illinois. Despite the fact that she has come to New York and made an important career, Clara's "pornographic fantasy" centers on the specter of miscegenation—"that image of a dark man raping a valuable white woman" (7). She automatically assumes that Gina's house party was composed of "street people," and that Gina has had sex with this black Frederic, who was seen lying on top of her on Clara's silk-cushioned couch, wearing combat boots no less. Clearly black Frederic, not upper-class white European Gina, is to blame for "spraying the whole place with sexual excitement" (71). Giving full vent to her outrage against the dark underclass presence that menaces her precariously maintained upper middle-class white world, she fumes, "These people came up from the tropical slums to outsmart New York, and with all the rules crumbling here as elsewhere, so that nobody could any longer be clear in his mind about anything, they could do it" (73). When she says to Gina, "And don't try to tell me he's being accused because of his color," Gina responds to this racist outburst with considerable irony: "I didn't try. People *are* nasty about the Haitians" (70).

When Ms. Wong, Clara's Chinese confidante, tactfully tries to point out that Clara herself has black friends in the house and is personally friendly with the colored lady who works there, Clara counters: "Ms. Peralta is no stranger. She brings her children here at Thanksgiving, and they eat with the girls at the same table. And why not?" (62). She does finally concede, however, that this might be confusing to the European girl. Furthermore, while her white friends and dubious ex-husbands, one of whom was a Mafia crook, need no special credentials to enter Clara's morally and socially confused life, the colored Ms. Peralta can only come into her home because she is triple-bonded and guaranteed by an agency. Seeing at least a tip of the iceberg of her own racial constructions, Clara defensively snarls, " 'I can see that this is a mixture that might puzzle somebody just over from Europe for the first time. My husband and I are not rashists' (This was a pronunciation Clara could not alter)" (62).

Finally, she designates Frederic as a "disgusting girl-fucker who used her [Gina] as his cover to get into the house and now sticks her with this theft" (71). Later, Clara too will become a thief in defrauding the insurance company over the lost ring. Her overall cultural assessment is doubly ironic in light of her own spotted sexual history: "I didn't think well of her [Gina's] Caribbean romance, or sex experiment. Just another case of being at sea amongst collapsing cultures" (89). Miscegenation, that oldest of American cultural taboos, is the site of the collapse of white culture. Not surprisingly, Clara's idea of a concession is comic in its unmitigated racial intolerance: "Inasmuch as Gina might have prevailed by reasonable means over him, Clara was ready to revise her opinion of Frederic too (On her scale of ten, she could upgrade him from a less than zero to one)" (84). Gogmagogsville, as depicted in *A Theft*, is an Africanized social jungle in which underbred black studs prey on well-bred white women. "Unless heaven itself were to decree that Gogmagogsville had gone far enough, and checked the decline — time to lower the boom, send in the Atlantic to wash it away" (65) thinks Clara. Presumably in Clara's fundamentalist paradigm, only the flood primeval or the apocalypse will foreclose black predatoriness and subsequent cultural chaos in white America.

Oriental Ms. Wong also becomes a foreign suspect "other of color." Clara's alter ego, priestly confessor, and confidante, Ms. Wong, for all that she is a New York lady, is finally primitivized by Clara as an "inscrutable chinee." As Clara's crumbling sense of self wanes, Ms. Wong's foreignness looms larger in her increasingly guilty and paranoid imagination. It occurs to Clara that her many revelations about the intimacies she has shared with Ms. Wong about her lover, Ithiel Regler, may have made him seem entirely too attractive. Perhaps Ms. Wong may become the sexual rival, the Chinese courtesan: "How long has the little bitch been dreaming of having him for herself! No way! . . . But I have to spin her off very slowly, for if I cut the relationship, she's in a position to hurt me" (92). However, Clara knows that somehow in overvaluing upper-class, intellectual, white, male Ithiel and the ring symbolizing their relationship, she has failed to properly value many kinds of "others" in her American world. With all her false racial and social class categories crumbling, she experiences a dissolving and a breaking up inside of her sense of her own social importance in Gogmagogsville. "She hurried, crying, down Madison Avenue, not like a person who belonged there but like one of the homeless, doing grotesque things in public, one of those street people turned loose from an institution. The main source of tears came open" (109). In this novella, the Object itself is the mirror in which the (racial) subject sees only an illusion of herself. Interestingly, in *The Actual* (1997) and *Ravelstein* (2000), Bellow seems to have sidestepped racial issues.

Like so many other mainstream white American authors, Bellow has used the Africanist persona as a reflex mechanism through which his white protagonists meditate on a forbidden, feared shadow self that, while it moves some protagonists with fear, longing, and fascination, also reveals the parasitic dependency of white identity on blackness. As Bellow and his protagonists use blackness for meditations on physical terror, cultural boundarylessness, internal loneliness, incompleteness, power, powerlessness, evil, and the collapse of culture, they fantasize that barbarism and the primeval forest is African, and Other to them. Even when they penetrate their own mirrors and locate the dreadful primeval forest within self and whiteness, they register great difficulty at socially or imaginatively entering that very blackness they are estranged from. In the meantime, the Bellow novel has recirculated the same old Conradian primitivist tropes of blackness.

Walter Shear suggests that this is directly attributable to Bellow's liberal notion of the intellect, its vulnerable sensitivity to a world of Otherness, and its tendency to despair.[15] Critic Venkateswarlu points out that Bellow's political positions and his angles of vision on contemporary American reality are expressed in given cultural domains. To get at the genesis of Bellow's critique of the generation of the sixties in *Mr. Sammler's Planet* for instance, he argues, is confusing, since in this book perceptions of the New Left are piled in together with the other insanities of the sixties, as well as with the horror and legacy of the Holocaust. He concludes that Bellow's critique of sixties radicalism "gets submerged in an overall critique of Western decadence."[16] Hence Bellow's novels perpetuate and legitimate misconceptions in the guise of predictable, generalized artistic arguments (129–130). It is certainly true that in his later years, Bellow has evaded really grappling with racial issues by sliding off into an idealist nonracially nuanced role of liberal humanist defender of high culture and Western values.

As an increasing number of postcolonialist critics, linguists, theorists, cultural historians, and philosophers address the issue of racial ideologies in white-authored colonialist discourse, we begin to understand the discursive operations of that metaphorical veil Du Bois first named for us in *Souls of Black Folk*. On one side of this veil, this critical narrative asserts, whiteness is given primacy, is considered originary, names itself as subject and its black other as object. On the other side of the veil lies a blackness that is secondary, and which receives its name "nigger." It is under that linguistic sign that all other white-generated pejorative racial language is unified and organized. This veil, which is in reality a two-way mirror, says Du Bois, allows those within the veil near enough to the fabric to afford a clear view of what lies beyond. However, those viewing from without see only the seeming opacity of the veil, which is of their own fabricating. In the Bellow novel we never see real Africans or African Americans for two reasons: in one set of novels they never appear at all, a matter of significance since Bellow styles himself as a social realist whose canvas is either Chicago or New York. In the other set of novels in which they do appear, they are obsured behind a thick veil of dread-filled primitivist tropes.[17]

Critic Frank Lentricchia suggests that this happens in white writers like Bellow because literary and linguistic "hegemony . . . is fundamentally a process of education carried on through various institutions of civil society in order to make normative, inevitable, even 'natural' the ruling ideas of ruling interests" (Venkateswarlu, "Ideology," 174). The mainstream American literary canon is just such an institution. Edward Said explains that such representations are "embedded first in the language and then in the culture, institutions, and political ambiance of the representer."[18] In a "dialectic of self-fortification and self-confirmation," culture achieves its hegemony over society and the state through a constantly practiced differentiation of itself from what it believes to be not itself."[19] The net effect of this mainstream construction of "constantly practiced differentiation" on the national psyche and on the construction of the educated and uneducated American reader is profound, writes Jacques Lacan, because "consciousness is the sum of the effects of speech on a subject, at the level at which the subject constitutes himself out of the effects of the signifier."[20]

Thus it is this liberal humanist, white consciousness, such as Saul Bellow's, which in a double move conceives of itself as "civilized" and there-fore not "nigger" while simultaneously reinforcing and perpetuating the niggerhood of those behind its veil. Hans Robert Jauss suggests that such a descriptive system "constitutes the paradigmatic level . . . [the] image fields . . . [and] associations called forth by certain words which have ad-equate connotative potential and evoke in the reader a self-contained sphere of ideas which are often recognized when just one single element of such a system is presented."[21] Bellow's reflexive use of a constantly evoked Africanized wilderness for American cultural diversity, and his invocation of cultural "niggerhood," is just such an element. Jean Paul Sartre describes this as the language of colonialism in which "colonists" pass "linguistic tokens among [them-selves] in conversation, not to pass along information or to mean, but as signifier[s] of [their] serial relations of race and power, as signs that [they] belong."[22] Aldon Lynn Nielsen explains that these linguistic "tokens" such as Bellow has used form a system of "interlocking self-reinforcing grids . . . [which] evoke in the reader a self-contained sphere of ideation which is recognized when just one

single element of such a system is evoked." He reminds us, It cannot provide
a Wittgensteinian view of the world (certainly Bellow's desire),

> because its intent is never to know the object but always to try to
> create and recreate the subject. Such a racial object is now [that]
> which cannot participate fully within culture, the one who is
> held to be an ahistorical creature with no tradition of art, and
> more particularly, burdened with an intuitive, unreflecting sen-
> suality, latent criminality, and few civilized instincts despite what
> trappings of white culture he or she might mimic.[23]

Hence the constitution of such whiteness has been to a large extent the
province of literature, and it operates by calling up the specter of the dreadful
not-white Other through its own guilty dread (Sartre, *Dialectical Reason*, 321).

Perhaps it is the matter of guilty white dread that offers the best explanation for Bellow's literary uses of frightening blackness. As Ursula K. Le
Guin explains:

> If you hold a thing to be totally different from yourself, your fear
> of it may come out as hatred, or as awe, or reverence.... If you
> deny any affinity with another person or kind of person ... if you
> declare it to be wholly different from yourself—as men have
> done to women, and class has done to class, and nation has done
> to nation—you may hate it, or deify it; but in either case you
> have denied its spiritual equality, and its human reality. You have
> made it into a thing to which the only relationship is a power
> relationship. And thus you have fatally impoverished your own
> reality. You have, in fact, alienated yourself. (Morrison, *Playing
> in the Dark*, 38)

In Bellow's defense, all of us who are white writers, readers, and critics
engage in "impoverishing of our own reality" through the uncritical and
continued recirculation of such racial tropes. Bellow is only one of a huge
number of white American writers to engage in these racial constructions.
Francois Lyotard notes with dismay that "any attempt to reform language
comes up against the circle that it is our tool, the only tool we possess, for
the purpose of transforming it."[24] Hans-Georg Gadamer observes, "escaping
from the sphere of influence of our education which is linguistic and of our
thought which is transmitted through language, as well as the doubt about
our capacity for openness to a reality which does not correspond to our
opinions, our fabrications, our previous expectations ... is unlikely" even
though it is with "increasing urgency, we are led to ask, whether there may
not be hidden in our experience of the world a primordial falsity ... [leading]

down a path whence there is no other issue than destruction."[25] At the heart of Bellow's novels is just this primordial falsity vis-à-vis Africanity.[26] All too frequently Bellow's racial subjects have used the female or Africanist persona as a reflex mechanism through which they meditate on a forbidden, feared shadow self of white masculinity, for meditations on physical terror, cultural chaos, internal loneliness, and the decline of Western culture. The historical fact of four hundred years of black presence on the North American continent is registered here.

Saul Bellow's nearly forty years of unremitting reactionary disgust with contemporary literary studies, critical theory, and multiculturalism is a growing bewilderment to this generation of readers increasingly sensitive to Bellow's misogynous depictions of women and his primitivist dread-filled images of blackness. Such critics will not be satisfied with Bellow's crabby, evasive, racist remarks, or his unconvincing attempts to defend his recurrent use of blackness as a metaphor for Western and American cultural collapse. As more critics and readers feel an ethical obligation not to avert their eyes from the literary construction of the racial subject and the racial object and the white literary master narrative out of politeness and deference to an icon of American literary culture, the subject will increasingly shape twenty-first-century assessments of Bellow's place in American literary history.

Notes

1. Adrienne Rich, "When We Dead Awaken: Writing as Re-vision," *College English* 34, no. 1 (1972): 18, 161.

2. Indigo Girls, "Ten Thousand Wars," on the album *Nomads, Indians, Saints* (New York: Epic, 1990).

3. Paul Lauter, ed., *The Heath Anthology of American Literature* (Lexington: D.C. Heath and Company, 1990), 958.

4. Saul Bellow, "Interview," *Playboy* 44, no. 5 (1997): 59.

5. Saul Bellow, *Dangling Man* (New York: Vanguard, 1944).

6. Saul Bellow, *The Victim* (New York: Vanguard, 1947).

7. Saul Bellow, *Henderson the Rain King* (New York: Viking, 1959).

8. Toni Morrison, *Playing in the Dark* (Cambridge: Harvard University Press, 1992), 59.

9. Saul Bellow, *Mr. Sammler's Planet* (New York: Viking Press, 1970).

10. For the most up-to-date and inclusive treatment of the subject of Jewish-black race relations in North America, see Emily Miller Budick, *Blacks and Jews in Literary Conversation* (Cambridge: Cambridge University Press, 1998).

11. Emily Budick, "Race, Homeland, and Identity," in *Blacks and Jews in Literary Conversation* (Cambridge: Cambridge University Press, 1998), 121.

12. Joshua L. Charlson, "Ethnicity, Power, and the Postmodern in Saul Bellow's *Mr. Sammler's Planet*," *The Centennial Review* (Fall 1997): 529–536.

13. Saul Bellow, *The Dean's December* (New York: Harper, 1981).

14. Saul Bellow, *A Theft* (New York: Penguin, 1989).

15. Walter Shear, "Bellow's Fictional Rhetoric: The Voice of the Other," in *Saul Bellow and the Struggle at the Center*, ed. Eugene Hollahan. *Georgia State Literary Studies* 12 (New York: AMS, 1996): 189–202.

16. D. Venkateswarlu, "Ideology in Saul Bellow's *Mr. Sammler's Planet*," in *Jewish-American Writers and Intellectual Life in America*, series in American Literature (New Delhi: Prestige, 1993), 174–180.

17. I am indebted to Aldon Lynn Nielsen, *Reading Race: White American Poets and the Racial Discourse in the Twentieth Century* (Athens: University of Georgia Press, 1988), 1–2 for such a clear expression of this dynamic.

18. Edward Said, *Orientalism* (New York: Vintage 1979), 272.

19. Edward Said, *The World, the Text, and the Critic* (Cambridge, MA: Harvard University Press, 1983), 12.

20. Jacques Lacan, *The Four Fundamental Concepts of Psycho-Analysis*, ed. Jacques Alain Miller, trans. Alan Sheridan (New York: Norton, 1981), 126.

21. Hans Robert Jauss, *Aesthetic Experience and Literary Hermeneutics*, trans. Michael Shaw (Minneapolis: University of Minnesota Press, 1982), 264.

22. Jean Paul Sartre, *Critique of Dialectal Reason*, ed. Jonathan Ree, trans. Alan Sheridan-Smith (London: Verso Editions, 1982), 322.

23. Aldon Lynn Nielsen, "To What Extent Does Language Preform Thought?" in Hans Georg Gadamer, *Truth and Method*, trans. Joel Weinsheimer and Donald G. Marshal (New York: Continuum, 19), 491.

24. Ursula K. Le Guin, "American SF and the Other," quoted in *The Language of the Night: Essays on Fantasy and Science Fiction*, ed. Susan Wood (New York: Putnam, 1979). Rpt. in *The Harper and Row Reader*, ed. Wayne C. Booth and Marshall W. Gregory (New York: Harper, 1984), 369.

25. Aldon Lynn Nielson, *op cit.* Georg Gadamer, "To What Extent Does Language Preform Thought?" In *Truth and Method* (New York: Continuum, 1993), 491.

26. Francois Lyotard, in Peter Dews, "The Letter and the Line: Discourse and Its Other in Lyotard," *Diacritics* 14 (1984): 40–49.

Works Cited

Bellow, Saul. *The Actual*. New York: Penguin, 1997.

———. *Dangling Man*. New York: Vanguard, 1944.

——. *The Dean's December.* New York: Harper, 1981.

——. *Henderson the Rain King.* New York: Viking, 1959.

——. *Mr. Sammler's Planet.* New York:Viking, 1970.

——. *Ravelstein.* New York: Viking, 2000.

——. *A Theft.* New York: Penguin, 1989.

——. *The Victim.* New York: Vanguard, 1947.

Budick, Emily. "Race, Homeland, and Identity." In *Blacks and Jews in Literary Conversation.* Cambridge: Cambridge University Press, 1998.

Buell, Lawrence. "Introduction: In Pursuit of Ethics." *Publications of the Modern Language Association of America* 114 (January 1, 1999): 7–20.

Charlson, Joshua L. "Ethnicity, Power, and the Postmodern in Saul Bellow's *Mr. Sammler's Planet." The Centennial Review* (Fall 1997): 529–536.

Dews, Peter. "The Letter and the Line: Discourse and Its Other in Lyotard." *Diacritics* 14 (1984): 40–49.

Du Bois, W. E. B. *The Souls of Black Folk.* New York: New American Library Signet Classic, 1969.

Gadamer, Hans Georg. "To What Extent Does Language Preform Thought?" In *Truth and Method.* New York: Continuum, 1993.

Indigo Girls. "Ten Thousand Wars" on the album *Nomads, Indians, Saints.* New York, Epic: 1990.

Jauss, Hans Robert. *Aesthetic Experience and Literary Hermeneutics.* Trans. Michael Shaw. Minneapolis: University of Minnesota Press, 1982.

Lacan, Jacques. *The Four Fundamental Concepts of Psycho-Analysis.* Ed. Jacques Alain Miller. Trans. Alan Sheridan. New York: Norton, 1981.

Lauter, Paul, ed. *The Heath Anthology of American Literature.* Lexington: D.C. Heath and Company, 1990.

Le Guin, Ursula K. "American SF and the Other." In *The Language of the Night: Essays on Fantasy and Science Fiction.* Ed Susan Wood. New York: Putnam, 1979. Rpt. in *The Harper and Row Reader.* Ed. Wayne C. Booth and Marshall W. Gregory. New York: Harper and Row, 1984.

Morrison, Toni. *Playing in the Dark.* Cambridge: Harvard University Press, 1992.

Nielsen, Aldon Lynn. "To What Extent Does Language Preform Thought?" In Gadamer, Hans Georg. *Truth and Method.* Trans. Joel Weinsheimer and Donald G. Marshal. New York: Continuum, 1993.

Rich, Adrienne. "When We Dead Awaken: Writing as Re-vision." *College English* 34, no. 1 (1972): 18–30.

Roediger, David. *Black on White: Black Writers on What It Means to Be White*. New York: Schocken, 1998.

Said, Edward. *Orientalism*. New York: Vintage, 1979.

——. *The World, the Text, and the Critic*. Cambridge, MA: Harvard University Press, 1983.

Sartre, Jean Paul. *Critique of Dialectal Reason*. Ed. Jonathan Ree. Trans. Alan Sheridan-Smith. London: Verso Editions, 1982.

Shear, Walter. "Bellow's Fictional Rhetoric: The Voice of the Other." In *Saul Bellow and the Struggle at the Center*. Ed. Eugene Hollahan. Georgia State Literary Studies 12 (New York: AMS, 1996): 189–202.

Venkateswarlu, D. "Ideology in Saul Bellow's *Mr. Sammler's Planet*." In *Jewish-'American Writers and Intellectual Life in America*. Series in American Literature. New Delhi: Prestige, 1993.

Warren, Robert Penn. *Who Speaks for the Negro?* New York: Random House, 1965.

11

The Jewish Journey of Saul Bellow: From Secular Satirist to Spiritual Seeker

Sarah Blacher Cohen

Some time ago, a Fuller Brush man came to Saul Bellow's door and tried to sell him his wares. When he got nowhere with him, he finally demanded, "Won't you even take it as a gift?" Bellow replied, "I've been given the gift of life, and it's more than I know what to do with" (Kazin, *Contemporaries*, 221).

Indeed Saul Bellow has inherited many gifts from many sources. He was born of Yiddish-speaking, Russian immigrant Jews, who settled in the Jewish ghetto of Lachine, Canada, and the Jewish West Side of Chicago. Yet he was loathe to identify any connections between the legacies of his Jewish background and his gifts as a writer. Meeting with little success as a new novelist, he claimed to be a Jew who happened to be a writer. Later when he became nationally and internationally acclaimed, he claimed to be a writer who happened to be a Jew.

But the artistic gift Saul Bellow acknowledged with the least amount of self-conflict and vacillation was his lavish talent as a comic writer. Throughout his career, he expressed his preference for the use of the comic in his works: "Obliged to choose between complaint and comedy, I choose comedy, as more energetic, wiser and manlier" (Harper, "Saul Bellow," 62). As an antidote to despair, he uses comedy to interrupt, resist, reinterpret, and transcend adversity.

The strength of his comedy and the function it performs varies in each novel he has written. In the early ones, the sullen *Dangling Man* and *The Victim*, Bellow's comedy acts as a shaky defense, trying to stave off distrust and melancholy. As an uneasy moratorium from the gloom, it does not free his heroes from their long-term hostilities. In *The Adventures of Augie March*, comedy serves not only as a tonic for the dispirited, but also as a miraculous alchemist that transforms the common into the precious. Although Augie recognizes the disfigurement of the present, his antic sense enables him to re-create a golden age out of the "dwarf end of times" (60). In *Seize the Day*, a compassionate treatment of the beleaguered little man, comedy is a shield, employed more by Bellow than by Tommy Wilhelm, to protect him against his ubiquitous harassment. It is also used as a subtle cosmetic to cover up Wilhelm's blemishes and make him more endearing. In *Henderson the Rain King*, the comedy resembles a flashing saber brandished by Henderson, the mock miles gloriosus, both to defend and undercut his vaunted image of himself and to attack his brute opponents. While it does not succeed in eliminating Henderson's self-lionizing or in slaying the iniquitous lions of the world, his nimble and clumsy thrusting and parrying are alone worth the price of admission. In *Herzog*, comedy acts as a "balance and a barricade" (62) which the morose hero introduces to counter and combat his own depressive tendencies and the apocalyptic pronouncements of the reigning cognoscenti. It is also a boomerang that ultimately returns to strike him with the knowledge that man does not live by wisdom alone. In *Mr. Sammler's Planet*, comedy appears as a confectionery to accompany the bitter views of an angry old man. While Bellow does not think these bitter views need sweetening, he assumes not all of his readers will be able to swallow them without his customary jocular treats.

"Comedy tends to present a glass in which we glimpse ourselves (albeit distorted for humorous effect), whereas satire, as Swift wryly put it, presents a glass in which we tend to see the others' failings, but seldom, willingly, on our own" (Stedmond, *Comic Art*, 89). *Mr. Sammler's Planet* is, in the above sense, more satiric than comic. Arthur Sammler, a variant of the Plautine *senex iratus*, dwells on the failings of rascally youth, arrogant blacks, and willful females, but is reluctant to acknowledge his own failings. A sworn upholder of Apollonian values, he stridently lashes out at the Dionysian excesses of the times—"the right to be uninhibited, spontaneous, urinating, defecating, belching coupling in all positions, tripling, quadrupling" (33).

Many elements of Bellow's golden age of humor have in *Mr. Sammler's Planet* appreciably diminished in luster and have in certain areas become downright rusty. A superb example of what Northrop Frye designates as "second-phase satire," or literature assuming the responsibility of social analysis, the novel succeeds in "breaking up the lumber of stereotypes, fossilized beliefs, superstitious terrors, crank theories, pedantic dogmatisms, oppressive fashions, and all other things that impede the free movement . . . of society" (*Anatomy of Criticism*, 233). All of this upheaval is brought about by the verbal torrents of the septuagenarian Sammler, which in their caustic satire most often strike their mark. Yet many of the readers who made *Herzog* a best seller did not fancy Sammler's dour scoldings and would have preferred more witticisms than weltschmerz. But to require more jests and fewer jeremiads is to misunderstand Bellow's overall intent, for *Mr. Sammler's Planet* is his book of lamentations about the difficulties of being a humanist in this world.

This book of lamentations is influenced by Bellow's Jewish background, since it contains traces of the exhortative kind of satire and irony unique to the Prophets, especially Amos and Jeremiah, who, with matchless skill, lay bare the weaknesses and follies of the stiff-necked Israelites. Bellow's often circuitous way of ascertaining what is ludicrous is akin to the tortuous wit found in the Talmud and Midrash, the commentaries on Jewish oral law. His defiant topical satire resembles that of the "affected Jewish minority" whom Goebbels denounced for originating "jokes that cease to be jokes when they touch the holiest matters of national life" (Goldman, "Boy-man," 6).

Bellow is not only a satiric writer who employs what Northrop Frye terms "militant irony" to accomplish the purported aim of conventional satire—the reform of the corrupt or inane status quo through ridicule. As he ages and, correspondingly, his protagonists age in his novels, he is not solely consumed with making trenchant exposés of society's corruption and inanity. He embarks upon a religious journey, seeking an elusive spirituality. Thus, Augie March, more latter-day transcendentalist than Jew, goes on a pilgrimage to relocate the axial lines of "truth, love, peace, bounty, usefulness [and] harmony" (454), whose embrace will remove man's "dread of fast change and short life" (455). He attempts to affirm there are meaningful stays against dissolution.

Unlike the spiritually limber Augie March, Tommy Wilhelm is a spiritually rigid Schopenhauer, caught in the throes of a midlife crisis, who spends the day plumbing his lower and upper depths. When Tommy Wilhelm is particularly distraught, he, like Sholom Aleichem's Tevye the dairyman, has a heart-to-heart talk with God. Only Wilhelm's address is not in the form of an "edifying rabbinic discourse" which is "comically impudent and sophisticated" (Kristol, "Jewish Humor," 433). Expressing himself in slang, Wilhelm acknowledges his fallibility and humbly appeals to God for help: "Let me out of this clutch and into a different life. For I am all balled up" (26). When Wilhelm is walking in an underground corridor and feels a sudden overpowering love for humanity, he bursts out in a rhapsodic hymn of praise for all "the imperfect and lurid-looking people" (84). He is soon embarrassed by his sentimental remarks and attempts to minimize his "onrush of loving kindness" (85). He discredits his effusive statements by crudely terming the experience "only another one of those subway things. Like having a hard-on at random" (85).

By contrast, *Henderson the Rain King*, Bellow's middle-aged explorer of a comic-book *Heart of Darkness*, is the zany combination of the Christian "fighting Lazarus" (217), the Jungian quester of the Dark Continent, and the Jewish *luftmensch,* borne aloft by his own flight of fancy and high-flown idealism. Henderson endeavors to prove that "chaos doesn't run the whole show," that this is "not a sick and hasty ride, helpless, through a dream into oblivion, [that] it can be arrested by a thing or two" (175). Despite King Dahfu's Reichian lion therapy, Henderson has come to know that he cannot escape from the endless cycle of "fear and desire" (298), the ineluctable condition of every living human being. Nor can he escape from his inevitable end, no matter how wily his stratagems or defiant his will. Yet he still affirms "there is justice, and . . . much is promised" (328), and that "whatever gains were made were always due to love" (339). However, Bellow does not end the novel on such a euphoric note. Henderson is not described in regal, leonine terms. He is, instead, associated with the wretched, time-abused trained bear, Smolak, with whom he rode the roller coaster in his youth. Like Augie, who concludes at the end of his quest that "imperfection is always the condition as found" (260), Henderson realizes now what Smolak instinctively knew then: "that for creatures there is nothing that ever runs unmingled" (339). Even so, Henderson, that "absurd seeker of high qualities" (Steers, "Successor," 38), is still a firm believer in American do-goodism and in his sixties will enroll in medical school to cure society of all its ills.

Herzog is Bellow's most deft vaudevillian of the mind, but as his full name—Moses Elchanan Herzog or "the man of heart chosen by God"—suggests, he is Bellow's most overtly Jewish protagonist. Returning to the mountains whence cometh his help, Herzog, the "old Jew-man of Ludeyville" (49), proclaims, "What a struggle I waged! Left-handed, but fierce. But enough of that—here I am. Hineni!" (309–310).

Herzog, notes Earl Rovit, utters the word that Abraham repeated three times in Genesis 22. First, when the Lord summons him to sacrifice Isaac as a burnt offering; second, when Isaac calls for his attention to question him about the sacrifice; and third, when the Angel of the Lord interrupts him before he can use his knife on his bound son ("Saul Bellow," 94). Erich Auerbach has indicated that "Hineni," meaning, "behold me" is not meant to indicate the actual place where Abraham is, but a moral position in respect to God who has called to him—"Here I am awaiting thy command" (*Mimesis*, 8). Thus Herzog calls himself present and ready to perform the duties assigned him: to obey his covenant with God and carry out the terms of his contract with his fellow human beings.

At his Berkshire sanctuary, he has ceased being a "junkie on thought" (Bellow, *Last Analysis*, 10). No longer placing such a high premium on intellectuality for its own sake, Herzog comes to understand that the power to recognize real and human facts has equal weight with ideas. This does not mean that Herzog has totally given up his intellectual endeavors, but he assures us he will never again be consumed with the solitary cerebral life and thereby lose his grasp of ordinary reality. Recognizing he can achieve meaning not in isolation but in the company of other people, Herzog vows, "I mean to share with other human beings as far as possible and not destroy my remaining years in the same way" (322). Freed of self-absorption, he is ready to dedicate himself to others and to God:

> To God he jotted several lines. How my mind has struggled to make coherent sense. I have not been too good at it. But have desired to do your unknowable will, taking it and you, without symbols. Everything of intensest significance. Especially if divested of me. (325–326)

Immersing himself in the holiness of God, Herzog is also ready to accept the eventuality of his own death, not with rancor, but with "a holy feeling" (340). With the same spirit of comedy with which his mother had tried to prove to him that Adam was created out of dust, and with the same "wit you can have only when you consider death very plainly" (233), Herzog declares, "I look at myself and see chest, thighs, feet—a head. This strange organization I know it will die" (340). Even though his face is "too blind," his mind "too limited," and "his instincts too narrow," Herzog opts to make do with his flawed being during his brief span of survival.

Herzog ends up being one of Bellow's representative Jews whom he defines as "not gods, not beasts, but savages of somewhat damaged but not extinguished nobility" (Bellow, "Arias," 5). A little lower than the angels, he is defined by Nathan Scott as the "contingent, imperfect, earthbound creature" whose function it is to "awaken in us a lively recognition of what in fact our true status is" ("Bias of Comedy," 19).

At the novel's end, we leave Herzog in his Eden, no longer the self-conscious Thinking Man but the more natural Man Thinking, accepting his humble beginnings and end. "Not more than human, nor less than human but exactly human" (Bellow, *The Victim*, 59), his still small voice is communing only with God and nature.

That still small voice seeking spiritual understanding of Jewish immigrant families is heard again in Bellow's 1967 short story, "The Old System," made up of a frame story narrated by and about a scientist of heredity, Dr. Samuel Braun. He is another of Bellow's cerebral protagonists suffering from an overdeveloped brain and an underdeveloped heart. While his December ruminations about his own misspent life and his witty castigations of the decadence of the times make for ruefully amusing reading, they do not powerfully absorb the reader. What is emotionally compelling is the inner tale Dr. Samuel Braun tells: his recollection of his warring immigrant family:

his cousin Isaac Braun, the embodiment of the ethical ideals and spiritual values of the Jewish old system, and fat cousin Tina, an assaulter of these values.[1]

Lillian Kremer likens the fictional Isaac to "his biblical namesake, the patriarch Isaac," who "settled among the Philistines at Gerar . . . and succeeded so well as to incur the envy and wrath of his neighbors" ("Saul Bellow's Remembrances," 15). Similarly, she claims that the prosperous fictional Isaac incurs the "envy and wrath" of his sister Tina, whose name and behavior is, for Bellow, emblematic of the Philistines, though a twentieth-century American variation of the ancient tribe. As a contemporary Philistine, Tina is depicted as a huge pagan force, a female Goliath, wanting to sexually vanquish her young Israelite cousin, the innocent cerebral Sammy. She also wants to usurp the family inheritance from her older brother Isaac by attacking him for his old-fashioned sentimentality and piety. According to Kremer's interpretation, Tina is an allegorical figure in a morality play whose function is to "evoke the historic antagonism between the biblical Israelites and Philistines" which, in turn, informs "the contemporary conflict of religious devotee and non-believer (17)."

Hurt by Tina's jealousy over his financial success and her continual rejection of his Yom Kippur attempts at reconciliation, Isaac complies with Tina's final wishes. He adheres to the ethical strictures of the Williamsberg Rebbe, whose "universal calm judgement of the Jewish moral genius" (77) bids him give his own sister the $20,000 she requests from him to visit her at her deathbed. However, cancer-ravaged Tina, rejecting his money, is able to embrace a Judaism that denigrates empty materialism and brings spiritual renewal. In the hospital room, sister and brother forgive one another, weep together, and reaffirm their love.

In his memory, scientist Dr. Samuel Braun wavers between skepticism and faith. He then intones his conflicted form of a Kaddish over them:

> Oh, these Jews—these Jews! Their feelings, their hearts! Dr. Braun often wanted nothing more than to stop all this. For what came of it? One after another you gave over your dying. One by one they went. You went. Childhood, family, friendship, love were stifled in the grave. And these tears! When you wept them from the heart, you felt you justified something, understood something. But what did you understand? Again, nothing! It was only an intimation of understanding. A promise that mankind might—might, mind you—eventually, through its gift which might—might again!—be a divine gift, comprehend why it lived. Why life, why death.
>
>   And again, why these particular forms—these Isaacs and these Tinas? When Dr. Braun closed his eyes, he saw, red on

black, something like molecular processes—the only true her-
aldry of being. As later, in the close black darkness when the
short day ended, he went to the dark kitchen window to have a
look at stars. These things cast outward by a great begetting spasm
billions of years ago. (82–83)

In *To Jerusalem and Back: A Personal Account*, Saul Bellow has, like
Dr. Samuel Braun, vacillated in his Jewish journey from skepticism to belief.
In his 1976 book, Bellow starts out as armchair anthropologist commenting
on the comic oddities of the Hasidim riding in the plane with him to Israel.
He is amused by their attempts to convert him to the true faith. Though he
tries to convince them that he is a thoroughgoing intellectual, they plead
with him to share their kosher sandwich, to pray with them, to visit them in
their observant homes. When they leave, however, he is certain they will
never cross paths again. Yet as Bellow is more and more enthralled by the
seductive holiness of the promised land, he writes, "I feel that the light of
Jerusalem has purifying powers and filters the blood and the thoughts; I
don't forbid myself the reflection that light may be the outer garment of
God" (93).

Such mystical statements about God are more plentiful and more
pronounced in Bellow's most spiritual novel, *Humboldt's Gift* (1975). In
it two worlds are at odds with each other, identified by John Clayton as
the external "World of Distraction" with its comic, manic, oppressive
energy, and the "Inner World, the World of Love . . . full of quiet mystery" and tantalizing depth ("Humboldt's Gift," 31). Humboldt calls this
"inner world" the "home world," with every one mourning its loss, including the souls banished from it. Similarly, Bellow, in his Nobel Prize
speech, talks about his characters, torn between the world of objects, of
actions, of appearances and that other world from which true impressions
come, "where one can hear 'the essence of things' " (325).

To escape from the noxious world of distraction where people live and
die meaninglessly, Charlie Citrine, Bellow's protagonist in *Humboldt's Gift*,
draws on the wisdom of the modern mystic Rudolf Steiner. Under his recent
influence, Citrine seldom thinks of death in the same way as Bellow's earlier
death-evading protagonists. Instead of envisioning the grave as an imprisoning tomb or "dreading at eternity of boredom" (221), Citrine often felt "un-
usually light and swift-paced, as if [he] were on a weightless bicycle and
sprinting through the star world." Moreover, Humboldt's gift of money and
its message that "we are not natural beings but supernatural beings" (347)
contributes to Citrine's spiritual maturation.

Bellow's most recent novel, *Ravelstein*, is still consumed with the spiritual, but it is more Jewish in its focus. Its eponymous hero, patterned after

University of Chicago professor Allan Bloom, tells Chick, the octogenarian protagonist, patterned after Bellow himself: "It's impossible to get rid of one's origins. It is impossible not to remain a Jew" (179). Ravelstein also convinces the assimilationist Chick of the inescapability of his Jewish fate. Unlike Augie March, who proudly asserts, "I am an American, Chicago born" (3), Chick is forced to conclude, "As a Jew you are also an American, but somehow you are also not" (23). Or when a minor Jewish character receives a heart transplant from a non-Jew, Chick has to restrain himself from asking him how "a heart originally Christian or Gentile, with its shadow energies and its rhythms," could "adapt itself to Jewish needs or peculiarities, pains and ideas?" (148).

Ravelstein also becomes, for Chick, the prototype of Bellow's comic Jewish man who engages in the rueful and whimsical struggle to combat the internal and external agents of his destruction. Like Sholom Aleichem's Tevyeh, he employs the "humor of verbal retrieval, the word triumphant over the situation" (Samuel, 186). Though there "is nothing funny about Tevye the dairyman as a character and nothing funny ever happens to him, he turns the tables on tragedy by a verbal ingenuity; life gets the better of him, but he gets the better of the argument" (184). So it is with Ravelstein, who uses not Tevye's folkloric Jewish humor of verbal retrieval, but his own mingling of highbrow and lowbrow vaudevillian Jewish humor to dull the pain of progressive illness and mock mortality itself.

> Ravelstein, shutting his eyes . . . flung himself bodily backward into laughter. In my own different style, I did the same thing. As I've said before, it was our sense of what was funny that brought us together, but that would have been a thin, anemic way to put it. A joyful noise—*immenso giubilo*—an outsize joint agreement picked us up together. (118)

This laughter about death enables Ravelstein, the younger, and Chick, the elder, to contemplate their inevitable end with a certain élan vital. It is also their only dependable life preserver, buoying their sinking spirits. And ultimately, it is their miraculous boomerang, catapulting them into higher spheres.

However, the fact that they laughed together doesn't mean that they laughed for the same reasons. The big joke for Ravelstein was that his most serious ideas, previously shunned by the academy, were put into a book which the lay public loved and, like Bloom's *The Closing of the American Mind*, made him a millionaire. And the rueful joke for Chick, Bellow's *senex*, is that he outlives Ravelstein, his *juvenis*, reversing the comic conventions of youth triumphing over old age.

But beyond the grave, Ravelstein is far from gloomy. "Ravelstein looks at me, laughing with pleasure and astonishment, gesturing because he can't be heard in all this bird noise. You don't easily give up a creature like Ravelstein to death" (233).

It appears that Bellow at age eighty-seven does not easily give himself up to death. Nor does he easily give up his Jewish identity. Though he has balked over the years at being labeled a Jewish writer, he acknowledges that his creative power "simply comes from the fact that at a most susceptible time of my life, I was wholly Jewish. That's a gift, a piece of good fortune with which one doesn't quarrel" (Kulshrestha, "Conversation," 15). So, too, at the end of *Ravelstein*, Chick acknowledges "his good fortune." His final discovery in the novel confirms Baudelaire's belief that "life is a hospital in which each patient believes that he will recover if he is removed to another bed." Throughout his life, Chick has gone from bed to bed to keep on living. He has currently landed in a Jewish bed to nourish his soul.

Note

1. The New York State Writers Institute and the University at Albany's College of Humanities and Fine Arts cosponsored the world premiere of *Saul Bellow's Stories on Stage*, a program of two plays, *The Old System*, adapted by English professor and playwright Sarah Blacher Cohen, and *The Silver Dish*, adapted by Chicago playwright and author Joanne Koch, at the Lewis A. Swyer Theatre, The Empire Center at the Egg in Albany, New York, on March 27 and 28, 1993.

Authors William Kennedy and Cynthia Ozick were literary cochairs of the event, at which Cynthia Ozick presented introductory remarks about the nature of adaptation for the theater in its relation to these works of Saul Bellow.

Just as six characters have been in search of an author, so, too, *Saul Bellow's Stories on Stage: The Old System and The Silver Dish* are in search of theaters, producers, and actors to present them. To make this connection, please get in touch with Sarah Blacher Cohen, English Department, The University at Albany, SUNY, 1400 Washington Avenue, Albany, New York 12222. Her phone number is 518-489-8759. Her e-mail is drsbcohen@aol.com.

Works Cited

Allen, Mory. "The Flower and the Chalk: the Comic Sense of Soul Bellow" (Ph.D. diss., Stanford University, 1969)

Auerbach, Erich. *Mimesis*. Princeton, NJ: Princeton University Press, 1953.

Bellow, Saul. *The Adventures of Augie March*. New York: Viking Press, 1953.

———, ed. "Arias." In *The Noble Savage*, 4–5. New York: Meridian Books, 1961.

———. *Henderson the Rain King*. New York: Viking Press, 1959.

———. *Herzog*. New York: Viking Press, 1964.

———. *Humboldt's Gift*. New York: Viking Press, 1975.

———. *The Last Analysis*. New York: Viking Press, 1965.

———. *Mr. Sammler's Planet*. New York: Viking Press, 1970.

———. *Mosby's Memoirs and Other Stories*. New York: Viking Press, 1968.

———. "Nobel Prize Address," In *The American Scholar*, 46 (Summer, 1977): 325–326.

———. Ravelstein. New York: Viking, 2000.

———. *Seize the Day*. New York: Viking Press, 1956.

———. *To Jerusalem and Back: A Personal Account*. New York: Viking Press, 1976.

———. *The Victim*. New York: Vanguard Press, 1947.

Clayton, John, "Humboldt's Gift and the Flight from Death." In *Saul Bellow and His Work*, ed. Edmond Shraepen, 31-48. Brussels: Free University of Brussels, 1977.

Frye, Northrop. *Anatomy of Criticism*. New York: Atheneum, 1965.

Goldman, Albert. "Boy-man, Schlemiel: The Jewish Element in American Humour." In *Explorations*, ed. Murray Mindlin and Chaim Bermant, 3–17. London, 1967.

Harper, Gordon L. "Saul Bellow—The Art of Fiction: An Interview." *Paris Review* 37 (Winter, 1965): 48–73.

Kazin, Alfred. *Contemporaries*. Boston: Little, Brown and Company, 1962.

Kremer, Lillian S. "Saul Bellow's Remembrances of Jewish Times Past: *Herzog* and 'The Old System.' " Unpublished essay, pp. 1–21.

Kristol, Irving. "Is Jewish Humor Dead?" In *Mid-Century*, ed. Harold U. Ribalow, 428–437. New York: Beechhurst Press, 1955.

Kulshrestha, Chiranton. "A Conversation with Saul Bellow." *Chicago Review* 23, no. 4, and 24, no. 1 (1972): 15–17.

Rovit, Earl. "Saul Bellow and the Concept of the Survivor." In *Saul Bellow and his Work*, ed. Edmond Shraepen, 89–102. Brussels: Free University of Brussels, 1977.

Samuel, Maurice. *The World of Sholom Aleichem*. New York: Schocken Books, 1943.

Scott, Nathan, A. "The Bias of Comedy and the Narrow Escape into Faith." *The Christian Scholar* 44 (Spring, 1961): 9–39.

Stedmond, John M. *The Comic Art of Laurence Sterne*. Toronto: University of Toronto Press, 1967.

Steers, Nina A. "Successor to Faulkner?" *Show* 4 (September, 1964): 36–38.

12

Philip Roth and Jewish American Literature at the Millennium

Bonnie Lyons

The brochure for the American Literature Association conference from which this volume of essays emerged asked the participants to address the future of Jewish American and Holocaust literature within the study of American literature, to envision the future audience for this literature and the scholarship that attends it, and to ponder its place on the maps of ethnic and cultural studies. Large orders. Even this announcement avoided several big questions. The very term "Jewish American"—sometimes hyphenated and with the emphasis on American—points to hotly disputed issues. Is this literature in fact more Jewish than it is American? What happens if we consider it against a background of Kafka and Babel rather than Melville and Faulkner? Moreover, since the parameters of American literature itself are now being radically questioned, even the size and shape of this category "American literature" into which we attempt to place Jewish American literature is fairly problematic. To say nothing of the even larger question of the viability of literary studies as such. If the academy continues to concede authority to cultural studies, the study of Jewish American literature as a subcategory of literary studies may well be marginalized, and possibly totally undermined.

Because of recent rapid changes in the academy, including the almost total displacement of deconstruction by gender/race/class analysis, the rise of queer theory, and the increasing dismissal of approaches to literature not overtly political, and a growing contempt for the very idea of art, it is impossible to predict with any confidence what the future of Jewish American literature, Holocaust literature, or indeed literature of any kind will be.

So instead of predicting the future from some imagined satellite-high authoritative overview, I look in this essay at a particular author and focus even more narrowly on a single book by that author, and use that analysis to sketch

out directions Jewish American literature seems likely to follow. I believe Philip
Roth is right now our most significant Jewish American writer and that to study
his work therefore seems a constructive approach to the field. Moreover, his
most recent novel, *American Pastoral*, is particularly illuminating in connection with the overall questions about the direction of the field, for reasons I
hope to show.

Instead of thirteen ways of looking at a blackbird, here, based on a
reading of *American Pastoral*, are five ways of looking at the near future of
Jewish American literature. First, Jewish American literature will situate itself self-consciously in the context of European texts. In Roth's case, *American Pastoral* is explicitly engaged in a dialogue with Tolstoy's *The Death of
Ivan Ilych*. Second, Jewish American literature will continue to respond
distinctively to American myth and reality. In this case, *American Pastoral* is
centrally concerned with just this theme, as the title indicates. Third, Jewish
American literature will be a meditation on the distinctively Jewish preoccupations with time, memory, history, and loss—all, however, with a postmodern
spin. *American Pastoral* is sharply focused throughout on the radical problematic of contemporary relativism and nihilism. Fourth, Jewish American
literature will explore the extraordinary variety and complexity of Jewish life
in an evolving American culture. In this case Roth focuses on a radically
assimilated Jew. Finally, I foresee that Jewish American literature will become, in this postmodern age, more involved in the complexities of self-
referential intertextuality. That is, with the author's own internal dialectic
within his developing oeuvre. *American Pastoral* is a novel in overt dialogue
with Roth's earlier novels responding thematically in particular to both *The
Counterlife*, through the organizing ideas of the pastoral, and oppositions
and counterlives, and to *Sabbath's Theater* through a protagonist who seems
an explicit antithesis to that novel's Mickey Sabbath.

Part One

Early in *American Pastoral*, the narrator Zuckerman—who is of course a
narrator/protagonist in several earlier Roth novels and is one "take" on Roth's
own alter ego—describes meeting his blue-eyed, blond athletic boyhood
hero Seymour "the Swede" Levov for dinner. Unable to see beneath the
surface of what Zuckerman calls Swede's "simple-seeming soul" exuding
sincerity,[1] Zuckerman posits the idea that the Swede just might be what he
appears to be—a simple, happy man—and he compares his complicated
speculations about the Swede to what he calls "the tendentious meaning that
Tolstoy assigned to Ivan Ilych" (30), condemning Tolstoy's fiction as a "heart-
less expose" that clinically depicts what it is to be ordinary. Zuckerman even
quotes Tolstoy's central line: "his life had been most simple and most ordi-

nary and therefore most terrible" (31), and then qualifies Tolstoy's judgment by saying, "Maybe so. Maybe in Russia in 1886," and in a paragraph consisting of one sentence italicized except for the crucial "for all I knew" announces: *"Swede Levov's life,* for all I knew, *had been most simple and most ordinary and therefore just great, right in the American grain."* A novel that summarizes, quotes and overtly disputes an earlier piece of literature is clearly asking to be read in dialogue with it—as a piece of Jewish American literature talking back to a piece of Russian fiction written a hundred years earlier.

The heart of Tolstoy's novella is the assertion and fictive proof of that monumental moral judgment "most simple, and most ordinary and therefore most terrible" (31). Conversely, Roth's novel ends with two questions: "And what is wrong with their life? What is less reprehensible than the life of the Levovs?" (423). *The Death of Ivan Ilych* is a brilliant and above all clear indictment of a life lived wrongly, told by an omniscient narrator who not only knows the crucial questions but also knows the answers. What Tolstoy's fiction lays out for the reader is just what *American Pastoral* refutes—including the underlying religious and fictional certainties. The question of irony, which any dispute with a classic like *Ivan Ilych* is bound to raise, is never resolved, and readers finally have to form their own judgments.

The moral vision of Tolstoy's fiction is absolutely clear. Living "a decorous life approved by society," Ilych fails to tap the three Tolstoyan wellsprings of human life: work, love, and understanding. Although an incorruptible judge, Ilych values the power, money, and prestige of his work rather than the work itself and treats people who come before him impersonally, without empathy. His marriage is merely a social contract, and until his deathbed recognitions he lacks spiritual insight. The novella is structured so that the moral choices are simple, the positive and negative characters are polarized, death is privileged as the moment to achieve wisdom, and the possibility of literally seeing the light is at once the climax of life and of the fiction. Tolstoy's novella begins by depicting the selfish unemotional response to Ivan Ilych's death by his colleagues and his wife's feigned grief, then summarizes his life including a symbolic fall. This is then followed by an extended dramatization of his deathbed agony and his recognition that he has lived his life wrongly. The novella ends with his triumphant religious insight about God and love. In a *New Yorker* review of *American Pastoral,* Louis Menand argued that Roth's novel is "a traditional realist novel" (which is to say a fiction like Tolstoy's), and concluded that although *American Pastoral* is open to many interpretations, Roth's novel asks one question—"what went wrong in the life of Seymour Levov"—and offers one answer—that Levov was, in his words, "blindsided by the culture of permissiveness" and that the novel exposes "the corruption of American life by liberal permissiveness." Menand argues that with a title like *American Pastoral* the negative "outcome

is foreclosed," but "the moral is not."[2] But I see the novel quite differently, for
to think of *American Pastoral* as having a moral is to see it as like *The Death
of Ivan Ilych*, while the ending, which consists of two questions, the avoidance
of an omniscient narrator, and the absence of any unquestionably moral characters, undermines that analysis.

Part Two

American Pastoral is also Jewish American literature taking on America; it is
Roth's most overt, extended response to both the American dream or idea
and actual American history in this century, a fin de siècle look at America
especially in the past fifty years. While Zuckerman is writing the novel in
1995, the America he dramatizes is mostly America from World War II
through Vietnam and Watergate. That is, America at the "greatest moment
of collective inebriation in American history" (40), America in an "exuberant
heyday, at the peak of confidence, inflated with every illusion born of hope"
(87) descending into bleak disillusionment and self-disgust. We see the boundless hopes, optimism, and moral certainty of the World War II victory over
the clear evil of Fascism coupled with the emergence of America as an
overwhelming world power followed less than thirty years later by a morally
troubling and divisive war, political corruption, rage, and cynicism. The very
title of the book, as opposed to titles with the protagonist's name, like *Portnoy's
Complaint, Zuckerman Bound, Sabbath's Theater*, demonstrates the central-
ity of "America" to the novel and suggests that a whole period of American
history can be seen as a collective pastoral, a beautiful and fragile bubble
bound to break.

   As symbolic center of its depiction of America, *American Pastoral*
focuses on the terrible decline of Newark from bustling, vital center of
industrial energy to a ravaged, crime-ridden city whose major industry is
car theft. Newark's decline, complete with race riots, disappearing industry,
and uncontrolled crime, is the domestic parallel to the national and international decline of America epitomized by Watergate and Vietnam.

   In Swede Levov, Zuckerman celebrates a worker's pride in possessing
specialized knowledge, the satisfaction of making something well, and the
American economic dream—the possibility of a worker becoming a small
businessman through courage, tenacity, and grueling hard work. By describing the Levov family business, Newark Maid, with extraordinary specificity
and detail, the novel endorses the Swede and his father as qualified workers
and self-made men who rose from their poor, immigrant, working background via their ingenuously simple motto "we work at it." While through
the Levovs the novel celebrates certain old-fashioned virtues of a productive

rather than consumerist America, some changes in American life are depicted as having no moral significance. Gloves are simply no longer popular. American workers find it more and more difficult to compete with cheap labor abroad. Such things happen and no moral decline is implied.

In addition to dramatizing contrasting periods of American life, the novel gives voice to opposing visions of America. In particular, Levov counterpoints his daughter Merry. Levov embodies a traditional patriotic love of America as the land of opportunity, freedom, and tolerance. Johnny Appleseed is his secret hero, Thanksgiving his beloved holiday. Merry, in contrast, despises her father's America and sees it as soulless, consumerist, and imperialist; in her eyes America economically exploits most of its own citizens and is an international tyrant. These irreconcilably conflicting views provide the novel's central tension.

The handling of time in *American Pastoral* is also complex. The most recent vision of America, of the 1990s, comes early in the novel when Zuckerman describes his high school reunion. There we see a generally happy and prosperous America—successful professional children and grandchildren of impoverished immigrants. But the novel itself ends much more darkly, with two long climactic scenes set on one day in 1973. In the first of these, Levov locates his daughter, who five years earlier had bombed the Old Rimrock general store to protest the Vietnam war, killing the local doctor. Heartbrokenly he learns that her subsequent bombs have killed three other people and that she has gone on to become what she is now—an unwashed Jainist fanatic. In the second climactic scene, during a dinner party that same night, Levov discovers that his much-loved wife is having an affair with their architect and friend Orcutt, and that a female friend hid Merry after the Rimrock bombing and never told him. When he hears his father scream "No," Levov imagines that Merry has returned home and that "this veiled intruder reeking of feces" (421) has killed her grandfather by telling him about her deadly bombs. Had the novel ended with this horror, one could read it as a parable about generational discord and the American dream changing into a nightmare. The actual ending is much more complicated both in tone and vision, however. Merry does not show up at all; instead we have a grim scene in which the architect's alcoholic wife, whom Levov's father is patiently trying to feed, responds by trying to poke out his eye with a fork. Thus the novel ends with an act of stupid, drunken apolitical violence. This is in turn made more monstrous by a female academic friend who witnesses the scene and laughs with relish at this "rampant disorder" (423). Something much darker and more nihilistic than what Menand calls "liberal permissiveness" is being excoriated here.

Part Three

The take on Jewishness in *American Pastoral* is in striking contrast to much of Roth's earlier work. While Zuckerman was aptly accused of having "Jew on the brain" in *The Counterlife*,[3] here Roth focuses on a man who has left his Jewish background behind like an old coat he discovered no longer fit and just never wore. That is, there is no struggle, no rejection, no repudiation—it's an effortless shrugging-off. *The Counterlife* ends with Zuckerman's insistence on circumcision and his philosophical defense of this ancient defining ritual, but in *American Pastoral* Swede's daughter is secretly baptized. The very secrecy suggests Swede would have opposed the ceremony, but she is in fact baptized and taken to Mass by her Catholic grandmother; meanwhile, Swede remembers the boredom of Hebrew school and wishing he was playing baseball instead. Passover, often the main emotional religious pull of childhood for disaffected Jews, has no resonance for the Swede; the all-American nondenominational Thanksgiving with its Puritan turkey is his favorite holiday. Although his father prevented him from marrying the first shiksa he was attracted to and tried unsuccessfully to block his marriage to Dawn, Swede never senses that his father had any real understanding of Judaism as a religion or commitment to it. The spiritual center of his father's world is an inseparable trinity: business, Newark, and America.

The neighborhood adulation felt for Swede also suggests complex and ambivalent attitudes toward Jewishness within the Jewish community. While Swede never denies his Jewishness, never considers converting or even trying to pass as a non-Jew, what the Jewish community most admires about him is that he is so unlike an ordinary Jew, as evident in his nickname. He is admired for his extraordinary athletic ability, not his mind, and because of his seemingly non-Jewish character. Early in the novel Zuckerman asks, "Where was the Jew in him?" and admits that "in our idolizing the Swede and his unconscious oneness with America, I suppose there was a tinge of shame and self-rejection" (20). The process of Jewish life in America here involves relinquishing residual Jewishness: each Jew "out of the desire to go the limit in America . . . gets rid of the traditional Jewish habits and attitudes" (85).

Swede's verbally aggressive brother cynically summarizes Swede's and Dawn's life, saying, "she's post-Catholic, he's post-Jewish, together they're going to go out there to Old Rimrock to raise little post-toasties" (73). In focusing on a non-Jewish Jew like Swede, the novel depicts the American movement toward homogenization and assimilation, toward the relinquishing of ethnic and religious identities. It is noteworthy that the change is widespread and general—not just Dawn and Levov. When his father and her Catholic father get together and talk about their boyhoods, Zuckerman says,

"They are on to something even more serious than Judaism and Catholicism—they are on to Newark and Elizabeth—and all day long nobody can tear them apart" (400).

One of the many explanations suggested for Merry's catastrophic acts is the Swede's insistence on marrying for love and his belief that he could raise a healthy child connected neither to Judaism nor to Catholicism. At one point he concludes despairingly, "His father was right . . . They raised a child who was neither Catholic nor Jew, who instead was first a stutterer, then a killer, then a Jain" (386). But the novel presents many possible causes for the unhappy effects, and in fact it works to undermine the whole idea of simple, direct causation. Merry is not depicted as just a stutterer and killer and Jain, she is also an adorable and adored child, a brilliant student, an extraordinarily sensitive girl who is genuinely moved by others' suffering.

Whereas in earlier novels Zuckerman was obsessed with Jewishness, in *The Counterlife* he accuses Jews praying at the Wailing Wall of kissing God's ass. Conversely, in *American Pastoral*, Swede, who finds nothing of interest in Judaism or Jewishness, possesses nonetheless a deep if nondenominational religious feeling of gratitude—of being *blessed*. Early in the novel when Zuckerman is supposedly hearing the "facts" about the Swede's life from his brother Jerry, Jerry tells him that at a family dinner the Swede made a toast saying, "I'm not a religious man, but when I look around this table, I know that something is shining down on me" (69–70). Later, when Zuckerman creates his fictional version of Swede's life, he has Swede using the exact same words—"Something is shining down on me" (201)—when he joyfully watches Merry and Dawn hard at work together rescuing the prize bull they are raising. This religious feeling of gratitude for earth's bounty is the heart of his identification with the emblematic figure of *American Pastoral* in the novel, Johnny Appleseed, who "wasn't a Jew, wasn't an Irish Catholic, wasn't a Protestant Christian— nope, Johnny Appleseed was just a happy American" (316).

Part Four

History, time, memory, and loss are quintessential themes of Jewish literature, including Jewish American literature. From the "If I forget thee O Jerusalem" to the Holocaust museum button instructing the wearer "Remember," Jewish thought emphasizes the sense that human beings are the sum of their memories and that to forget this is analogous to murder. This concern with memory and history has always marked Jewish American literature and contrasts with much twentieth-century mainstream American literature. What is new is the insistent postmodern questioning of history, the sense that what is called history is simply the biased report of the victors, that no knowledge, especially historical knowledge, is objective, that we are condemned to subjective and thus untrustworthy versions of unrecoverable events. This recent problematization of history touches Jewish writing in particularly unsettling ways. Just to name two: revisionist historians of Zionism have sharply divided Israelis between those who praise them as iconoclastic truth tellers and those who see them as self-hating Palestinian apologists. Meanwhile, revisionist denials of the Holocaust have left many Jews and Jewish writers keenly aware of the dangers of denying the possibility of objective historical knowledge.

Louis Menand has called *American Pastoral* "a historical novel about the period of the Second World War to Watergate," arguing that unlike chronicles such as *Rabbit Run*, in which the protagonist's life "is a series of scrapes and fender benders," historical novels like *American Pastoral* "are about head-on collisions." But the novel is much more complex than that. Quite unlike a historical novel, *American Pastoral* again and again reminds the reader that he or she is not being given the past, but only scraps of memories plus an imagined fictional construction by a narrator who, as all Roth readers know from his earlier fiction, is a "fictive proposition" himself. Thus the first of the three sections is titled "Paradise Remembered," not "Paradise," and the idiosyncratic, selective, and unreliable nature of memory is a major theme in Zuckerman's storytelling itself. Even before Zuckerman begins to imagine the Swede's history, an old friend at his high school re-union tells him how much the interest Zuckerman's father took in him affected his life; Zuckerman, however, is unable to corroborate his friend's memories and says, "yet what I had missed completely took root in him and changed his life" (55). He then goes on to generalize that what "each of us remembers and forgets is a pattern whose labyrinthine windings are an identification mark no less distinctive than a fingerprint." After listening to Swede's brother tell the facts (if there are facts) of Swede's life, Zuckerman concludes with a typical Rothian paradox, "Anything more I wanted to know I'd have to make up" (74). So, although Zuckerman reports doing research into Swede's life, he is overt about his portrait being one vision of Swede Levov—he says such things as "I lifted the Swede up onto my stage" (89)—and questions whether his frankly fictional approach is less "true" than Swede's brother's version would be: "Whether the Swede and his family come to life in me any less truthfully than in his brother—well, who knows?" (77).

Here the comparison with Tolstoy's novella is again instructive: by ending *The Death of Ivan Ilych* with Ivan's epiphanic dying moments, Tolstoy brings together two supposed sources of truth: the last words of a fiction as a summary truth and the end of a life as the time when one can cut through the superfluous and superficial to reach the deeper, hidden truth. But Roth slyly undermines the idea that proximity to death brings truth. When Zuckerman last saw the Swede, months before Swede's death, the Swede insisted his recent prostate operation had been successful although he knew the cancer had metastasized, and he also backed off from telling Zuckerman about Merry and the Rimrock bombing, the central event of his family's life.

While Zuckerman is not the overtly dominating figure in this Rothian fiction, that he is telling the story is central to the novel's structure, meaning, and tone, including its preoccupation with time, history, and memory. Early in the novel, while describing that last meeting with the Swede, Zuckerman drops a quiet psychological bombshell, saying that he himself is recovering from a prostate operation. Significantly, he lies to the Swede, attributing the operation to friends of his, saying, "One ended up impotent . . . the other's impotent and incontinent," but he tells the reader what he never told the Swede: "the person I had referred to as 'the other' was me" (28). By writing about the Swede, Zuckerman chooses, in his words, "to inhabit this person least like" himself (74), which is to say the Other in psychological and sociological terms. But in fact the reader recognizes that by writing about the Swede, Zuckerman is writing about someone who is both like and unlike him. Zuckerman's memories and imagination are inseparable from his re-membering and creating of the Swede's history. In *The Facts* Roth said of his own father, "his repertoire has never been large: family, family, family, New-ark, Newark, Newark, Jew, Jew, Jew. Somewhat like mine" (16). And in *American Pastoral*, Roth's alter ego Zuckerman and the Swede are linked through all three. Moreover, the extraordinarily moving elegiac tone of much of the novel expresses Zuckerman's own self-characterization; early on he mentions that his catastrophic prostate operation came "in the wake of all the other isolating losses, in the wake of everything gone and everyone gone" (65). It hardly seems surprising that as a man now seeking solace "nowhere but in sentences," Zuckerman would be drawn to narrate, that is, give verbal form to, the story of his boyhood hero who himself experienced terrific losses and died from the same disease that recently ravaged Zuckerman's own body.

In the opening pages of the novel, when Zuckerman leaves his forty-fifth high school reunion, classmates give him a commemorative mug con-taining half a dozen rugeluch wrapped in their school colors. Rapidly devouring the Jewish delicacies full of memories of his mother and his childhood, he hopes to banish what Proust says vanished for Marcel at the savor of the madeleine: "the apprehensiveness of death" (47). But Zuckerman has no such luck, and the apprehensiveness of death is as ever-present in *American Pastoral* as it was in *Sabbath's Theater*.

The dual epigraphs to the novel, the first from Johnny Mercer's popu-lar 1940s song, and the second a phrase from William Carlos Williams, both point to the novel's central concern with time and history. While the novel thematizes pastoral as dream, it also stresses that fiction making itself is ultimately a kind of dreaming. In Zuckerman's words, "To the honeysweet

strains of 'Dream' I pulled away from myself, I pulled away from the reunion
and I dreamed . . . I dreamed a realistic chronicle" (89), a paradoxical description of *American Pastoral* itself. The Williams epigraph, "the rare occurrence of the expected," reflects the novel's exploration of the desire for life
to be comprehensible and predictable and life's stubborn failure to provide
just that assurance. Structurally and thematically, the novel suggests that
while we deeply desire order, and art requires shapeliness, life, the sea in
which we swim and the matter of art, provides neither. Early in the novel,
Zuckerman despairs of human beings understanding each other and of writers
reaching truth. In his words, trying to understand another person's life is "an
astonishing farce of misperception" and "That's how we know we're alive:
we're wrong" (63). When Jerry, Swede's brother, who is a surgeon, tells
Zuckerman that "the operating room turns you into somebody who's never
wrong. Much like writing," Zuckerman adamantly disputes it, saying, "Writing turns you into somebody who's always wrong. The illusion that you may
get it right someday is the perversity that draws you on." Here Zuckerman is
not very far from from Beckett's famous "I can't go on. I'll go on."

Similarly, Zuckerman asserts that the Swede "had learned the worst
lesson life can teach—that it makes no sense" (81). And in the closing pages
of the novel Zuckerman concludes that Merry's effect on her father's life was
to make him see the prevalence of chaos and disorder—"he had thought
most of it was order and only a little of it was disorder. He'd had it backwards.
He had made his fantasy and Merry had unmade it for him" (418). Yet
despite the frailty of order, the impossibility of truth telling, the problems of
history and subjectivity, the fallibility and idiosyncrasies of memory—
Zuckerman still chooses to write the novel, to take the pains to shape a work
of art, and dreams a realistic chronicle in which the worst and cheapest
response to chaos and meaninglessness is nihilistic laughter.

Part Five

With Philip Roth, as with other significant Jewish American writers, analysis
of one work leads to a recognition of the interplay with other works by the
same author, the discovery of significant, repeated individual strategies and
themes. The central repeated theme in the case of *American Pastoral* is the
pastoral idea itself, which is also pivotal in *The Counterlife*, where the pastoral idea is at first toyed with as possibility, then repudiated as unhistorical,
hence un-Jewish. Indeed, in the last words of that novel, Zuckerman defines
the idea of pastoral as the *dream* of a unified, unconflicted world where each
person is free to be himself. There both major characters have their own
pastoral dream place or places. What Basel is to the Henry of part one, Judea
is to the Henry of part two, and Gloucestershire is to Nathan—are all vari-

ants of pastoral. The repudiation of the pastoral dream is based on the fact that it "cannot admit contradiction or conflict" (322) and is therefore no more than a dream of the return to the womb, a flight from history.

In *The Counterlife* the focus is on the highly individual nature of personal pastorals, while *American Pastoral* depicts the Swede as an embodiment of a distinctively collective American phenomenon. In a sense the whole period of American history following World War II is seen as a national idyll shattered by race riots, Vietnam, and Watergate, as well as Merry's murderous bombing. Not only is the handling of the pastoral theme more cultural and less idiosyncratic in *American Pastoral*, but the tone is distinctly different. In *The Counterlife*, much of the reader's pleasure is intellectual, and Nathan Zuckerman as narrator finally seems separate from and superior to the "fictive propositions" he generates, less implicated, less touched by the revelation of their unreality. In contrast, *American Pastoral* works on a much more emotional level, and from the beginning Zuckerman asks the reader to see the Swede as a tragic hero; or, in his words, "To embrace your hero in his destruction . . . to let your hero's life occur within you when everything is trying to diminish him, to imagine yourself into his bad luck, to implicate yourself not in his mindless ascendancy, when he is the fixed point of your adulation, but in the bewilderment of his tragic fall—well, that's worth thinking about" (88). In every way, including the depiction of the extraordinary tenderness of the Swede with his daughter, *American Pastoral* prevents the reader from seeing him as a simple-minded, self-deluding escapist who needs and deserves to be awakened from a mindless dream. Likewise, the sweetness and energy of the earlier America are so densely evoked that it is impossible simply to dismiss and disdain them. Thus the pastoral which is wittily and ironically deflated in *The Counterlife* is here mourned as tragic loss.

From his earliest book, *Goodbye, Columbus*, with its assimilated Jew versus alienated Jew, thinking and fictionalizing through oppositions has been a predominant strategy in Roth's fiction. *American Pastoral* has the Rothian pattern of two antithetical brothers. The Swede and Merry are also dialectical antagonists in their diametrically opposed responses to America and in their opposite temperaments—the father seeks moderation and conciliation, the daughter demands extremes and violent responses. But the most interesting opposition of all is external to the novel: the Swede as a counterpoint to Mickey Sabbath. Like *American Pastoral*, *Sabbath's Theater* is preoccupied with time, loss, and death, but the wild anarchic Mickey embodies something like the irrepressible id, the part of the self that revels in destroying false conventions and unmasking social norms, the part that feels most alive in the unsocialized, transgressive sexual appetite. For Mickey the final battle is between Eros and Thanatos, and he challenges death with his cock. His vitality is full of fury and hatred toward everything that domesticates and contains, for to him these render existence lifeless. Through the Swede, Roth explores the opposite approach to life and embodies an alternative life principle, a counterlife. Moderate and balanced, "ecstatically complicitous" with his wife and only his wife, the Swede is the ego living, or attempting to live, in harmony with the superego, recognizing the need for living with joy and love within rules. While Mickey's misbehavior gets him thrown out of academia, the Swede's tolerant and charitable response to academia neatly exposes the entire recent oppositional stance in American university life today: "the academic world, the intellectual world, where always to be antagonizing people and challenging whatever they said was apparently looked on with admiration. What they got out of being so negative was beyond him; it seemed to him far more productive when everybody grew up and got over that" (p. 341).

To conclude: what will Jewish American literature be like in the next century? Judging from *American Pastoral*, it is likely to be talking back to European literature, face-to-face with American myth and reality, meditating on time, history, and memory, eyeballing varieties of Jewish life, and mulling over its authors' earlier acts of imagination. That it will continue to exist and even to thrive seems likely. We are not just the people of the book; we are the people of many books.

Notes

1. Philip Roth, *American Pastoral* (Boston: Houghton Mifflin, 1997), 30.

2. Louis Menand, "The Irony and the Ecstasy: Philip Roth and the Jewish Atlantis." Review of *American Pastoral*, by Philip Roth. *New Yorker* 19 (May 1997): 88.

3. Philip Roth, *The Counterlife* (New York: Farrar, 1987), 316.

Works Cited

Menand, Louis. "The Irony and the Ecstasy: Philip Roth and the Jewish Atlantis." Review of *American Pastoral*, by Philip Roth. *New Yorker* 19 (May 1997): 88–94.

Roth, Philip. *American Pastoral*. Boston: Houghton Mifflin, 1997.

———. *The Counterlife*. New York: Farrar, 1987.

———. *The Facts: A Novelist's Autobiography*. New York: Farrar, Straus & Giroux, 1988.

———. *Sabbath's Theatre*. Boston: Houghton Mifflin, 1995.

Tolstoy, Leo. *The Death of Ivan Ilych*. London: Oxford University Press, 1971.

13

Malamud and Ozick: Kindred "Neshamas"

Evelyn Avery

Separated by gender, religious practice, and lifestyle, Bernard Malamud and Cynthia Ozick would appear to share little but their accidents of birth and choice of craft as twentieth-century Jewish American authors. Indeed, they even define themselves differently, since Malamud describes himself as a "writer who happens to be Jewish," while Ozick sees herself as a writer in the Jewish tradition.

Despite such differences, however, they share a deep respect, affection, and concern for each other's lives and writings as evident in their letters and interviews.[1] Moreover, their fiction reflects shared values, a common approach to their art, in spite of contrasts in style and subject matter. Linked by *Yiddishkeit*, compassion for the underdog, outrage against injustice, and commitment to truth, their fiction invites comparison. Works such as Malamud's "Silver Crown," *The Tenants*, and *The Fixer*, and Ozick's "Pagan Rabbi," "A Mercenary," "Usurpation," and *The Shawl* illuminate and enrich each other, verifying that their authors are kindred spirits.

Ozick's respect for Malamud's writing is apparent in "Usurpation," where she admits her envy of Malamud's "Silver Crown," which turns on magic, faith, and the possibility of redemption. The presence of Rabbi Lifschitz, a questionable "miracle" worker, and his illusory silver crown ironically underscore the importance of faith and love, without which the miraculous is impossible. Since the crux of the story is an arid relationship between Albert Gans and his dying father, only love—an act of faith—can transform the son and save the father. Instead, the guilt-ridden but shallow Albert seeks a quick, cheap fix from Rabbi Lifschitz, who will, for a fee, fashion a silver crown to heal the elder Gans.

Although the rabbi's intentions and the crown's existence are suspect, both Malamud and Ozick recognize their potential to inspire real magic, to alter Albert's feelings for his father and transmute hatred into forgiveness and even love. But in "The Silver Crown" there is no magic; the rabbi and the crown fail, for Albert's heart is bitter, his *neshoma* (soul) merciless, as he curses his father: "He hates me, the son of a bitch, I hope he croaks" (Malamud, 328). An hour later, Gans "shut[s] his eyes and expire[s]." While Cecilia Farr argues that "trust in magic destroys faith and the father" (Farr, 90), the reverse is true in "The Silver Crown," where magic can only work if love, which is essential to faith, exists. Repeatedly the rabbi asks Albert whether he loves his father and "believes in God" (Malamud, 310). Repeatedly Albert is evasive, describing their relationship as difficult. Although the rabbi hardly looks or sounds prophetlike, his first name, Jonas (Greek for Jonah), suggests he has suffered and accepted God.

While the rabbi may be a materialistic con man, he is capable of sacrifice and love, and is qualified to instruct Albert. Thus the Gans' sterile relationship is counterpointed by the rabbi's bond with his retarded daughter. Described as a "bulky, stupefying, fifteen year old," with an "unfocused face" and garbled words, Rifkele lives with her father, whose magic she hawks in the street (308). In Albert Gans' eyes, she is disgusting, a freak who makes him question the rabbi's ethics and judgment, but ironically Rifkele uplifts Rabbi Lifschitz, who views his daughter as God's perfect creation. In the end, rabbi and daughter "rush into each other's arms" when they witness Albert's blasphemy against his father. "Murderer," cries the rabbi as he and Rifkele embrace and Albert flees with a "massive, spike-laden headache" instead of the silver crown (328). Without love, Malamud and Ozick both recognize, death ensues; with love, however, life has meaning.

Although Ozick playfully considers brighter alternative endings with the father recovering, Albert reforming, or the silver crown materializing, her own stories are as magical and as "logically decisive" as Malamud's (Ozick, "Usurpation," 134). Thus "The Pagan Rabbi" contains many of the elements of "The Silver Crown"—obsessive emotion, absence of love, rejection of God's Law, and dire consequences. While teacher Gans cannot honor his father and seeks answers from a crown, Rabbi Kornfeld betrays his wife and seeks love from a tree, an act of suicide. A dialectic between man's soul and nature's sensuality, "The Pagan Rabbi" is a midrash on the dangers of paganism, the worship of the physical world, of hedonistic sexuality divorced from God and human love. Relinquishing faith, love, and responsibility, the rabbi succumbs to the *yaisha hora*, the idolatrous impulse that Ozick repeatedly warns against in her fiction. On the surface, Rabbi Isaac Kornfeld seems very different from Albert Gans, one an orthodox rabbi, the other a secular Jew, but their self-indulgent natures are similar, incapable of sacrifice and love.

Nourished by the holiest literature and the most profound secular works, Rabbi Isaac Kornfeld, whose name paradoxically evokes the biblical and pastoral, rejects the Law for nature and seeks his soul in a tree nymph.

In the process, he denies his wife and God, and in committing suicide, damns himself eternally. Like Malamud, Ozick depicts the dangers of idol worship, of investing faith and love in objects, whether a silver crown or a tree.

In a variation on the theme, both authors examine the impact of selfishness and crass ambition on a power struggle between Jews and blacks. Published a few years apart, Malamud's *The Tenants* (1971) and Ozick's "A Mercenary" (1974) seem to have usurped each other in their similar themes and conclusions. While settings, characters, and plot details differ, black and Jewish rivalry crushes friendship and eventually life itself. In both works, the Jew dominates intellectually and culturally, threatening the black ego, until deposed by black rage.

Thus in *The Tenants*, Harry Lesser, a published author struggling with his second novel, is challenged by Willie Spearmint, a self-taught black writer who vies with him for literary supremacy and a Jewish woman's affections. Because the Jew mentors the black, correcting his grammar and critiquing his work, equality is impossible and violence inevitable.

Set against a jungle background in a crumbling tenement, the novel evokes the wilderness and passion of Africa, where the Jewish intellect is no match for African fervor. In a lesser dreamscape, he is married to Mary Kettlesmith by a tribal chief on the "dark continent" while his nemesis, Willie Spearmint, is simultaneously wed to Irene Bell (née Belinsky) by a rabbi. Malamud's intentions seem clear. If ethnic differences can be muted, perhaps a clash can be avoided or, better yet, if Jew and black can wed professionally and romantically perhaps their people can thrive together. Unfortunately, even the dream ceremony is undermined by misunderstanding. In an increasingly nightmarish reality, the two writers stalk each other, driven by literary envy, romantic rivalry, and base fear until the verbal dueling erupts in violence, with each attacking the other's most vulnerable site, Spearmint's brain and Lesser's manhood.

A pair of unequals, black and Jew are doomed from the beginning, a truth Cynthia Ozick realizes in "A Mercenary." The settings alternate between Africa and New York, somewhat evocative of *The Tenants* except that Africa is not just a dream, but an exotic-cannibalistic backdrop to the deadly battle between Morris Ngambe, a prominent tribal member, and his Oxonian assistant, Stanislav Lushinski, a Polish Jewish Holocaust survivor. A paid diplomat for a tiny African nation, Lushinski enjoys the tropical fruits, including the plentiful "black-brown nipples." But despite his privileged position, Lushinski cannot forget he is a Jew, although "he was cold to Jews, and labored to identify as an 'African.'" Likewise, Ngambe, half Lushinski's age, possessing an excellent British education and European experience, distrusts the West and Lushinski, but is attached to both.

The stage is set for the African and the Jew, both "impersonators," to expose each other's real identities. In "New York, a city of Jews," Ngambe views "their neighborhoods, their religious schools, their synagogues, societies and an avalanche of books" and then surveys nearby "the streets of Blacks, victims with African faces, lost to language and faith" ("A Mercenary," 50). From his perspective, the contrast is evident—economically, culturally, religiously, the Jews are the "haves" and the blacks the "have nots." Nor can individuals successfully reinvent themselves, especially when they possess the dense ethnic histories of the Holocaust or colonial experiences. Thus, Ngambe and Lushinski are fated to play out their roles. Back in the "white African villa," Lushinski receives a threatening note from Ngambe, who calls him a Jew, a traitor, and appeals to his mother's spirit to destroy the imposter.

Although the tribal father heads the family and community, Ozick empowers Ngambe's mother, who, after her bizarre "unkosher" death, which blends her nursing milk with blood, becomes a source of worship. Still worse off, Lushinski had been orphaned when his Aryan-looking, assimilated parents had been executed by Nazis, leaving Stanislav to fend for himself. To survive, both youths had buried their pasts, donned masks, and in effect attempted to exchange identities, but their behavior has been no more than playacting.

In a Malamudian-style epigram, Ozick writes, "Every man at length becomes what he wishes to victimize. . . . Every man needs to impersonate what he first must kill" ("A Mercenary," 51). Eerily reminiscent of *The Tenants*, "Mercenary" climaxes in an invocation to evil as Ngambe beseeches his "divine mother" to return the Jew to "the merciless palms of [Polish] peasants and fists of peasants under the rafters . . . , against the stone and under the snow" (52). In short, the Polish Jew, dispatched by African sorcery, is transported back to the Holocaust, to the Jewish identity and fate he sought to escape.

Similarly, the Jew in flight is evident in Malamud's *Fixer* and Ozick's *The Shawl*, both Holocaust nightmares, though the former is set in early twentieth-century Russia, while the latter occurs primarily in Miami, forty years after the death camp experience. Commenting on *The Fixer*, Malamud acknowledged the Mendel Beilis case as the source for his novel but added that he "shap[ed] the whole to suggest the quality of the afflictions of the Jews under Hitler."[2] In short, *The Fixer* can be considered Holocaust literature.

Although different ages, genders, and backgrounds, Rosa Lublin (*The Shawl*) and Yakov Bok (*The Fixer*) endure similar suffering and even possess comparable characteristics. Both have undergone terrible physical abuse, one in a camp, the other in prison. Rosa, raised in a prosperous, assimilated Polish Jewish family, is doubly bitter over her losses, while Yakov, extremely impoverished, yearns for wealth and the opportunity to assimilate into gentile Kiev. Both are arrogant, blaming others for their tragedies. Thus Rosa believes her niece Stella to be responsible for her baby Magda's death while Yakov wrongly blames his wife Raisl for their childlessness. Both resist advice and comfort. Rosa accepts money from Stella but shuns her and only reluctantly allows Simon Persky, a would-be friend, to enter her life. Likewise, Yakov rejects his father-in-law's consoling words and initially condemns his wife when she visits the prison.

Of course, both characters will change, mature, and accept responsibility for life. But before Yakov can become a Jew, insisting on a public trial to clear his name and to expose Russian anti-Semitism, he must acquire courage to forgive his wife and acknowledge his fault in the failed marriage. He must embrace *Yiddishkeit* and recognize the decency of some Russians. Since Rosa occupies a more circumscribed world than Yakov, her task is similar but more focused. Thus, she must relinquish the worn blanket that serves as her baby, admitting that Magda is dead, murdered in the camp. She must view her niece realistically and gratefully accept the overtures of other human beings who may come from "inferior" backgrounds but who are "menschen."

In each work, the protagonists are educated to become more understanding and virtuous. Clearly, Malamud and Ozick share the same values and speak the same language. Whether in "The Silver Crown," *The Tenants*, or *The Fixer*, the heroes struggle to control their basest instincts. When they fail, as in the instances of Albert Gans and Harry Lesser, we mourn with the author. When they succeed, as does Yakov Bok, we applaud their sacrifice and ultimate righteousness. As a longtime Malamud enthusiast, Cynthia Ozick expresses similar ideals. While some of her characters, Rabbi Kornfeld and Stansilav Luchinski, succumb to their passions, Rosa Lublin reminds us that redemption is possible even forty years after the Holocaust. Although Yakov Bok's fate is uncertain in the Tzar's court and Rosa Lublin's future is somewhat problematic, we are reminded that their nobility resides in the struggle for freedom, an ongoing process.

At Bernard Malamud's funeral, a rather secular affair attended by hundreds, Cynthia Ozick mourned the loss of a great Jewish writer and friend. In the midst of the tributes to Malamud's genius, his contribution to literature, his personal relationships, Ozick rose and, facing the mourners, recited the *Shema*, the holiest prayer in Jewish worship, which binds the Jew to God. Although she knew that Malamud was not observant, Ozick had to affirm that his *neshama* was Jewish, that Bernard Malamud was a member of the tribe. The mourners' surprised response assured her that the Hebrew prayer was not only fitting testimony, but also a necessary reminder of Malamud's identity.[3]

Notes

1. Several Malamud-Ozick lettters have been reprinted in *The Bernard Malamud Society Newsletter* 6 (1996). Telephone interviews between Ozick and Avery, December 1995 and August 1996.

2. Alan Cheus and Nicholas Delbanco, *Talking Horse: The Life and Writing of Bernard Malamud* (New York: Columbia University Press, 1996), 89.

3. Ozick's description of the funeral appears in the letters and interviews cited in note 1.

Works Cited

The Bernard Malamud Society Newsletter 6 (1996).

Cheus, Alan and Nicholas Delbanco. *Talking Horse: The Life and Writing of Bernard Malamud*. New York: Columbia University Press, 1996.

Farr, Cecilia Konchar. "Lust for a Story: Cynthia Ozick's 'Usurpation' as Fabulation." *Studies in American Jewish Literature* 6 (1987).

Malamud, Bernard. *The Fixer*. New York: Farrar, Straus, Giroux, 1966.

———. "The Silver Crown." In *The Stories of Bernard Malamud*. New York: Farrar, Straus, Giroux, 1983.

———. *The Tenants*. New York: Farrar, Straus, Giroux, 1971.

Ozick, Cynthia. "A Mercenary" in "Usurpation (Other People's Stories)." In *Bloodshed and Three Novellas*. New York: Alfred A. Knopf, 1976.

———. *The Pagan Rabbi and Other Stories*. New York: Schocken, 1976.

———. *The Shawl*. New York: Alfred A. Knopf, 1987.

———. "Usurpation (Other People's Stories)." In *Bloodshed and Three Novellas*. New York: Alfred A. Knopf, 1976.

14

Myth and Addiction in Jonathan Rosen's "Eve's Apple"

Suzanne Evertsen Lundquist

Any discussion of the female body ought to be grounded in personal experience.

—Janet Burstein, Drew University

I call it "personal voice criticism."

—Carole S. Kessner, SUNY Stony Brook[1]

Studied alive, myth . . . is not an explanation in satisfaction of a scientific interest, but a narrative resurrection of a primeval reality, told in satisfaction of deep religious wants, moral cravings.

—Bronislaw Malinowski, *Magic, Science and Religion*

The specific struggles we undergo with our addictions are reflections of a blessed pain. To be deprived of a simple object of attachment is to taste the deep, holy deprivation of our souls. To struggle to transcend any idol is to touch the sacred hunger. . . . It is a willing, wanting, aching venture into the desert of our nature, loving the emptiness of that desert because of the sure knowledge that God's rain will fall and the certainty that we are both heirs and cocreators of the wonder that is now and of the Eden that is yet to be.

—Gerald G. May, *Addiction and Grace*

I became interested in Jonathan Rosen's novel *Eve's Apple* when I heard Rosen speak on the history of the *Forward* (an American Jewish newspaper out of New York) at the annual Jewish American Literature Conference in Boca Raton, Florida in 1999. I admired his presence; he was confident, knowledgeable, and had a sophistication about him that drew me to believe in his motives for doing scholarship. When I heard that he had also published a novel in 1997, and that furthermore it had something to do with Eve, the woman whose subtitle is the mother-of-living, I was intrigued and determined that I would not only read the novel but write about it. Little did I know when I volunteered to speak on the text that it was about eating disorders—a very distasteful topic. And yet, this novel has become important to me in ways that few have. Indeed, for me the academic is also personal.

I first read *Eve's Apple* when I was in the Netherlands visiting my daughter. She had a baby in June and the delivery was difficult—she lost two liters of blood and required several transfusions plus an immediate operation once the baby was born. During her pregnancy, she selected with care every mouthful of food for her son. But she also complained that she was constantly hungry throughout the nine months. As a result, she went from a size four to a size she wouldn't reveal. Her sixty-plus pounds of weight gain, however, alarmed all three of my daughters. The second time I read the book, I was home in Utah. My second son had just been released from the hospital after a fifteen-month stay for various complications due to brain chemistry disorders. When he was first admitted to the hospital, he was terrified of eating anything. He lost seventy-two pounds in less than two months. The hospital staff had him on a twenty-four-hour watch to ensure that he not only took his medications but that he did not purge the medications or his meals. I also suffer from a disease called PCOS—a condition related to the failure of the insulin in my body to convert certain foods into energy. I likewise have never come to terms with my body, even though, philosophically, I can discourse at length about the major mind/body split we have inherited from Western thought—a separation that has long privileged the spirit, mind, or intellect over the body. Is there any wonder, then, that Rosen's novel would be of interest to me?

Essentially, this novel suggests that "A" is not only for apple, but also for addictions and anorexia. And furthermore, the text suggests that the West's problems with food are inseparably connected to the book of Genesis. Given the various historical interpretations of the forbidden fruit, it is no surprise that women, and therefore all living, have an uneasy relationship to what they eat.

The blurb on the jacket claims, "Part psychological mystery, part poignant love story, *Eve's Apple* brilliantly captures our passionate longing for knowledge, connection, and acceptance." It continues:

Ruth Simon is beautiful, smart, talented, and always hungry. As a teenager, she starved herself almost to death and though outwardly healed, inwardly she remains dangerously obsessed with food. For Joseph Zimmerman, Ruth's tormented relationship with eating is a source of profound distress and erotic fascination. Driven by his deep love for Ruth and haunted by his own painful secrets, Joseph sets out to unravel the mystery of hunger and denial. Blind to everything but his insatiable appetite for Ruth, Joseph is determined to save her, at all costs.

Embedded in this summary of the text are ample clues to the obsessive nature of both characters. And then the names themselves thrust the text into mythological realms: Eve, Ruth, Joseph. And Joseph's sister, who suicided when she was just sixteen, is also named Evelyn or Evie for short.

A quick glance at the meaning of these names and the stories they refer to furthers the implications of the mythological import of Rosen's novel. The creation of the first woman in the Hebrew Bible is an episode, according to Michael Fishbane, that suggests Adam is the mother of all living, rather than Eve. The mythic image of Eve emerging from Adam's flesh "reflects a male fantasy of self-sufficiency" (199). However, "the subsequent narrative," Fishbane advocates,

> introduces a more realistic perspective. Thus, after the woman has succumbed to the wiles of the snake, eaten of the tree of the knowledge of good and evil, and shared it with her husband, she is acknowledged as a source of new life—albeit with negative overtones, since the narrative stresses the punishment of pain that must be borne by Adam's mate and all her female descendants during pregnancy and childbirth.

When Rosen writes, "All knowledge has about it a pornographic lure" (102–103), he underscores the erotic nature of the Genesis tale. Eve equals one who needs to be controlled inasmuch as she brought the knowledge of good and evil into the world because of something she ate. And somehow, erotic desire comes into the mix. To complicate matters, all women suffer because of Eve's choices.

Two facts about the name Ruth revealed in Jack M. Sasson's article on "Ruth and Naomi" apply directly to Rosen's selection of a name for his leading lady. First of all, Sasson tells us that "some Semiticists claim" that the name Ruth "derives from the root *rwt*, which permits the meaning 'fertilized one' " (491–492). The irony of such a meaning is twofold in this novel. First of all, women with severe anorexia don't have menstrual cycles and, therefore, can't get pregnant. Consequently when Ruth claims to be pregnant, she is perpetuating a con on Joseph. And second, "That Ruth was the ancestress of David the king (and hence of the Messiah)" (491), makes the contemporary Ruth's anorexia even more problematic. Thus the names of Eve and Ruth in relationship to creation and futurity are clearly evocative in terms of eating disorders.

Similar reflections apply to Rosen's choice of a name for his protagonist. Certainly Joseph's sojourn in Egypt creates the possibility that those who have wounded family members can repent and be forgiven. And Joseph's relationship to overcoming the famine facing his family in the Genesis tale also makes Rosen's choice of names emblematic. Nonetheless, Rosen's Joseph is as sick as his Ruth. To understand the death and near death of the two women that matter to him most, Rosen's Joseph ingests information from numerous sources. Characteristic of consumptive or codependent individuals, Joseph's behavior mirrors the conduct of those afflicted persons in his circle of care.

Mythological and psychoanalytic theories apply to this text. However familiar these theories might be to those in academia, directed to this text they take on consequential relevance. No matter how weary of theory we are beginning a new century, understanding cultural causes for life-threatening maladies remains necessary. And even if we are tired of the French having critical sway, we must gain insight from whatever resources are available to us. Pierre Brunel tells us that "It would be impossible to exaggerate the part played by Pierre Albouy and his remarkable essay, *Mythes et Mythologies dans la Litterature francaise* (1969) in fostering" our understanding of "literary myth" in "contemporary comparative studies" (xiii). Albouy makes an important distinction between the concept of "theme" and "literary myth." For Albouy,

> the literary myth consists of the story implied by the myth—a story "that the author can treat and alter with great liberty"— and of the new meanings that are then added to it. If there is no extra meaning added to what has been handed down by tradition, there is no literary myth, just a theme or subject.

By myth, I mean those sacred narratives that are considered true, living, and paradigmatic to members of those cultures to whom they relate— the Old and New Testaments, the Koran, the *Mahabharata*, and so forth. Furthermore, most sacred narratives are cautionary; they warn readers and hearers of the behaviors that bring sorrow into the world. And many contemporary novels, by extension, continue the sacred narratives.[2] Indeed, in correlating the symbiotic relationship between anorexia and the story of Eve in the Bible, Rosen is adding iconoclastic meaning to the study of Genesis.

Myth as the house of important psychological insights is also not a new approach to literature. Certainly, Jungian analysis is derived from just such insights. However, we have developed further comprehension of the connections between addictions and myth since Jung. In fact, we are currently engaged in a paradigm shift with regard to myths and obsessions—particularly developed in the works of Anne Wilson Schaef. In *When Society Becomes an Addict*, Schaef defines paradigm shift as "the buildup of information and the subsequent, drastic introduction of new information" (148). A paradigm shift "involves being wrenched out of where we are and forced to go somewhere else." This can conceivably be said to be the condition that Joseph finds himself in by the end of *Eve's Apple*. In fact, in order to find out as much as he can about Ruth's anorexia, Joseph spends an inordinate amount of time at the New York Public Library reading every reference to anorexia that Flek, the retired therapist in the novel, refers him to. The shear volume of information Joseph gains from the books he reads as well as from Fleck and his own crises brings Joseph to a paradigm shift in his understanding of his own cultural and familial contexts.

In addition, Schaef's definitions of "addiction" and "addictive systems" are also provocative:

> An addiction is any process over which we are powerless. It takes control of us, causing us to do and think things that are inconsistent with our personal values and leading us to become progressively more compulsive and obsessive. (*When Society*, 19)

Moreover, "A sure sign of an addiction is the sudden need to deceive ourselves and others—to lie, deny, and cover up." Schaef, herself a therapist, has developed her theories over a long period from both her personal and professional experiences. She notes that addictions are "progressive" and that "they lead to death unless we actively recover" from them. Schaef divides addictions into two major classes: "substance addictions and process addictions." Schaef tells us that addictions keep us from knowing ourselves. We externalize our interests and project our needs onto objects or others. Our sensory input is distorted, we cannot receive information clearly, and we con people when we are addicts. Furthermore, even though we know that something is wrong with us, we blame others "for what is happening. . . . An addiction absolves us from having to take responsibility for our lives" (22), says Schaef. Ruth, in her aversion to food, could be identified as a substance addict and Joseph in his obsessive need to heal Ruth could clearly be called a process addict.

"People with food-related addictions talk in terms of 'burying' what is going on inside of them and 'stuffing' their feelings. Food (or the avoidance of food) is perceived as a 'cure' for anger, depression, fear, anxiety, and other unpleasant feelings," adds Schaef. Certainly Ruth's resentment of her parents and her need for their unconditional love and acceptance are partially responsible for her anorexia.

In addition, Joseph secretly reads Ruth's diary, avoids telling Ruth about his visits to Flek and to the library, and is abnormally or erotically attached to Ruth's body. Process addictions occur when "one becomes hooked on a process—a specific series of actions or interactions" (22). Accumulating money, gambling, sex, work, religion, and worry are examples of process addictions. What becomes alarming, however, is that process addictions are systemic. This means that all facets of a culture participate in promoting addictive behaviors. Several unconscious assumptions are fundamental to addictive systems: (1) that one's system of thought (i.e., Western civilization) is the only, or true system; (2) that one's system is "innately superior"; (3) that the system produces knowledge and understanding; and (4) "that it is possible to be totally logical, rational, and objective" (*When Society* 7–8). The fact that our particular Western, Judeo-Christian system is also fundamentally dualistic—male and female, dominant and submissive, controlling and controlled—adds kindling to the mind/body dualism found in *Eve's Apple*.

Flek defines Joseph's systemic awareness in this manner:

> Can't you see, Joseph? You're not just trying to save Ruth. You're trying to solve the riddle of female sadness itself. You're trying to solve the self-destructive urge of humanity. You're trying to crack the mystery of the body. Take it from someone who once tried to do these things for a living: it isn't possible. You've been hunting the white whale and it isn't going to end well if you don't take care of yourself. (173)

And Joseph recognizes that his own process addiction might be systemic when he says:

> I felt myself growing more and more desperate. Like a gambler, I could not keep away from the library. The less I found the more I wanted. I'd go through one stack of books, cash them in at the return desk and get another. Chemical, cultural, historical, biological—each explanation offered a partial view but nothing I found in the library gave me the key. Was it gender? Genes? Genesis? The story in the Garden of Eden still expressed the paradox best: we reach for the apple because we want more. And we have wanted more since we reached for the apple. (202)

The entire novel is full of Joseph's research and speculations. And Rosen, in crafting the novel, leaves almost nothing to the imagination. Often the novel resembles a scholarly paper more than a tale. And yet, the long quotes from actual texts are absorbing. In determining what kind of eating disorder Ruth has, for example, Joseph quotes long passages, in his notebook, from the *Diagnostic and Statistical Manual* of the American Psychiatric Association (133–138).

As Joseph builds his research base, he discovers from John A. Sours' book *Starving in a Sea of Objects* that "high intelligence has always been linked with anorexia nervosa" (139). And indeed, Ruth is very bright. In fact, she is an art student at the New School. Many of the works that Joseph reads come from a list given to him by Flek. Flek himself has a vested interest in issues about the body. In his youth, he was a victim of polio and, as a result, has spent the majority of his life in a wheelchair. When Joseph tries to determine how far back anorexia dates from, he finds a partial answer in a book Flek recommends called *Holy Anorexia*, by Rudolph M. Bell. Bell claims that

> cloistered women of medieval Italy starved themselves to gain authority and independence, the book argued that fasting was a way for powerless women to rebel against the patriarchal world they lived in. They could exercise dominion over their own bodies and the control they gained over food somehow translated into a sort of mystical authority that helped them in their quest for sainthood. (140)

Again, such information relates directly to Ruth's condition. When Joseph queries Ruth about her beliefs concerning the soul, she confesses, "Maybe the best part of us is the invisible part" (143). She asks Joseph if the soul is "part of our body, or separate? Where does it go afterward? Does it weigh anything?" (142). This conversation is generated during one of Ruth's cleaning frenzies. She asks Joseph where all the dust comes from and, to her disgust, he tells her it comes primarily from dead skin cells.

On that day, Joseph quoted an observation of Sours in his notebook: the anorexic, says Sours, "treats her body as though it were a threatening entity which, like a demon, needs to be controlled at all times. As her flesh falls away, her soul is revealed, made free again" (143). Although Joseph has rejected the belief that there is a religious side to anorexia, Ruth's focus on her soul leads him to the possibility. Flek advised Joseph earlier that he must begin his quest for knowledge "at the beginning. . . . In the Garden of Eden. 'The day that thou eatest the fruit thereof thou shalt surely die,'" Flek observes. "Food has been causing trouble ever since" (127). Clearly the message, "If you eat, you will die," is fundamental to this biblical narrative. In fact the word "eat" is the most often repeated word in the story—with some twenty uses. But, in the beginning, Joseph dismisses biblical origins of Ruth's malady. The correlation between myth and illness seems remote to Joseph.

Typical interpretations of the Eden narrative are untenable: Eve equals one who can be beguiled by evil (the serpent) in the form of forbidden food. Robert Alter's new translation of Genesis, however, suggests that it is no longer viable to rush to pejorative conclusions. "In the Hebrew here, the phonetic similarity is between *hawah*, "Eve," and the verbal root *hayah*, "to live." It has been proposed that Eve's name conceals very different origins, for it sounds suspiciously like the Aramaic word for "serpent." However, suggests Alter, "could she have been given the name by the contagious contiguity with her wily interlocutor, or, on the contrary, might there lurk behind the name a very different evaluation of the serpent as a creature associated with the origins of life?" (15n). Certainly such a discussion could be useful to the daughters of Eve and their partners.

Flek also tells Joseph that all his research is not going to save Ruth. His focus is on intellectual understanding rather than on the body. "The body is our one great book," claims Flek (128).

> Unfortunately it is written in a language we no longer under-stand. All other books, even our most cherished, are merely ef-forts to understand our one great book, which holds the secret of ourselves. . . . Our most brilliant writers haven't come any closer to the body than those chalk outlines policemen make on the ground after a murder. The body is our true Bible. All other books are commentary. (128)

Flek then warns Joseph, "You've been studying Ruth, it's clear, but you have a lot to learn and you can't do it by tracing her life endlessly in the air. You can't do it by going to the library." Joseph's model for learning, however, is at once medical, psychological, and rational rather than mythological.

Even Joseph has no conception of his *own* body. Some of the most troubling portions of this novel are the long sections in which Joseph dis-cusses, in minute detail, his sexual encounters with Ruth. It is as though having Ruth's naked body on top of his is a way of stroking his own body—a way of returning Ruth's body to his, to Adam's. Joseph muses, "She was melting into me, dissolving back into my flesh. God opened Adam's body and plucked out Eve and now he was putting her back. But then Ruth toppled beside me, separate again, panting faintly" (225). Ruth's body is not only the object of Joseph's desire, it is an extension of his sexual fantasies. Early in the novel, Joseph confesses, "I wished to learn something from

Ruth, to study her, ill, for Ruth knew something or *embodied* something that I sensed, vaguely, was of vital importance to me" (18). The key word here is "embodied." Joseph fails to realize, here, that his real need is for the body, for something incarnate. That Joseph also confuses his preoccupation with Ruth as "love" is doubly alarming.

Again, Anne Wilson Schaef has insights into this malady. In her book *Escape from Intimacy: Untangling the "Love" Addictions*, Schaef explains that any focus on the other that bypasses an actual person in order to gain a personal fix is a way of avoiding intimacy. She suggests that "we seem to use a simple cause-and-effect mentality to think about psychological problems. This approach makes it easy to fall into the illusion that if we just understand why people are the way they are then we . . . can fix it" (7). And furthermore, says Schaef, "the very process of 'understanding' may be a way to 'protect one's supply.' " The "prerequisites for intimacy," claims Schaef, are: "Loving someone (being a lover); / While staying with yourself and; / Fully participating in your own life." Joseph doesn't, therefore, actually have an intimate relationship, a loving relationship, with Ruth. He is a graduate from Columbia, teaching English, by default, to Russian immigrants, while he lives with Ruth who, incidentally, pays the major portion of the rent from money she gets from her father. After Joseph's condom is punctured during a sexual encounter, Ruth claims to be pregnant. Rather than view this revelation as a sign of health in Ruth or the opportunity to have a coupled, truly creative future together, Joseph says he isn't ready to father a child. He is, however, willing to accompany Ruth to an abortion clinic.

During one of their several conversations, Flek tells Joseph,

> Rich girls don't have children, they have eating disorders, but they are guided by the same principle. They use their bodies to try to negate the body, to exercise power over it. They think they will free themselves and gain control, only to find themselves prisoners. The body in this culture is the weapon and the wound. (169)

Could the same be said of Joseph? Certainly his refusal to take responsibility for the probability that sexual intercourse might lead to new life might indicate that Joseph is equally alienated from his own body. Joseph is also constantly agonized by migraines—a manifestation of his own unresolved issues. And when Ruth leaves him for a couple of months to study art in France, Joseph is painfully lost. So lost he even has a sexual encounter with one of his colleagues from ETNA, a place where "no one . . . was what he wanted to be"—including Joseph. "What is your wound?" Flek asks Joseph (173). "When are you going to speak about that?" And furthermore,

Flek entreats Joseph, "why are you so afraid to talk about your sister?" Joseph responds, "I failed her. . . . I'm not going to fail Ruth."

To *not* fail, in this novel, is to come to terms with the body, to be embodied, to be environed, to be in families, to be open, honest, and intimate. According to Schaef, intimacy is a complex of interactions and conditions:

> Knowing and being known by another
> Sharing information openly
> Stroking
> Not necessarily romantic or sexual
> Being alive and sharing that sense of aliveness
> Being intimate with the self first
> Experiencing life together—developing a common history
> Involves all the senses
> Not brought about by techniques
> Not confined to time and space—one can remain intimate
>   without contact, allowing the other to go away when she
>   or he needs to
> Magical, beyond language, a hologram
> Varied—one kind does not diminish another kind; there is
>   enough
> Playful and fun—sharing mistakes and foolishness
> Much talking, no analyzing
> A lot of paradoxes—requires being together yet not having
>   to be; requires working at, yet cannot be worked at
> A gift (*Escape from Intimacy*, 137–138)

Neither Joseph nor Ruth, for much of the novel, are able to approximate such intimacy. Certainly Joseph's and Ruth's retreat from their families, their inability to be honest with each other, and their near collapse when separated support the notion that these two might fail, might fall. And this is the prospect set forth in *Eve's Apple*. The entire novel is divided into seasons: winter, spring, and summer, with a look toward fall. What the end of the work implies, however, is a new kind of fall and not the Fall described in Genesis. This new fall, however, needs to lead to a new kind of consciousness that is fully present and embodied. This new fall is also contingent and depends on a multifaceted notion of relationship.

When Ruth returns from France she regrettably requires hospitalization; she is skin over bone—the image of a concentration camp internee. Joseph, thankfully, has made a partial metamorphosis in her absence. The possibility of such a transformation is what Rosen's novel intimates. At this point, Rosen makes nothing explicit; the relationship exists almost solely in potential.

What Rosen's novel does make explicit, however, is the substance of the import of Joseph's journey. His journey is toward life and commitment and away from death and estrangement. Flek tells Joseph that women "try to abort, not the child in them, but the woman in them. And nothing is more danger-ous than human beings in revolt against their own natures" (170). But abortion is both a male and female decision. If Ruth and Joseph can revise their rela-tionship and move toward well-being, their achievement is "bound up with the whole of human history." Joseph himself begins to play with the implications of the general nature of his particular dilemma. He thinks that perhaps "Stalin's Great Purge had been preceded by a Great Binge." And he asks,

> Were the bodies in Hitler's ovens, like the children baked by the witch in *Hansel and Gretel,* part of an ancient grotesque war on physical existence conducted on a mass scale? Were all the great punctuating horrors of modern times linked to our war against our bodies, a war that technology . . . greatly intensified? (170)

When Joseph reads Kenneth Clark's *The Nude: A Study in Ideal Form,* he realizes all the various attitudes about the body we have inherited through time. Art transforms the body into something alien to nature. "The naked body was the body as it actually appeared in nature—lumpy, bumpy, wrinkled, gross. The nude was what artists made of that body, an ideal representation" (158). And every historical period has a different idea about bodily perfec-tion. As Joseph realizes our evolution from preferring chubby goddesses to the "popsicle stick" and "Celestial Venus" figures, to the "rumpled flanks" of Rubens' women and so forth, he fails, at first, to take note of the represen-tations of men in Clark's book. When he returns to the book to see what the paintings actually say about the body, he discovers various conceptions of gods bound up in notions of the body as well. Joseph asks,

> Had I ever seen a fat Jesus the way one saw fat Buddhas? And what was Jesus doing on the cross if not fulfilling a western wish to destroy the body once and for all? Is this why the image was still so compelling after 2000 years? As for the Jewish God, he didn't have a body at all. And yet we were said to be made in God's image. (171)

For those grounded in religious narratives as explanations for human purpose and destiny, Joseph's questions are, at the least, disturbing. Moreover, when he asserts that our conception of God "might be part of the problem," he advances the literary myth he is creating. When Joseph queries, "Was the idea that God lay outside nature, separate from our bodies and the living world, destructive?" he certainly is asking for an answer worthy of our sincere consideration. With so many bewildering questions, what could possibly be the nature of Joseph's reformation? Joseph's sister committed suicide. Previous to her death, Joseph came upon a letter in her drawer that indicated her despair caused by the failure of their family to actualize her image of a true immigrant family. She wrote, "I'm so sorry. . . . I don't seem to know how to be happy" (294) and finally ends with, "Joseph, make them happy"—meaning make his parents happy and at home in an America where families disintegrate. Because Joseph, as a young boy, failed to grasp the magnitude of his sister's despair, he now feels unrelenting guilt.

During a bout with remorse, Joseph thinks of his aborted child. "I thought, for the first time, that people really do have souls and that a soul had been summoned and dismissed. I felt it beating against me like a moth, as real as Ruth was real, though unseen" (295). He determines that if the child had lived, it would have been a girl, a daughter, and that she would have been named Evelyn-Evie. "What else did we come into the world for but to create new life? To undo death. And I had failed. I had sacrificed my child." Despite the fact that Ruth never was pregnant, these thoughts are coming from a Joseph who is becoming more aware, more accountable. When Ruth returns home, she admits her pregnancy was a fantasy—a wish to be fertile. Their separation and reunion brings about a confrontation of motives between them. And it is a fruitful encounter. Ruth requires hospital care; and they both attend to her return to Twin Oaks and her original therapist, Dr. Ranki. While Ruth is hospitalized, Joseph plans to visit his parents. Joseph admits, "I had chosen Ruth to dramatize all my troubles, much as she had chosen food. We both needed to let the world back in" (309).

This is where the novel ends: with Ruth and Joseph "dreaming of a new beginning." Joseph even dreams of himself and Ruth establishing a small café, called Eve's Apple, in an old Jewish immigrant neighborhood in New York. And yet, such neighborhoods no longer exist. What the novel *Eve's Apple* does not deal with is how one lets the world back in, or what such an opening can mean.

I now want Rosen to write a sequel, *The Book of Joseph and Ruth*. Where in all of canonized scripture is there a book carrying the name of a couple who can celebrate a sacred marriage? Certainly we have alternative myths—Isis and Osiris, Psyche and Eros, Tristan and Iseult, and numerous other mythological couples—that suggest what it takes to live in a coupled world. Certainly the Bible's prototypical celebration of gendered love, the Song of Songs, is not a pregnant text. I long for a new book to be added to the Testaments. Can there be a new creation? Or will scriptural books always suggest that we are continually moving toward an apocalypse? Few fine novels create an image of healthy human intimacy over time. Too many end at a beginning. I want Rosen to read Robert Johnson's *We*, Sam Keen's *A Passionate Life*, Morris Berman's *Coming to Our Senses*, Gerald May's *Addiction and Grace*, and Anne Wilson Schaef's *Beyond Therapy, Beyond Science*. Together, these texts suggest what it takes to overcome the isolating, addictive behaviors so typical of the modern era.

Certainly, mythology tries to establish harmonious or covenant relationships between the creators, communities, land, and an individual's potential. And addictions are what detract from such harmony. Perhaps Gerald May is accurate when he asserts, "To be deprived of a simple object of attachment is to taste the deep, holy deprivation of our souls. To transcend any idol [addiction] is to touch the sacred hunger God has given us" (181). In addition, obsessions can lead us to recognize our "willing, wanting, aching venture into the desert of our nature." Such awareness might help us heal and, therefore, help us become accountable "cocreators of the wonder that is now and of the Eden that is yet to be." Perhaps it has taken these several millennia for us to realize that the Fall was actually about the tragic separations humans create in their self-centered, competitive compulsion to know. Have we taken our human dominion to mean that we are not dependent on our environment or communities for our well-being? Have we adopted a radical individualism that prevents us from ever seeing our flawed ideologies? Have we accepted mythological misinterpretations as truth? That is, can we rethink Eden?

Consider what Ruth and Joseph might make of Sam Keen's notion that

> We cannot ask the question of the relation between person and land [Joseph's letting the world in] as if we were talking about two separate entities, one of which owns the other, any more than I can ask how I should relate to my body. The mystery of my carnality is that I am inseparable from my body. The mystery of my humanness is that I am inseparable from the humus. (236)

Could it be that the mind, spirit, body, earth, man, animal separations and hierarchies are language based rather than biologically grounded? Is what we call spirit actually matter? Keen tells us,

> In the strictest sense, it is not accurate to speak about the lover's body. No noun can capture the pulsing commonwealth of cells that make up any living thing. We exist as verbs, always in process. Each singular-plurality is a vibratory center in constant intercourse with other vibratory centers. There are no isolated events or entities in the universe. (199)

And yet, as anyone who lives with addictive personalities knows, no amount of explaining such an interactive universe can cause life-process changes in another. How do we extricate ourselves from addictive systems? Anne Wilson Schaefs' *Beyond Therapy, Beyond Science* tries to speak of such possibilities. "To love is to be about the task of healing," remarks Keen. Furthermore,

> The Lover's vocation is to lure others (and that part of the self that nurses old injuries and fears, takes pride in autonomy, and harbors the illusion of self-sufficiency) into re-cognition of their true being and their true allegiance. It is to practice the art of forgiveness and to expand the circle of care. (191)

Love, then, is inclusive rather than exclusive. Joseph has researched the causes of Ruth's anorexia. He can define the problem. As with any work of literature, however, the content is preemptive. No amount of speculation about the future lives of characters can alter the fact that the book is already given and, therefore, unalterable by our conjectures. We can only ask what we, together, need to realize in order to come to a new consciousness and, therefore, a new way of being in the world? *Eve's Apple*, however, can be a stimulus into this important inquiry.

Notes

1. Janet Burstein, Carole S. Kessner, and I presented papers on Jonathan Rosen's *Eve's Apple* at the Jewish American and Holocaust Literature Symposium on October 22, 1999, in Boca Raton, Florida. Their comments came to me as a result of their interest in my personal approach to my topic. Both scholars agree with me, to use Kessner's name, that personal voice criticism is essential when doing ethnographic work.

2. See Mircea Eliade's "Survivals and Camouflages of Myths," in *Myth and Reality* (New York: Harper and Row, 1975) 163–193, for a discussion of the relationship between myth and the novel.

Works Cited

Alter, Robert, trans. *Genesis*. New York: W. W. Norton, 1996.

Brunel, Pierre. "Preface." In *Companion to Literary Myths, Heroes and Archetypes*, ed. Pierre Brunel, ix–xvi. London: Routledge, 1996.

Fishbane, Michael. "Eve." In *The Encyclopedia of Religion*, ed. Mircea Eliade, 607–608. New York: Macmillan, 1987.

Keen, Sam. *The Passionate Life*. San Francisco: Harper San Francisco, 1984.

May, Gerald G. *Addiction and Grace*. San Francisco: Harper, 1988.

Rosen, Jonathan. *Eve's Apple*. New York: Plume, 1997.

Sasson, Jack M. "Ruth and Naomi." In *The Encyclopedia of Religion*, ed. Mircea Eliade, 491–492. New York: Macmillan, 1987.

Schaef, Anne Wilson. *Escape from Intimacy: Untangling the "Love" Addictions*. San Francisco: Harper & Row, 1989.

———. *When Society Becomes an Addict*. San Francisco: Harper, 1987.

15

Evolving Paradigms of Jewish Women in Twentieth-Century American Jewish Fiction: Through a Male Lens/ Through a Female Lens

S. Lillian Kremer

Part One

The radically divergent portraits of Jewish women in mid and late twentieth-century Jewish American fiction are, more often than not, a reflection of the gender of the author. Jewish women are rarely adequately contextualized either historically or culturally, but are frequently the subject of satire and calumny in texts written by men. Assertive, highly verbal, clever Jewish women are frequently caricatured in mid and late twentieth-century male-authored American fiction as "pushy" and unfavorably compared with restrained, docile, "real" American women, that is, gentile women. Often, as in Philip Roth's fiction, Jewish women are either manipulative mothers or lovers, or spoiled daughters. The Jewish mother is routinely transformed from Yiddish literature's self-sacrificial enabler to American literature's selfish, pathologically domineering, guilt-inducing castrator of husbands and sons. Sophie Portnoy,[1] the apotheosis of the typical "smothering mother," is obsessed with controlling every aspect of her son's life, as is the overprotective, overbearing, quick-tongued mother in Bruce Jay Friedman's A Mother's Kisses.[2] Similarly subject to the barb of male invective in high and popular culture is the daughter of the Jewish mother, the denigrated "Jewish American Princess." Brenda Patimkin of Goodbye, Columbus and the daughter of Newark's zipper-king in My Life as a Man are satirized as self-centered, materialistic, and sexually manipulative, all stereotypes of the Jew in love with money, revisioned from a misogynistic perspective.

I do not assert that all Jewish male writers are guilty of misogynistic stereotyping. There are complex, even admirable, female characters in the fiction of Jewish men. Henry Roth's 1937 masterpiece, *Call It Sleep*, celebrates the Jewish mother, an immigrant with enormous reserves of strength, who provides love and security for her sensitive, intelligent, terrified son and her psychotic husband.[3] Bellow's female portraits are not merely satiric. They are culturally and historically contextualized. For instance, Herzog's adoring mother and the sustaining wife of "The Old System" garner honor as traditional Jewish women.[4] Although Sorella Fonstein shares the physical grotesquery Bellow often attributes to women, she is nevertheless the fiction's moral registrar.[5] Malamud's beautiful lady of the lake, Isabella della Seta, takes the moral high ground over her American would-be lover, who hides his Jewish identity to win her love.[6] Potok's women are consistently portrayed respectfully for their intellectual achievements and communal service. More often, however, Jewish women are represented in mid and late twentieth-century male authored texts as materialistic and self-centered, manipulative, overprotective mothers and emasculating lovers, sexually frigid or alluring as the exotic Other. Prior to the proliferation of fiction by Jewish American women, rarely was a Jewish female protagonist presented as a significant social or political activist, Judaically literate, a religious or spiritual thinker, a moral mentor, or even shaped by the vagaries of Jewish history.

Female Jewish writers create protagonists borne of the life they know and *against* the literature on which they, and their readers, have been nurtured. They write against the grain of Jewish and gentile misogynist representations, creating fiction that focuses not on the Jewish woman's surgically bobbed nose and ample breasts, or on her capacity for colorful invective, but on the fullness of her being, her intellect, her concern for social and political justice, and her ethical stance. The results, then, are female protagonists manifestly shaped by a distinctive history and culture. In contrast to male-created Jewish women who seem oblivious to Jewish culture and history, women's fictional portraits are of fully developed, complex protagonists who, as Joyce Antler observes, are concerned with "the pull between assimilation and tradition; loss of identity; the exploration of unfamiliar cultures; the search for the moral meaning of Judaism and Jewish life; anti-Semitism; feelings of marginality (as Jews and/or as women); generational conflict; the importance of social commitment, and of writing itself."[7] The women writers who are the subject of this study introduce identifiable Jewish subjects and themes in their fiction, which is marked by diversity and inclusivity of Jewish experience. They introduce female protagonists who are influenced by the particularity of Jewish languages, history, religious philosophy, and traditions. Their fiction reflects increased visibility of Jewish women who are deeply involved in Jewish life at every level of experience, ranging from the historical to the spiritual, including women in the roles of Holocaust survivor, Jewish feminist activist, religious penitent, and religious leader, who are occasionally transported to an Israeli setting where they explore the fullness of their Jewish identity. But more commonly they confront their multiple identities as American Jewish women.

In Jewish American women's writing, the maternal figure has undergone a series of transformations and is presented primarily from her daughter's point of view and occasionally through self-reflection. The immigrant mother who honored her European ways, although often appreciated as an enabler, did not appeal to her American daughter as a role model because the daughter's primary goal was assimilation, as in Anzia Yezierska's *The Breadgivers* or "The Fat of the Land." Encouraged by their mothers, second-generation Jewish women sought better lives fashioned on the American middle-class model. An unfortunate component of assimilation was rejection of the assertiveness European Jewish women developed as they worked outside the home to support their scholar-husbands and children. This pattern, as Sonya Michel notes, engendered "self-hatred among women of the first generation and conflict among those of the second and third." The second-generation women are reviled by their literary sons, and more recently but less vehemently by their daughters, "those very same third generation women whom culture has stereotyped as 'Jewish American Princesses.' "[8] The generational quarrel these daughters have with their mothers is often directed to the mothers' practical insistence on marriage and interference with courtship, for the daughters' self-definition is less frequently associated with marriage.

Far more arresting as literary characters and human beings than the simplistic caricatures of the domineering, guilt-inducing Jewish mother and her "Princess" daughter are the female protagonists crafted by Jewish feminists. Intelligent, assertive women are the protagonists in short stories and novels celebrating the enormous changes in American women's lives in recent decades. Strongly influenced by the values of Judaism and feminism, Jewish women are fashioning new paradigms. Immigration, with its concomitant themes of assimilation and acculturation to American society resulting in diminished Jewish life, and third-generation rediscovery or rededication to Judaism and Jewish community are among the recurrent contextual frames privileged in fiction by Jewish women and men. A major divergence is evident in works tempered by female gender sensibilities designating radically different roles for women in revisioned narratives influenced by contemporary feminism.

Jewish feminists are reversing the pattern of male precursors privileging acculturation and the work of Jewish women whose characters' tangential Jewishness provides a rich source of humor but little of Jewish substance, characters whose Jewish identities are limited to their names and whose stories revolve around their sexuality and amorous relationships. Writers intellectually and politically motivated by Judaism and feminism create new models: female characters who either return to or reevaluate traditional Judaism and seek entrée into the religious life that had been exclusive male territory, characters who grapple with secular feminism's critique of Judaism and patriarchal orthodoxy. In dramatic contrast to Roth's knife-wielding Mrs. Portnoy and his Judaically ignorant Mrs. Patimkin, as well as Bellow's issuers of colorful curses, sweet-tempered mavens of sponge cake and chopped liver, and adoring mothers of sons, Jewish feminists delineate young women who are essentially mute on shopping and cooking, and relatively restrained on matters of child worship. Instead, they think predominantly about their own religious ambivalence or their spiritual seeking. They are Jewishly and secularly educated, at ease with Judaica and with Western high culture. These authors contest the marginal communal roles of women in orthodox society as well as misogynist stereotypes found in high and popular culture. Most protagonists of contemporary Jewish feminists resist traditional orthodoxy and advocate communal and spiritual gender equality. They strive to liberate women from behind the *mechitzah* and deliver them into the main sanctuary where they may read the Torah from the synagogue dais.

A precursor of contemporary Jewish feminists, Anzia Yezierska relates not only the physical hardships of immigrant women and the forces that impede their opportunities for happiness, but portrays their spiritual starvation within orthodoxy. In a 1925 novel, *Breadgivers*, a work acclaimed by Jewish and gentile feminists for its attack on Jewish patriarchy despite its limited literary value, the author introduces the critique Jewish women will register against patriarchy in later decades. The subtitle, *The Struggle of a Father of the Old World and a Daughter of the New*, maps the protagonist's course in generational and gender conflict. Sara resists her father's expectations of gender socialization, perceiving him as "a tyrant from the old country where only men were people,"[9] an old world Torah scholar who would circumscribe the dreams of daughters in the conviction that every woman should be a self-sacrificial nurturer of men and children. In spirited rebellion, she escapes patriarchal dominance to seek autonomy, a better life through education and assimilation. Sara is typical of Yezierska's women who struggle against the physical and spiritual ghettos of their childhood to pursue assimilation and acculturation. Yezierska's theme of Jewish women's intellectual and social advancement resonates in the more sophisticated and finely honed prose of Cynthia Ozick, Tova Reich, Nessa Rapoport, Rebecca Goldstein, and Allegra Goodman, among others, in work enhanced by Judaic erudition and discourse that these better educated women bring to their writing.

Displacing the view that male experience is the normative Jewish experience, that the experiences of Jewish women and men are essentially identical, women have introduced gender issues to challenge the paradigm of ordering and representing Jewish experience according to male norms concomitant with the assertion that the male paradigm is universal. The Jewish woman who emerges in postwar women's texts is most frequently portrayed as an acculturated American with Jewish sensibilities intact. Representative of Jews who transferred traditional Jewish messianic longing to secular messianism are Tillie Olsen's and Grace Paley's Jewish socialists and secular utopians, whose lives evidence the economic hardships of working-class Jews who are inextricably linked to the fate of all exploited workers in capitalist societies. Olsen said she conceived Eva of "Tell Me a Riddle" as "a celebration of fervent Jewish revolutionaries during the early years of the century and of a time of boundless hopes and richly humanist fervor."[10] Yiddish-inflected speech, interest in Russian and Yiddish writers, rejection of Orthodox Judaism's viability for the modern era while retaining Yiddish socialism's battle for justice and revolutionary zeal all contextualize the character within the historic experience of Jewish socialists and add breadth to the literary portrayal of Jewish women. As Olsen herself explained in a recent interview, this background, which she calls *Yiddishkeit*, taught her "knowledge and experience of injustice, of discrimination, of oppression, of genocide and of the need to act against them forever and whenever they appear," and endowed her with "an absolute belief in the potentiality of human beings" (73).

Part Two

Beyond the literary representation of immigrant and assimilationist experiences characterizing Jewish women's history, contemporary writing also foregrounds the two critical events of twentieth-century Jewish history—the Holocaust and the establishment of Israel—that have dramatically impacted the lives of Jewish women. European-born Ilona Karmel and Elzbieta Ettinger write of their Shoah experiences of incarceration, hiding, and resistance. Among the American-born writers who have become, to employ Norma Rosen's apt phrase, "witnesses through the imagination," are Susan Fromberg Schaeffer, who conducted many interviews with survivors for her representation of women's Holocaust encounter in *Anya*; Norma Rosen, who incorporated documentary materials from the Eichmann trial in *Touching Evil*; Marge Piercy, who traced the metamorphosis of her protagonist from Jewish self-denier to Holocaust-wrought Zionist in *Gone to Soldiers*; and Cynthia Ozick, who projected two sides of Holocaust survivorship in Rosa Lublin of *The Shawl* who suffers from the classic symptoms of survivor syndrome, and her antithesis, Hester Lilt of *The Cannibal Galaxy*, a model of one who fulfills a survivor's mission as she dedicates herself to the restoration of Judaism and the midrashic mode of textual commentary.

Further evidence of historically contextualized portraits in fiction by Jewish Americans are Holocaust survivors, immigrants of a vastly different sort from those in Yezierska's world, who are frequent centers of consciousness in postwar fiction. Unlike earlier immigrants who arrived in this country full of hope, eager to assimilate to American life, and joyous despite their poverty, Susan Fromberg Schaeffer's Anya Savikin[11] and Cynthia Ozick's Rosa Lublin[12] are deeply wounded, suffering the aftereffects of physical and psychological battering in ghettos and concentration camps, enduring the anxiety associated with being fugitives in Nazi-occupied Europe, and adjusting to postwar life bereft of family and friends. The economic ambition of pre-Holocaust immigrants is neglected by survivors who are disinterested in the material beyond mere sustenance. The desire to integrate into American society, so typical of earlier immigrants, is supplanted by the tendency to remain apart, to live in survivor enclaves where others will understand the hell they have experienced. The fiction focuses emphatically on various types of survivors: survivors plagued by the Holocaust trauma still intruding into their lives; survivors reliving wartime horrors in daytime memories and nighttime dreams; and those experiencing guilt, disturbances of self-image, professional and educational limitations, and social alienation. Anya Savikin and Rosa Lublin, for instance, withdraw from the larger society to inhabit a small apartment and hotel room respectively and operate neighborhood antique shops, Anya hearing the voices of her beloved parents beckoning her, and Rosa imagining lives for her infant daughter who was hurled to her death against an electrified concentration camp fence.

Departing from the psychiatric literature that is devoted to survivors who remain traumatized by their Holocaust experiences, and the imaginative literature that explores survivor syndrome, American Jewish Holocaust fiction also portrays survivors who are well-adjusted to contemporary life and are dedicated to bearing witness and preserving Judaism and the Jewish people. Illustrative of this pattern is Cynthia Ozick's midrash-designing logician in *The Cannibal Galaxy*.[13] Hester Lilt resists full assimilation, not because she is broken, but because she is engaged in a mission to preserve Jewish traditions, language, history. Similarly, Marge Piercy's Jacqueline Levy-Monot, having been transmogrified by the Shoah from an ardent French citizen into a committed Zionist, rejects repatriation to France, a country that betrayed its Jewish citizens to the Nazis, in favor of emigration to and ardent support for a Jewish homeland.[14]

The quest for Jewish meaning in the works of second-generation writers constitutes a distinctive voice in Jewish American fiction, one that grapples with the legacy of Auschwitz and post-Shoah Jewish identity. As a result, the younger generation has turned to fictional representation of the generation who were "not there" but are intimately connected to the Holocaust as children of survivors. This paradigm shift in representation of Holocaust memory, as Alan Berger details in *Children of Job*, centers on the second generation's "own experience of the Shoah's legacy."[15] The children of survivors write both of their parents' suffering and of the impact of such witnessed suffering on their own psyches. Rebecca Goldstein's powerful short story, "The Legacy of Raizel Kaidish," is exemplary. This is a tale of an American child raised by a guilt ridden survivor-mother. Named for one of her mother's Buchenwald friends, a comrade whom she betrayed, Raizel Kaidish is educated according to a strict morality based on Shoah extremes that classifies people as saints or sinners, heroes or villains. She is brought up on the lessons of the concentration camp universe, "stark tales of cruelty and sacrifice, cowardice and courage."[16] Features of the camp environment and routine become more real to her than her American surroundings and existence. Gloria Goldreich's *Four Days* also focuses on a Holocaust mother-daughter relationship, and the mother's metamorphosis from passionately maternal protector during the Holocaust era to distanced maternal figure following her liberation and emigration to America — a transformation that confounds the daughter.[17] The Holocaust is also a dark undercurrent of Goldstein's novel, *The Mind-Body Problem*.[18] Unlike Norma Rosen's American gentile protagonist, whose sacrificial decision to remain childless in empathy for Jewish women bereft of their children by the Nazis,[19] or Susan Fromberg Schaeffer's survivor, whose refusal to have additional children is based on the lingering effects of Holocaust trauma, Goldstein's Renee Feuer is committed to procreation to enhance Jewish continuity, to defeat German genocidal goals, and to commemorate both the million and a half Jewish children slaughtered by the Nazis and all the unborn Jewish progeny.

Spared direct experience and knowledge of the Holocaust, Jewish American writers, whether of the contemporary generation or the second and third generation, articulate their recognition of the Shoah as a turning point in history, as a catastrophe that altered the way we perceive God and humanity. These writers have not only addressed the Holocaust as a central reference point in their fiction and established the Holocaust survivor as a recognizable literary persona, but have delineated the gender-specific experience of Jewish women in the ghettos and camps. By adding their voices to Holocaust testimony, these Americans join their European and Israeli colleagues to commemorate the dead, to preserve the collective memory, and to offer warnings for the future.

Although the establishment of Israel as a Jewish homeland — the second momentous event of twentieth-century Jewish history — has not fired the imagination of American writers as has the Shoah, it has recently gained a more prominent place in American fiction, periodically emerging in connection with Holocaust themes and more often, and more persuasively, as the setting for themes of self-exploration and spiritual seeking for American women. Esther Broner, Anne Roiphe, Nessa Rapoport, and Tova Reich are among the novelists who situate their spiritual seekers in Israel. Broner's feminists, in A Weave of Women, live together in Israel and create a feminist Jewish utopia, displacing Jewish women's silence with vibrant voice.[20] Roiphe's Lovingkindness takes the form of a religious-secular debate staged in Israel with two American women as contending forces. The elder, a 1960s-style feminist, argues on behalf of secular and universalist identification while her formerly debauched daughter affirms Israeli ultraorthodox religious life.[21] Nessa Rapoport does not rely on the structure of repentance and reconciliation but transports her protagonist to Israel, to augment her lifetime connection and commitment to Judaism. The most broad-ranging intersection of Jewish feminism and Jewish nationalism may be found, as Andrew Furman notes, in the fiction of Tova Reich. The principal Jewish American characters of her second novel, Master of the Return, have left their previous lives to join together in an ultraorthodox redemptive society. Rather than repudiate Orthodox Judaism, Reich "envisions its feminization."[22] The women seek Jewish redemption and a union that is more loving and mutually helpful than is the patriarchal model. The concluding destruction of the penitents' community house signifies that ultraorthodox Judaism should be rebuilt in Israel on "a feminist model of Jewish interrelationships" (188). As an astute political voice who has increasingly turned to both religious and political Jewish subjects, Marge Piercy closes her important World War II novel, Gone to Soldiers, with a passionate argument for a Jewish state. Among the strongest political responses of women's Holocaust literature is Piercy's defense of an independent Jewish state.

Part Three

In an analysis of modification in contemporary Jewish women's writing, Sylvia Barack Fishman argues persuasively that Jewish women who had for many years been "doubly marginal, disguising two primary aspects of their identity, are at last writing out of their full vision."[23] Recent fiction exploring spiritual identity signifies the end of a period when Jewish American writers feared that focus on their religious and cultural interests would hinder their acceptance by publishers and readers. Judaism and reaction to its varied interpretations is a rich vein being mined by secular and religious Jewish feminists. Secular feminists ask how a woman could be a feminist and simultaneously embrace a patriarchal religion that denies women full participation in ritual and prayer and subjects them to second-class status marked by practices like segregated synagogue seating. Miriyam Glazer encapsulates the alienation of fiction's contemporary Jewish women of the 1970s and 1980s, such as those who inhabit Anne Roiphe's world, as "marked by cultural transience, at home neither in time nor in space, their personal identities unstable or erased . . . fragmented characters riven by their own sense of Otherness, marginality, and incompletion."[24] She attributes this "instability of identity" and "cultural rootlessness" (83) to the problematic relationship of "Jewish" and "American" as they relate to gender in Roiphe's feminists who are repeatedly searching for "an end to spiritual, emotional, psychic, and physical exile" (85). Representative of the secular feminist critique, Roiphe's protagonist of *Long Division* argues against exclusion of women from orthodox ritual, phrasing her complaint in gendered images:

> Weep far away from the Torah, weep away from the holy center of the men's world, because the Lord God, Jehovah, the nameless name of all names, does not like menstruating women whose blood is after all their own. Weep for being unclean, weep for being born Jewish. . . . Weep because your sons will feel sanctified only in places their mother is forbidden.[25]

Complementing her understanding of the feminist rejection of the strictures of orthodoxy is Roiphe's converse comprehension. *Generation Without Memory* gives strong evidence of a contrary yearning "that mandate[s] a return to Jewishness, to acceptance of oneself as a Jew."[26] *Lovingkindness,* her most sustained articulation of contending arguments for and against woman's orthodox Jewish identity, pits a secular feminist mother against a daughter who has found redemption for her profligate American life in an Israeli yeshiva community. The mother is horrified, unable to fathom why her daughter is willing to resign autonomy for adherence to what she perceives to be a fossilized tradition, "clos[ing] yourself off in this Jewish particular, this walled city of convictions" (56–57). The penitent daughter just as vehemently repudiates the "melting pot" gentilization of the American Jew; privileging spiritual return, embrace of Jewish morality, and communal life. *Lovingkindness* and *The Pursuit of Happiness* extend Roiphe's encounter with Judaism as her characters discover in Israel a place where they can live according to their Jewish values, "where they can reclaim their historical ancestry and spiritual heritage all at once, despite the continued skepticism they encounter from their elders."[27]

Among the women who are exploring the intersection of gender and spirituality are Jewish lesbians who address the problematics of Otherness from lesbian and Jewish perspectives. A pioneer in this realm is Jo Sinclaire

(Ruth Seid) whose 1946 novel, *Wasteland,* interweaves Jewish and lesbian
themes in realistic portraits of a second-generation Jew who tries to conceal
his Jewish origins and a lesbian who confronts the perils of her sexual non-
conformity.[28] For some, according to Evelyn Torton Beck, "the experience of
coming out as lesbians was a crucial step toward . . . coming out as Jews."[29]
Although these writers reject patriarchal Judaism, they celebrate their Jewish
lives, the parts of the tradition they value and those they have revised or
created in a feminist mode. As Beck notes, some of these writers are struggling with denial, silence, erasure, while others take pride from their Jewish
identities and trace their secular political activism to its Jewish sources
such as the Bund and labor union movements. This is an active group
trying, among other causes, to urge lesbian feminism—and, by extension,
the larger feminist movement—to take anti-Semitism seriously, to recognize it as a form of racism and purge feminist writing and politics of anti-
Semitic caricatures and stereotypes. The questions many of these writers
pose in their fiction are formed around their dual identities as Jews and
lesbians: What does it mean to identify as Jewish lesbians? How are they
similar to and different from other Jews? How have they internalized the
myths and stereotypes about Jewish women? How have Jewish survival
skills influenced their thinking about lesbian survival? What are the Jewish
roots of their political radicalism?[30]

Irena Klepfisz's writing and her political activism evidence strong commitment to lesbianism and *Yiddishkeit,* to Jewish community and a just peace
in the Middle East. Shoah motifs dominate the writing of this child survivor
of the Holocaust, who represents herself "as the ultimate outsider, the Jew,
the lesbian, the survivor."[31] Similarly, Lesléa Newman, who has acknowledged feeling that in gay communities she is perceived as too Jewish and in
Jewish communities too gay, shares a concern of many Jewish intellectuals
and humanities scholars that the multicultural climate excludes Judaism.
Representative of the conciliatory theme of much of this writing is Lesléa
Newman's "The Gift," a tale tracing the childhood and young adulthood of
a self-hating Jewish lesbian. It is not until she rejects several lovers, one
exhibiting anti-Semitic sentiments and the other a Jew who attends a Christ-
mas party on the first night of *Hanukka,* that she reconciles her Jewishness
with her sexual identity in a relationship with a new Jewish lover. Emblematic of their finding community and support in return to their religious
heritage is a synagogue scene in which the two women sing the central
doctrinal prayer of Judaism, the Shema.[32] In prose that is rich in Yiddish
diction and intonation, each of these women confront homophobia and anti-
Semitism, with Newman crediting her freedom to write in Yinglish to Grace
Paley and appreciatively quoting Klepfisz's defense of Yiddish: "Language is
our only homeland."[33]

Religious feminists, while similarly critical of patriarchal orthodoxy for its exclusion of women from select rituals, nevertheless choose to remain within Judaism and effect institutional change. In a creative alliance of feminism and Judaism, the new female protagonist knowledgeably addresses Jewish texts, liturgy, and history. Echoing the rebellious voice of Anzia Yezierska, but reaching far beyond it to constructive confrontation and engagement, are the works of writers who progress from secular feminism to feminist Judaism, heralding a Jewish literary renaissance, one that takes American Jewish writing beyond the immigrant/assimilation/alienation themes of the golden era of American Jewish fiction. The critically acclaimed leader of this movement, Cynthia Ozick, eruditely and self-consciously writes about Judaism and Jewish history advocating affirmation, renewal, and redemption. She abjures the sociological observation of contemporary life that functioned as the predominant signifier of Jewish content in her predecessors' fiction. Ozick's writing reflects and contributes to the Jewish textual tradition in the mode her essay "Toward a New Yiddish" advocates. There she persuasively and eloquently argues for the creation of an English-language indigenous American Jewish literature that is "centrally Jewish in its concerns" and "liturgical in nature," not a "didactic or prescriptive" literature but one that is "aggadic" in style, "utterly freed to invention, discourse, parable, experiment, enlightenment, profundity, humanity."[34]

Rejecting literature that is merely self-referential as amoral, Ozick argues for redemptive writing that insists on freedom to change one's life, that celebrates creative renewal. Among the recurrent Judaic themes plumbed by Ozick and other writers who embrace Judaism are *tikkun* (repair) and *t'shuva* (redemption). Her Puttermesser stories reverberate with these principles. Progressing from the first narrative's representation of the repair theme is the lawyer's activism on behalf of Soviet Jews, her work for political reform, and her dream of bettering the world. The final narrative returns to the protagonist's interest in social justice, this time the liberation of Soviet Jews, and to her preoccupation with Jewish ideas, and concludes with a paradisal vision. As Puttermesser studies Hebrew and Judaic texts she discerns a civilization, a value system, a distinctive culture, and she forges a link to the history and texts of the Jewish people.[35]

One of the most significant indices of the revitalization of American Jewish writing is its incorporation of and play on classical Jewish sources. Text-centeredness, as Harold Bloom makes evident in *Agon*, is the essence of Jewish learning. Writing infused with precursor literary and ideational concepts reveals the contemporary pertinence of those influences and extends the cultural breadth of American literature. Ozick advocates the validity of the midrashic narrative mode for "transmittal [rather than disjunction, displacement, revisionism], signifying the carrying-over of the original strength" of a work of art.[36] By combining the *tikkun* theme with an intertextual approach, she effectively adapts the golem myth to underscore Puttermesser's quest for social justice. "Puttermesser and Xanthippe" owes its twelve-part structure to the pattern of construction and destruction employed in the Gershom Scholem essay, "The Idea of the *Golem*," that Puttermesser has been studying. Repelled by the corruption and mediocrity of city government, Puttermesser breathes life into a creature fashioned from the earth who will do her bidding and effect reform. Following the commandment of Deuteronomy, "Justice, justice shalt thou pursue," Puttermesser's golem implements an urban reform plan and assists in her master's ascent to the mayoralty. Indicative of the contemporary writer's appropriation of, and contribution to, the literary heritage is her extension of the golem's beneficence to a nonsectarian population and her endowment of the creature with female gender and sexual and procreative desires. Like the legendary golem that became a destructive agent despite its creator's intent, Xanthippe eventually rejects her role as an instrument of reform, leading Puttermesser to invoke the ritual of reversal to destroy her golem. These intertextual connections that characterize Ozick's midrashic mode lift the narrative to intellectual, aesthetic, and moral heights surpassing many acclaimed Jewish novels of alienation and sociological insight.

Paralleling Ozick's narrative method and her original gendered reconstruction of a Jewish legend to accommodate the contemporary situation, Tova Reich offers a feminist perspective on the *Akedah* legend (the binding of Isaac) to conclude *Master of the Return*. In this contemporary rendering of a Jewish mother agonizing over the disappearance of her son with a surrogate father who claims the child for religious ritual, Reich introduces the sacrificial theme from the perspective of the mother rather than those of father and son. Reich's Sarah resents her husband's dominance over the child and his subservience to the demanding deity. The contemporary mother, a product of modern psychology, realizes that she and the child will remain emotionally scarred: "The child that was returned . . . was not the same as the one she had lost, nor was she the same woman who had lost the child. That child had been sacrificed, and that woman's soul had burst out of her and surrendered."[37]

Rarely, if ever, have Jewish religious values and textuality been as fundamental and intrinsic to American literary work as they are in texts of contemporary Jewish feminists like Esther Broner, Nessa Rapoport, Rebecca Goldstein, and Allegra Goodman. Increased attention to Jewish tradition and liturgy appears in the work of women composing new fictions to articulate their claim for a place in what has been a patriarchal tradition. Esther Broner has achieved "a radical feminist reordering of social and fictional hierarchies, . . . [new methods for incorporating] the inheritance of Yiddish and Hebrew themes and tones in an experimental fictional mode that celebrates the female hero."[38] Her women explore alternative female-centered spirituality. They reclaim ancient rituals and fashion new ones expressing women's spirituality, and write feminist prayers and services, new Sabbath worship, and a woman's Haggadah. Their rituals parallel, but are distinguished from, Jewish male rituals in order to demonstrate women's Jewish cultural identity and authenticity. Of the best young Jewish women writers who are equally at ease in Western and Yiddish high culture, Rapoport, Goldstein, and Goodman have no need to introduce the pious as exotics or as penitents traumatically motivated to religiosity. Their protagonists' given is *Yiddishkeit* and distinctively Jewish lives. Products of Judaically educated confident writers, these characters are steeped in Jewish learning. They quote Torah and Talmud in the original languages and they opine on the sages' commentaries and midrashim. These women are critical insiders rather than alienated outsiders. These writers confidently present Jewish culture as the focus of their characters' lives, allude to classic Jewish texts, and infuse them into their American fictions.

Goldstein's *The Mind-Body Problem* chronicles a Jewish feminist's break with orthodoxy, defying its clearly distinguished gender roles and masculinist biases to pursue personal freedom and autonomy in secular humanism, only to discover there an even more restrictive and less benevolent world. Goldstein's protagonist appears, acts, and thinks like a man in order to be regarded as an intellectual. She must mask her female mind and body to be accepted as a professional. Albeit critical of orthodoxy's marginalization of women, she nevertheless craves the spirituality she admires in orthodox Judaism. During the course of her career as a philosopher, she continues to seek the spiritual and laments her presence in the company of "Jewish goyim" whose sons are circumcised by doctors, who are unaware of "what it is to yearn for the coming of the Messiah" (Goldstein, *Mind-Body Problem*, 277). She is, as Sylvia Barack Fishman put it, "drawn to the sweetness of traditional Jewish life but repelled by its distorted view of women."[39] Her restoration to Jewish life, signaled by her invocation of the *Kol Nidre* and *Ne'elah* prayers, is not to religious piety as much as it is to Jewish history, to the continuity of the Jewish people.

Responses to Judaism and Jewish culture across three generations of Jewish women is the subject of Goldstein's fifth work of fiction, *Mazel*, which earned her the Edward Lewis Wallant Award for Jewish American fiction. Soon thereafter she received a MacArthur "genius" award. In this brilliant novel, Goldstein examines the continuity and rupture of Jewish women's association with orthodoxy in the Old World and the New, in three complementary venues: the prewar shtetl of eastern Europe; cosmopolitan Warsaw on the eve of the Shoah; and American post-Holocaust suburbia.

The novel travels full circle, dramatizing the modern European woman's resistance to orthodoxy, followed by thorough assimilation in America and resurgence of commitment to Orthodox Judaism by an American intellectual of the third generation. Through the vehicle of multiple evolving narratives, the book is both a memorial for the murdered community of European Jewry and a celebration of Jewish continuity embodied in marriage and the birth of a daughter named in honor of matrilineal ancestors.[40]

Another fine, and earlier, representative of contemporary religious feminists is Nessa Rapoport's Judith Raphel, a young Orthodox woman who chooses allegiance to orthodoxy despite dissatisfaction with its patriarchal dominance and marginalization of women. *Preparing for Sabbath* scrutinizes the life, from childhood to adolescence and beyond, of this descendant of a long rabbinical line. Judith's spiritual quest is influenced by women, by her devout and intellectually gifted grandmother, by a great aunt she is said to resemble and who introduces her to a sympathetic Israeli poet with whom she studies, and finally by a young woman leading her to a Hasidic shul where she finds spiritual fulfillment. Faithful to her ancestral links, even as she forges new directions, Judith Raphel is an exemplar of the new Jewish woman of American fiction. Judith examines her social/sexual/spiritual attitudes and values with reference to Jewish ideals. She argues for political commitment because "Judaism says we're supposed to seek justice, it's our responsibility to guard and keep the earth, which means not abusing anything with life in it."[41] She withdraws from a romantic relationship with a non-Jew because he is outside the realm of her religious and cultural experience. She is empowered by her Jewish education to fight the battle for women's equality within Judaism and posits a learned critique of the exclusion of Jewish women from religious practice.

Like Ozick's characters, who are equally at ease in Western and Hebraic culture, Allegra Goodman's universe is populated by Judaic scholars in conference settings, rabbis and congregants embroiled in synagogue politics, traditional women content to worship behind a partition separating men's and women's sections in an Orthodox synagogue, and feminists demanding an equal role in the conduct of religious services, figures totally immersed in Jewish sensibility.[42] Unlike Malamud's Yiddish speakers, whose speech is characterized by inverted sentence structure, Allegra Goodman's Hawaiian Jews speak *mamaloshen*. Their English sentences are unapologetically peppered by Yiddish and Hebrew. Her women keep kosher kitchens; her young parents send their children to Orthodox day schools, her intellectuals debate religious law; her poets write in Hebrew and English. Goodman writes, as Gloria Cronin notes, "out of the richness of historical Jewishness, her community, and her literary, scriptural, and Jewish theological traditions."[43] In her effort to claim the religious and spiritual dimensions of Judaism for her fictional world, Goodman claims "to turn to old resources—the deep Jewish tradition beneath the self-deprecating Jewish jokes, the biblical language and the poetry welling up beneath layers of satire."[44]

A generation of Jewish American women writers has emerged that is freer than Saul Bellow initially was to explore the particularity of Jewish literature, religious experience, and history. This is a self-emancipated generation, liberated to express its artistic visions in Jewish terms; a generation unwilling to accept either the constraints of the immigration/assimilation theme or the popular early Roth school of social satire with its cast of stereotypical suburban Jews composed of domineering mothers, ineffectual fathers, pampered daughters, and whining sons. The literary school Saul Bellow initiated and Cynthia Ozick brings to fruition illuminates Jewish themes and judiciously appropriates precursors to extend the significant contribution of Jewish writers to American letters. Women have established a claim to Judaism in feminist terms by redistributing and inventing rituals and prayers, and have revitalized the Jewish American literary tradition by shifting focus from the paradigms established by Bellow, Malamud, and Roth to those of Cynthia Ozick, to work that she has characterized as "liturgical fiction," a program she envisioned for the preservation of Jewish writing in America in her brilliant essay, "Toward a New Yiddish."

The prophecies of Irving Howe and Leslie Fiedler that exhaustion of the immigration theme meant the death of American Jewish fiction have not been realized. Claire Satlof succinctly captures the objective and achievement of many Jewish feminists in her notice of their self-conscious attempt "to end the division of the world into a male-controlled spiritual realm and an everyday, profane woman's world."[45] Nessa Rapoport speaks for many American Jewish writers when she declares, "Having won our place in American culture, we are beginning to be confident enough to reclaim Jewish culture."[46] Jewish American writing is enjoying a renaissance, vitality in no small measure attributable to feminist Jewish writers who have claimed their rightful place as interpreters of the traditions and texts of their people, women who have shifted the focus of Jewish texts from the themes of assimilation and acculturation to the varieties of Judaism and Jewish experience, who are creating a flourishing literature, more assertive than it was in the 1950s and 1960s, and more overtly Jewish and feminine.[47]

Notes

1. Philip Roth, *Portnoy's Complaint* (New York: Random House, 1967).

2. Bruce Jay Friedman, *A Mother's Kisses* (New York: Simon and Schuster, 1964).

3. Henry Roth, *Call It Sleep* (New York: Avon, 1964).

4. Saul Bellow, *Herzog* (New York: Viking, 1964) and "The Old System," in *Mosby's Memoirs and Other Stories* (New York: Viking, 1968).

5. Saul Bellow, *The Bellarosa Connection* (New York: Penguin Books, 1989).

6. Bernard Malamud, "The Lady of the Lake," in *The Magic Barrel* (New York: Farrar, Straus, Cudahy, 1958).

7. Joyce Antler, "Introduction," in *America and I: Short Stories by American Jewish Women Writers* (Boston: Beacon Press, 1990), 2–3.

8. Sonya Michel, "Mothers and Daughters in American Jewish Literature: The Rotted Cord," in *The Jewish Woman: New Perspectives*, ed. Elizabeth Koltun (New York: Schocken Books, 1976), 279.

9. Anzia Yezierska, *Breadgivers* (New York: Persea Books, 1952), 295.

10. Tillie Olsen, quoted in Bonnie Lyons, "American Jewish Fiction Since 1945," in *Handbook of American-Jewish Literature: An Analytical Guide to Topics, Themes, and Sources*, ed. Lewis Fried (New York: Greenwood Press, 1988), 73.

11. Susan Fromberg Schaeffer, *Anya* (New York: Macmillan, 1974).

12. Cynthia Ozick, *The Shawl* (New York: Alfred A. Knopf, 1989).

13. Cynthia Ozick, *The Cannibal Galaxy* (New York: Alfred A. Knopf, 1983).

14. Marge Piercy, *Gone to Soldiers* (New York: Summit Books, 1987).

15. Alan L. Berger, *Children of Job: American Second-Generation Witnesses to the Holocaust* (Albany: State University of New York Press, 1997), 20.

16. Rebecca Goldstein, "The Legacy of Raizel Kaidish: A Story," in *America and I: Short Stories by American Jewish Women Writers*, ed. Joyce Antler (Boston: Beacon Press, 1990), 283.

17. Gloria Goldreich, *Four Days* (New York: Harcourt Brace Jovanovich, 1980).

18. Rebecca Goldstein, *The Mind-Body Problem* (New York: Dell Publishing, 1983).

19. Norma Rosen, *Touching Evil* (New York: Harcourt, Brace, and World, 1969).

20. E. M. Broner, *A Weave of Women* (Bloomington: Indiana University Press, 1978).

21. Anne Roiphe, *Lovingkindness* (New York: Summit Books, 1987).

22. Andrew Furman, *Israel Through the Jewish American Imagination: A Survey of Jewish American Literature on Israel 1928–1995* (Albany: State University of New York Press, 1997), 182.

23. Sylvia Barack Fishman, *Follow My Footprints: Changing Images of Women in American Jewish Fiction* (Hanover: University Press of New England, 1992), 52.

24. Miriyam Glazer, " 'Daughters of Refugees of the On-going-Universal-Endless Upheaval': Anne Roiphe and the Quest for Narrative Power in Jewish American Women's Fiction," in *Daughters of Valor*, eds. Jay L. Halio and Ben Siegel (Newark: University of Delaware Press, 1997), 80.

25. Anne Roiphe, *Long Division* (New York: Simon and Schuster, 1972), 58.

26. Anne Roiphe, *Generation Without Memory* (New York: Simon and Schuster, 1981), 172.

27. Carolyn Hoyt, "Anne Roiphe," in *Jewish American Women Writers: A Bio-Bibliographical and Critical Sourcebook*, ed. Ann R. Shapiro (Westport: Greenwood Press, 1994), 346.

28. Jo Sinclaire, *Wasteland.* (Philadelphia: Jewish Publication Society, 1987).

29. Evelyn Torton Beck, ed. *Nice Jewish Girls: A Lesbian Anthology* (Boston: Beacon Press, 1989), xvii.

30. These questions are among those Evelyn Torton Beck enumerates as common concerns of the writers anthologized in *Nice Jewish Girls* (xxxii).

31. Ronit Lentin, "Irena Klepfisz," in *Jewish American Women Writers: A Bio-Bibliographical and Critical Sourcebook*, ed. Ann R. Shapiro (Westport: Greenwood Press, 1994), 167.

32. Lesléa Newman, "The Gift," *A Letter to Harvey Milk* (Ithaca, NY: Firebrand Books, 1986).

33. Lesléa Newman, quoted in Gail Koplow, "Lesléa Newman: Writing from the Heart," *Sojourner* (August 1989), 8A.

34. Cynthia Ozick, "Toward a New Yiddish," in *Art and Ardor* (New York: Knopf, 1983), 174–175.

35. Cynthia Ozick, *The Puttermesser Papers* (New York: Alfred A. Knopf, 1997).

36. Cynthia Ozick, "Literature as Idol: Harold Bloom," in *Art and Ardor*, 194.

37. Tova Reich, *Master of the Return* (New York: Harcourt, Brace, Jovanovich, 1988), 239.

38. Cathy Davidson, "E. M. Broner," in *Dictionary of Literary Biography: Twentieth-Century American-Jewish Fiction Writers*, vol. 28, ed. Daniel Walden (Detroit: Gale Research, 1984), 26.

39. Sylvia Barack Fishman, "Rebecca Goldstein," in *Jewish American Women Writers*, ed. Ann Shapiro (Westport: Greenwood Press, 1994), 82.

40. Rebecca Goldstein, *Mazel* (New York: Viking, 1995).

41. Nessa Rapoport, *Preparing for Sabbath* (New York: William Morrow, 1981), 138.

42. Allegra Goodman, *Total Immersion* (New York: Harper and Row, 1989).

43. Gloria Cronin, "Immersions in the Postmodern: The Fiction of Allegra Goodman," in *Daughters of Valor*, 248.

44. Allegra Goodman, "Writing Jewish Fiction In and Out of the Multicultural Context,"in *Daughters of Valor*, 268.

45. Claire R. Satlof, "History, Fiction, and the Tradition: Creating a Jewish Feminist Poetic," in *On Being a Jewish Feminist: A Reader*, ed. Susannah Heschel (New York: Schocken Books, 1983), 187.

46. Nessa Rapoport, "Summoned to the Feast," in *Writing Our Way Home: Contemporary Stories by American Jewish Writers*, eds. Ted Solotaroff and Nessa Rapoport (New York: Schocken Books, 1992), xxx.

47. In contrast to male-edited anthologies of Jewish American writing that underrepresent women's writing, including: Azriel Eisenberg's *The Golden Land: A Literary Portrait of American Jewry, 1654 to the Present*, which contains excerpts from eighty-eight works, only eight of them by women; Irving Malin and Irwin Stark's 1964 breakthrough, *A Treasury of Contemporary American Jewish Literature*, which contains thirty-one pieces, two of them by women; and *The Rise of American Jewish Literature*, edited by Charles Angoff and Meyer Levin (1970), which lists twenty-two entries, none by women; Theodore Gross's *The Literature of American Jews* (1973) which includes the work of forty-one writers, six of them women; as well as more recent anthologies such as Abraham Chapman's *Jewish-American Literature: An Anthology* (1974), that included nine titles by women compared to forty-five male authors writing fiction, autobiography, and poetry; and Irving Howe's *Jewish American Stories* (1977) with a ratio of twenty-two male to four female entries. Even Dan Walden, who has been the godfather to many female Jewish American literary scholars, included five women compared to twenty-nine men in his anthology, *On Being Jewish: American Jewish Writers from Cahan to Bellow* (1974). There is now a flowering of anthologies either entirely devoted to Jewish women's writing or including a significant number of female-authored texts: Julia Mazow's *The Woman Who Lost Her Names: Selected Writings by American Jewish Women* (1980), Evelyn Torton Beck's *Nice Jewish Girls: A Lesbian Anthology* (1982), *The Tribe of Dina: A Jewish Women's Anthology* (1989) edited by Melanie Kaye/Kantrowitz and Irena Klepfisz; Joyce Antler's *America and I: Short Stories by American Jewish Women Writers* (1990), Sharon Niederman's *Shaking Eve's Tree: Short Stories of Jewish Women* (1990), Sylvia Barack Fishman's *Follow My Footprints: Changing Images of Women in American Jewish Fiction* (1992), and Ted Solotaroff and Nessa Rapoport's *Writing Our Way Home: Contemporary Stories by American Jewish Writers* (1992) with fifty percent inclusion of women writers, as opposed to earlier anthologies of Jewish writing such as Saul Bellow's *Great Jewish Short Stories* (1963) that includes work by eighteen men and one woman, Grace Paley.

Works Cited

Antler, Joyce, ed. *America and I: Short Stories by American Jewish Women Writers.* Boston: Beacon Press, 1990.

Beck, Evelyn, Torton, ed. *Nice Jewish Girls: A Lesbian Anthology.* Boston: Beacon Press, 1989.

Bellow, Saul. *The Bellarosa Connection.* New York: Penguin Books, 1989.

———. *Herzog.* New York: Viking, 1964.

———. *Mosby's Memoirs and Other Stories.* New York: Viking, 1968.

Berger, Alan. *Children of Job: American Second-Generation Witnesses to the Holocaust.* Albany: State University of New York Press, 1997.

Broner, E. M. *A Weave of Women.* Bloomington: Indiana University Press, 1978.

Cronin, Gloria. "Immersions in the Postmodern: The Fiction of Allegra Goodman." In *Daughters of Valor,* eds. Jay L. Halio and Ben Siegel. Newark: University of Delaware Press, 1997.

Davidson, Cathy. "E. M. Broner." In *Dictionary of Literary Biography: Twentieth-Century American-Jewish Fiction Writers,* ed. Daniel Walden, 26–28. Detroit: Gale Research, 1984.

Fishman, Sylvia, Barack *Follow My Footprints: Changing Images of Women in American Jewish Fiction.* Hanover: University Press of New England, 1992.

———. "Rebecca Goldstein." In *Jewish American Women Writers,* ed. Ann Shapiro, 80–87. Westport: Greenwood Press, 1994.

Friedman, Bruce Jay. *A Mother's Kisses.* New York: Simon and Schuster, 1964.

Furman, Andrew. *Israel Through the Jewish American Imagination: A Survey of Jewish American Literature on Israel 1928–1995.* Albany: State University of New York Press, 1997.

Glazer, Miriyam. In *Daughters of Valor,* eds. Jay L. Halio and Ben Siegel. Newark: University of Delaware Press, 1997.

Goldreich, Gloria. *Four Days.* New York: Harcourt Brace Jovanovich, 1980.

Goldstein, Rebecca. In *America and I: Short Stories by American Jewish Women Writers.* Boston: Beacon Press, 1990.

———. *Mazel.* New York: Viking, 1995.

———. *The Mind-Body Problem* New York: Dell Publishing, 1983.

Goodman, Allegra. *Total Immersion.* New York: Harper and Row, 1989.

———. "Writing Jewish Fiction In and Out of the Multicultural Context." In *Daughters of Valor,* eds. Jay L. Halio and Ben Siegel, 268–274. Newark: University of Delaware Press, 1997.

Hoyt, Carolyn. "Anne Roiphe." In *Jewish American Women Writers: A Bio-Bibliographical and Critical Sourcebook*, ed. Ann R. Shapiro, 342–349. Westport: Greenwood Press, 1994.

Koplow, Gail. "Lesléa Newman: Writing from the Heart," *Sojourner* (August 1989) 7A–8A.

Lentin, Ronit. "Irena Klepfisz." In *Jewish American Women Writers: A Bio-Bibliographical and Critical Sourcebook*, ed. Ann R. Shapiro, 165–172. Westport: Greenwood Press, 1994.

Lyons, Bonnie. In *Handbook of American-Jewish Literature: An Analytical Guide to Topics, Themes, and Sources*, ed. Lewis Fried. New York: Greenwood Press, 1988.

Malamud, Bernard. *The Magic Barrel*. New York: Farrar, Straus, Cudahy, 1958.

Michel, Sonya. "Mothers and Daughters in American Jewish Literature: The Rotted Cord," in *The Jewish Woman: New Perspectives*, ed. Elizabeth Koltun. New York: Schocken Books, 1976. 272–282.

Newman, Lesléa. "The Gift." In *A Letter to Harvey Milk*, 11–31. Ithaca: Firebrand Books, 1986.

Ozick, Cynthia. *The Cannibal Galaxy*. New York: Alfred A. Knopf, 1983.

———. "Literature as Idol: Harold Bloom." In *Art and Ardor*, 178–199. New York: Knopf, 1983.

———. *The Puttermesser Papers*. New York: Alfred A. Knopf, 1997.

———. *The Shawl*. New York: Alfred A. Knopf, 1989.

———. "Toward a New Yiddish." In *Art and Ardor*, 151–177. New York: Knopf, 1983.

Piercy, Marge. *Gone to Soldiers*. New York: Summit Books, 1987.

Rapoport, Nessa. *Preparing for Sabbath*. New York: William Morrow, 1981.

———. "Summoned to the Feast." In *Writing Our Way Home: Contemporary Stories by American Jewish Writers*, eds. Ted Solotaroff and Nessa Rapoport, xxvii–xxx. New York: Schocken Books, 1992.

Reich, Tova. *Master of the Return*. New York: Harcourt, Brace, Jovanovich, 1988.

Roiphe, Anne. *Generation Without Memory*. New York: Simon and Schuster, 1981.

———. *Long Division*. New York: Simon and Schuster, 1972.

———. *Lovingkindness*. New York: Summit Books, 1987.

Rosen, Norma. *Touching Evil*. New York: Harcourt, Brace and World, 1969.

Roth, Henry. *Call It Sleep*. New York: Avon, 1964.

Roth, Philip. *Portnoy's Complaint*. New York: Random House, 1967.

Satlof, Claire R. "History, Fiction, and the Tradition: Creating a Jewish Feminist Poetic." In *On Being a Jewish Feminist: A Reader*, ed. Susannah Heschel, 186–206. New York: Schocken Books, 1983.

Schaeffer, Susan, Fromberg. *Anya*. New York: Macmillan, 1974.

Sinclaire, Jo. *Wasteland*. Philadelphia: Jewish Publication Society, 1987.

Yezierska, Anzia. *Breadgivers*. New York: Persea Books, 1952.

16

After the Melting Pot:
Jewish Women Writers and
the Man in the Wrong Clothes

Miriyam Glazer

At an informal gathering in Los Angeles, a group of Jewish academics was discussing anthropologist Karen Brodkin Sacks' essay, "How Did Jews Become White Folks?"[1] The more we spoke, the more the air grew palpably tense, as if, whether we were admitting it or not, the narratives of our personal and professional lives were at stake. Did we see ourselves as "white"? Who among us did? Who didn't? In what specific projects and desires, inclusions and exclusions were we implicated, if we were or were not "white"? Like the *gens de couleur* of Louisiana, Jews of the nineteenth century had occupied an "in-between zone"; they were regarded as members of the "Oriental" or "Semitic" race. A court ruling had turned the *gens de couleur* into blacks.[2] Was it, as Sacks argues, the economic benefits of the G.I. bill that had catapulted thousands of Jewish men (and presumably their wives and children) into education, home ownership, and thus into the "whiteness" of the middle class? Or, rather, was it primarily white Protestant America's determination to see things in black and white—to simplify, stabilize, institutionalize the racial divide—that meshed with the Jews' eagerly embraced dissolution of difference and upward mobility in order to turn the Jewish members of the "Semitic race"—the "Israelites," the "Orientals"—into "whites"? Are Ethiopian Jews, or, for that matter, African American Jews, by virtue of their Jewishness, "white"?

Amid that afternoon's melange of opinions, anxieties, positions, a colleague of mine—an olive-skinned, traditionally bearded professor of Talmud—posed a question. "Maybe," he said, "most of the people in this room are white. But what are the boundaries of 'whiteness'? Is an ultraorthodox European-born Jew with *payes* and a *streimel* 'white'?"

Discomforting if momentary silence in the group. In the thick air, I heard in my inner ear the anxious Eli of Philip Roth's upper-middle-class 1959 suburban Woodenton pleading with the immigrant Orthodox yeshiva head newly arrived in town: "The world is the world, Mr. Tzuref. As you would say, what is, is. All we say to this man is change your clothes."[3]

The uncertainty we Jewish intellectuals felt about our own "whiteness" and the boundaries of whiteness—and the question of what we were if we weren't "white"—had, of course, complex autobiographical, political, socio-ideological, economic, and, in the end, gender and religious underpinnings. What we were really dealing with was how at "home" each of us experienced ourselves as being, or willed ourselves into being, on what Brownsville-born Alfred Kazin (presumably with an unintentional tongue in cheek) called "native" ground and what, indeed, we comprehended as our Jewishness. Did a proudly borne Jewish identity nourish our spiritual, intellectual, creative, and/or cultural life? Or did "Jewish identity" serve as a residual remembrance of brisket and bagels, an annoying ache, a rejected awareness, a rooted sorrow? Did it enrich our lives, and/or make us feel inevitably set apart, "split or contradictory" (in the terms of Donna Haraway), a sort of "half-breed" who understands "everyone because [belonging] completely to no one" (in those of Albert Memmi), or perhaps, in Homi Bhabha's phrase, "almost the same but different"?[4] At what point do Jews cease to be what Bhabha, theorizing postcolonial writing, calls a "reformed, recognizable Other," who embodies an "authorized version of Otherness"? (129). What, crucially, are the qualities, content, dynamics, of that specifically "Jewish" voice that Sarah Horowitz has eloquently described as having been "silenced" except insofar as the voice "mimics or reproduces the voice of normative culture and modulates itself in timbres pleasing and non-threatening to the larger society"?[5]

If in various complex ways Jewish men and Jewish women have both seen themselves and been seen as Others within androcentric gentile American culture, Jewish women, as I have contended elsewhere, have been the "Other of the Other." Jewish women are the embodied presence made invisible by their absence from Eurocentric masculinist cultural critiques. Jewish women have been excluded from male-centered religious life until recent years, when, within liberal denominations, we/they are permitted to imitate the ritual practice of men.[6] But in ways "almost the same" as postcolonial writers, that double remove also freed Jewish American women writers to explore and inscribe the knotted issues of Jewish positionality itself.

Looking back at the last two decades of Jewish American women's writing, one can chart three stages of that exploration. The first was that of the Jewish American woman writer's pursuit of the "American quest-romance" written within the cultural matrix of the prefeminist and illusorily inclusive "melting pot" era.[7] Whereas that same pursuit enabled Jewish male writers to be incorporated into the American literary tradition by positioning themselves as alienated antiheroes, no such "place ... space ... niche," in the words of Anne Roiphe,[8] was available to women–Jewish or otherwise. With the rise of the feminist movement in the secular arena and the subsequent problematizing of assimilation itself, however, gender issues within Judaism moved to the forefront. The late 1970s, 1980s, and early 1990s thus witnessed the production of narratives that no longer engaged the desirability of assimilation. Instead, novels written in the feminist era concentrated on revealing what Jewish critic Helene Cixous has called "the cracks in the overall system."[9] That is, narratives like Esther Broner's *Weave of Women*, Rhoda Lerman's *God's Ear*, or Tova Reich's *Master of the Return* were no longer written with the "gentile over the shoulder," nor even with the goal of being "almost the same but different." Rather, these novels recast as their narrative center hitherto marginalized women who are depicted as engrossed in religious exploration with the very Judaisms which had themselves been marginalized by the mainstream American Judaisms of their era—that is, with the mystical Judaisms that the people of Roth's postwar Woodenton would have denounced as dressed in the "wrong clothes." Whereas *God's Ear* and *Master of the Return* assume textual and thematic power through their dramatizations of that mystical tradition's exclusion of women, a novel like Marge Piercy's *He, She, and It*, which may be understood to represent a third stage, more closely reflects the theologies of the Jewish feminist movement emergent in the social arena by purposively misreading the mystical tradition and thus creating, by implicitly assuming, both a strong place for Jewish women and a central place for a revisioned Judaism.

By the mid-1990s, however, mysticism itself also began filtering increasingly into more mainstream Jewish American life, as evidenced by the mass marketing of "spirituality"—once a word rarely heard in Jewish circles—as well as the proliferation of classes and publications on the long-silenced Kabbalah, and the resurgence of interest in the nineteenth-century Hasidic master Nahman of Bratslav. If we are to wish for a Jewish American literature that functions not merely to mirror social reality but to serve as a creative irritant, spur, oppositional voice to that social reality, the increasingly popular "new spirituality" provokes a new question. If being costumed in the "wrong clothes" has become the latest fashion, what in turn becomes the new "wrong clothes"? That is to say, if the territory of the mystical margin has been annexed to the Jewish mainstream center, what, within Jewish American writing, has been marginalized in its stead?

The current popularity of new-age Hasidism and "Jewish spirituality" in Jewish communal life can also obscure the subversive power inherent in the novels of the feminist era. For while early assimilationist narratives dwell on the alienation and rootlessness, the disabling marginality, of Jewish women, those of the second stage reverse the pattern of most Jewish American literature in this century. Like postcolonial fiction that is no longer compelled to reenact how "things fall apart" (in the notable phrase of Chinua Achebe) or the crisis of identity within a colonized culture, the mise-en-scène in the second-stage novels is not so much a peripherally Jewish, predominantly American, culture, but rather an assertively Jewish one. In other words, the mise-en-scène is not one of the familiar and normative Jewish communities—an affluent suburb, for example—whose presence in the novel ever-so-ambivalently-Jewish readers can recognize as "almost the same but different" from their own "native" territory, a community at whose edges are the eccentrics who by the novel's end are either neutralized, dismissed, or, by having themselves changed, included. Nor is it an eccentric community whose too-Jewish quirks are tacitly neutralized for the reader by an appropriately alienated and assimilated Jewish American narrative voice. Rather, as in Lerman's brilliant comic-tragic *God's Ear* (1989) and Marge Piercy's cyberpunk feminist midrash *He, She, and It* (1991), the socially marginal has become the celebrated narrative center. In the former novel, that center becomes a traditionally devout if wildly unusual Hasidic community not at all problematized by the narrative because its leaders insistently wear "the wrong clothes." And in *He, She, and It* the "wrong clothes" turn into those worn by outsiders to the community.

As a passage in *God's Ear* reveals, such a strategy can become, in turn, an important and resonant critique of the status of the Jewish writer in America. At a crucial moment in the narrative, the side-curled Hasidic protagonist Yussel Fetner is invited to speak before the Reverend Bismark's Assembly of God adult education class for what the church intends to be an informative, polite, ecumenical evening. Though Yussel is initially skeptical, in the end he nonetheless agrees. Both the narrative voice, and that of Yussel Fetner, are instructive.

Reverend Bismark tentatively begins, "nervous and sincere." "We understand you all don't believe in the Messiah," he says. "Is that true?" And he continues, "Why did God make evil?" And "Have the Jews learned to live with the Holocaust?"

As Yussel begins to respond, he grows more and more excited. He feels as if he is in "Yeshiva again, soaring like an eagle, the answers rolling out, his father's words, his father's father's words, commentaries, commandments, stories, meanings" (283). The audience writes, underlines. But suddenly something interrupts him:

> Yussel soared. Maybe he was illuminating, enlightening. [But then in] the rear a woman closed her notebook, dropped it into

a shopping bag at her feet, took out a red-and-white checker-board sweater, started knitting, moved her lips to count stitches. Suddenly Yussel realized how many thousands of other fools had tried to teach them, tried to explain, begged them for pity, pleaded for a child's life. . . . How many stand-up comic saints had stood before them, hoping for a spark, a breakthrough behind the cataracts of distaste, begging for their lives. They nod, say Je-ew in two syllables, and murder you in your bed. Go home, ladies. Play duplicate bridge, make tomato aspic, hang curtains in your garage windows. "How many of you here think the Jews killed Jesus? Raise your hands."

Faces froze. (284)

Like a Jewish American novelist wrestling with how to inscribe Judaism and Jewish experience for an American readership, searching for the language of that experience, searching to translate that experience, Yussel has been called upon to "explain the Jews."At the very crest of his imagined glory as a "light unto the gentiles," however, one gesture of indifference— a woman starting to knit—becomes enough to expose the emptiness of that designated role. As an implicit comment on the real status of Judaically affirming Jewish American writers on the American literary stage, Lerman's Yussel realizes that he is, after all, no light, but rather a court fool. No ecumenical evenings with Christian adult education classes, any more than trying to be "almost the same but different," can assuage the pain of historical memory. To embrace that history, to embrace difference, is to drop the mask of authorized Other whose voice, in the words of Sarah Horowitz recalled above, "modulates itself in timbres pleasing and non-threatening to the larger society." When Yussel rejects that role, he also rejects the social elimination of difference, one, for example, that has created such fictional hybrids as "Judeo-Christian" culture on the American landscape. He thus feels compelled to name the source of real difference: "How many of you," he bursts out, "think the Jews killed Jesus?" Just as Lerman has chosen to write a novel in which the men in the wrong clothes occupy the narrative center, so her protagonist Yussel refuses any longer to be the accommodating representative Jew. At one incisive stroke, Yussel transforms himself into the Other who is inappropriate and inappropriated.[10]

"Grammar is [also] politics by other means" (Haraway, *Simians*, 3). With his *payes*, skullcap, and "inappropriate" question, with his "commentaries, commandments, stories, meanings," Yussel Fetner thinks thoughts and speaks in a Jewish-Yiddish-English modulated voice that is beyond the margins not only of "normative culture," but of mainstream Jewish American literature as well. Lerman's transcription of Yussel's language, indeed, is closer to that of the early writers Anzia Yezierska and Abraham Cahan than it is to contemporary Jewish Americanese. But its function in its modern context is profoundly different. Unlike the Yiddish-inflected English used by the early writers simultaneously to mark their Jewish immigrant protagonists as green-horns, separate themselves from their characters, and thereby establish themselves as writers on the American literary stage, American-born Yussel *chooses* his language, giving up his career as an insurance salesman to rejoin (not without initial reluctance) his father's Hasidic sect. As in much postcolonial writing, *God's Ear* appropriates English to *celebrate* "the spirit that is one's own": particularly in its rhythms, the language of *God's Ear* becomes a carrier of specifically Jewish cultural, historical, and linguistic experience.[11] Indeed, just as Yussel Fetner's question harrows the soil of the supposed "dialogue" between Christians and Jews, Lerman ruptures the assimilationist literary tradition that portrays Jewish "difference" while it simultaneously marginalizes or eliminates the source of true difference—not a "Jewishness" which during most of the twentieth century could be bleached into an apparent "universality," but rather the Judaism, which cannot. The radical contribution of *God's Ear* is just this shift of axis. Margin and center are reversed, and accommodative "Judeo-Christian" culture is displaced, while a mystically compelling, midrash-quoting Hasidic community in the midst of the American Midwest is turned into the narrative norm.

Throughout the novel, the locus of narrative consciousness is not an unease with Jewishness, an anxiety about being Jewish, a persistence in imagining a judging gentile over the shoulder—what postcolonial critics call "cultural denigration" (Ashcroft et al., *Empire Writes Back*, 9)—a denigration characteristic of much Jewish American literature of the twentieth century. It is, rather, on what prevents the scion of a Hasidic dynasty, a man in the wrong clothes for the citizens of assimilationist Woodenton, from even more fervently binding himself to God—in Jewish terms, from "circumcising his heart." What blocks the arteries of Yussel's feeling heart is implicit in Lerman's description of Yussel's recalling his "father's words . . . father's father's words": it is the absence in his consciousness of the words of women. "I know who you are," declares angry Lillywhite Stevie to Yussel. "You're five thousand years old. You won't look at me. I see you everyplace I go and you won't look at me" (204).

For in *God's Ear* the man in the wrong clothes meets all the Jewish American women of fiction who failed to find their "place . . . space . . . niche" in the assimilationist culture of the States. Lerman's Lillywhite has been what Anne Roiphe's protagonist in *Long Division* (1972) calls a "wandering Jewess." Emily Brimberg Johnson compares herself to the "Daughters of the American Revolution," daughters of the land of "countrytisofthee." Unlike them, she says, she is a wandering Jewess . . . belonging only peripherally to one culture or another, a grandmother who collected china, knowing alien boots could and would smash it all to bits in a week, a century later. Perhaps contemporary Jewish women should form their own society. Daughters of Refugees of the Ongoing-Universal-Endless-Upheaval. We could meet on boats, three miles out to sea, and not allow anyone whose ancestors had lived in less than four countries to join.[12]

Jewish American women's narratives are replete with such "wandering Jewess[es]": Lillywhite Stevie has drifted to London, Kathmandu, and Tibetan refugee camps, "avoid[ing] Israel" (173); there is also Marjorie Weiss in *Torch Song*; the women of Tova Reich's *Mara* and *Master of the Return*; Rita of Lynn Sharon Schwartz's "The Melting Pot"; the women "who were all travelers before settling down in each other's friendships" in E. M. Broner's *Weave of Women* (239); Rachel of Joanna Spiro's short story, "Three Thousand Years of Your History . . . Take One Year for Yourself," who finds herself shorn of identity when she returns to America after a summer in Israel. All of these characters are marked by a sense of existential exile.

In *God's Ear,* that exile symbolically culminates on the mountaintop refuge that overlooks Yussel's Hasidic community. From that mountaintop Yussel hears not the voice of God announcing his presence and bestowing covenant, but rather the voice of Lillywhite, singing out with such loneliness that she sounds like a "wolf cry in the wilderness" (118). Whereas Emily Brimberg Johnson felt she should be on a boat "three miles out to sea" from Daughters-of-the-Revolution America, in *God's Ear* it is that America which is on the margins: in the center now are women writers dreaming up the men in the wrong clothes. There is no redemption for Yussel Fetner until he finally hears and internalizes Lillywhite's song and acknowledges the diminishment and erasure of women both within Judaism and within his own heart, in a manner that restores a spiritual center to Lillywhite as well.

At the end of the novel, a Lillywhite whose own spiritual longings have finally been realized rejects Yussel's exclusively male interpretations of midrashic legend. She sees nothing pious in an often-told Fetner tale of a holy ancestor's sacrifice of his family's welfare for the sake of ritual purity. "I would have thrown him against the wall," she tells Yussel; "I think it is time to make up some new stories" (309). And that longing of Lillywhite's for the "father's words, father's father's words, commentaries . . . stories, meanings" to be recast to include the experience of women is precisely what is realized in Marge Piercy's novel *He, She, and It,* which appeared two years after *God's Ear.*

Piercy's novel is a complex enterprise. Set in the twenty-first century, it interweaves a futuristic cyberpunk *Blade Runner* landscape reminiscent of the novels of William Gibson; the Jewish legend of the creation of the golem through the mystical ministrations of sixteenth-century Rabbi Judah Loew of Prague; the retelling of that legend by Malkah ("Queen") who, as her Hebrew name implies, is spiritual leader of the Jewish "freetown" of Tikva ("Hope") founded on principles of "libertarian socialism with a strong admixture of anarcho-feminism, reconstructionist Judaism . . . and greeners" (418)—a town that occupies the "unclaimed margins" of a wholly dystopic American landscape; the programming by Malkah of Yod, a heroic cyborg whose name kabbalistically evokes that of the Divine, and who was built by the Tikva patriarch Avram, biblical resonance clearly intended; the journeying of Malkah's granddaughter Shira ("Poetry") back home to Malkah and to Tikva after a life in which she felt, in a manner reminiscent of those wandering Jewesses of earlier novels, "too physical . . . too loud, too female, too Jewish, too dark, too exuberant, too emotional" (7) in the territory controlled by her former employers, the hostile multinational corporation that had required blond hair and blue eyes for its employees; Yod's own journey into a quasi-humanity through a passionate relationship with Shira; his ultimate destruction, echoing the fate of Rabbi Judah Loew's golem; and, last but not least, subplots involving Shira's mother, the information pirate Riva ("Quarrel" in Hebrew) and Nili, an Israeli feminist freedom fighter and warrior whose name, an acronym for "*Nezah Yisrael lo Yeshaker*" ("the strength of Israel will not lie," I Samuel 15:29) is also the code name of Jewish secret agents who operated in Palestine during World War I.[13] In short, Piercy's *He, She, and It* is an epic attempt to retell the stories of the past—in this case that of the golem—as well as to reimagine through a feminist and kabbalistic lens vast expanses of Jewish history: the gendered Jewish experience of the diaspora from the sixteenth-century ghetto of Prague to the twenty-first-century refuge of Tikva on the edge of America. It seeks to redeem that experience through an honoring of both Jewish feminism and—rather literally here—a new-age Jewish mysticism.

But to redeem the feminine within Judaism, Piercy has to misread kabbalistic mysticism. For the wise, gifted, and compassionate crone Malkah the Queen is intended to embody both a fully realized womanhood and the divine feminine principle of Kabbalah, the Shekhinah—the figure that feminist Judaism has incorporated in place of the male Yahweh or "Adonai" ("Our Lord") in its liturgy[14]—a figure more familiar to mainstream Jews in her whittled-down guise as a kind of fairy godmother Sabbath Queen in English-language prayer books. On the one hand, Piercy's kabbalistic theology in *He, She, and It* allows her to restore powerful spiritual significance to Shekhinah; on the other, however appealing the Shekhinah may be to feminist Jews, in the kabbalistic tradition itself, as Elliot R. Wolfson has argued, the figure is only problematically female.[15] But if grammar is politics by another means, so is gendering. Piercy, after all, is making up "new stories."

Ultimately, in *He, She, and It* two constructs exist in eternal opposition: the material "slag heap" that has become an America so rabidly commercial that the loving and spiritual have gone underground, and Malkah's Jewish and feminist vision of a "holy and powerful light that shines through history" (26–27). At the end of the novel, Malkah chooses to travel toward that "hidden light . . . a fountain of light into which [she] can plunge [herself]"; she is seeking new eyes, and in both Malkah's and Piercy's vision, those new eyes, that "fountain of light" is ultimately to be found only among women. But not among women living even on the "unclaimed margins" of what is left of the States. In a way that provoked unease about the possibility of an authentic creative renewal of woman's spiritual and narrative vision in this country when the novel appeared in 1991, when Malkah leaves on her "vision quest," it is to Nili's post-nuclear-catastrophe Israel, where Palestinian and Jewish women now live in harmony without men, and "the black Jews of Ethiopia had a higher survival rate . . . than any other group" (435), that she goes. When the Divine Feminine returns to the reclaimed Promised Land, Jews who are "white folks" must be "protected under disguised wraps" to endure.

With Malkah's departure from the States and her *aliyah* to Israel went the end of this second stage of Jewish women's writing. Piercy's *He, She, and It* sought to retell an ancient story, one deeply embedded within Jewish tradition, to celebrate the "man in the wrong clothes" by reconceiving him as Shekhinah. By the end of the twentieth century, however, he seems to have disappeared from women's writing; on the American landscape, Jewish religious vision no longer seems to inform women's novels. The name of the exhibition created by the protagonist Sara in Erica Jong's *Inventing Memory* (1997) is "Dancing to America," the retelling of an entirely secular individual family's immigrant tale.

Notes

1. Karen Brodkin Sacks, "How Did Jews Become White Folks?" in *Race*, ed. Steven Gregory and Roger Sanjek (New Brunswick, NJ: Rutgers University Press, 1994), 78–102.

2. See Joe Wood, "Escape from Blackness: Once Upon a Time in Creole America," *Village Voice* 39, no. 49 (December 6, 1994): 25–34. See also the references to Jews as "Orientals" and as "Semites" in Diane Lichtenstein, *Writing Their Nations: The Tradition of Nineteenth Century American Jewish Women Writers* (Bloomington: Indiana University Press, 1992).

3. "Eli, the Fanatic," in *Goodbye, Columbus: and Five Short Stories* (Cambridge: Riverside Press, 1959), 274.

4. Donna Haraway, *Simians, Cyborgs, and Women: The Reinvention of Nature* (New York: Routledge, 1991); Albert Memmi, *The Colonizer and the Colonized*, trans. Howard Greenfeld (Boston: Beacon Press, 1967), xvi; Homi Bhabha, "Of Mimicry and Man: The Ambivalence of Colonial Discourse," *October* 28 (Spring 1984): 129.

5. From "Jewish Studies as Oppositional? or Gettin' Mighty Lonely Out Here," in *Styles of Cultural Activism: From Theory and Pedagogy to Women, Indians, and Communism*, ed. Philip Goldstein (Newark: University of Delaware Press, 1994), 155.

6. See my essay, "Orphans of Culture and of History: Gender and Spirituality in Contemporary Jewish-American Women's Novels," *Tulsa Studies in Women's Literature* (Spring 1994): 127–141.

7. See my " 'Daughters of Refugees of the Ongoing-Universal-Endless-Upheaval': Anne Roiphe and the Quest for Narrative Voice in Jewish-American Women's Novels," in *Daughters of Valor: Contemporary Jewish-American Women Writers*, ed. Jay Halio and Ben Siegel (Newark: University of Delaware, 1997), 80–96.

8. Anne Roiphe, *Torch Song* (New York: Signet, 1977), 89.

9. Helene Cixous, "Sorties: Out and Out: Attacks/Ways Out/Forays," in *The Newly Born Woman*, ed. Helene Cixous and Catherine Clement, trans. Betsy Wing (Minneapolis: University of Minnesota Press, 1986), 7.

10. I am indebted to Trinh Minh-has's formulation of the "inappropriated Other." See Haraway, "Introduction," *Simians*, 2.

11. See Bill Ashcroft, Gareth Griffiths, and Helen Tifflin, *The Empire Writes Back: Theory and Practice in Post-colonial Literatures* (London: Routledge, 1989), 38–39. The phrase "the spirit that is one's own" is Raja Rao's, *Kanthapura* (New York: New Directions, 1938).

12. Anne Roiphe, *Long Division* (New York: Simon and Schuster, 1972), 71–73. For an extended discussion of these "wandering Jewesses," see also my "Daughters of Refugees," cited above.

13. Rosie Rosenzweig incorrectly identifies the name Nili with "N'eilah," the closing prayer of Yom Kippur; if indeed, as she claims, Marge Piercy told her that the two words come from the same Hebrew root, Piercy is quite mistaken. See her "Marge Piercy's Jewish Feminism: A Paradigm Switch," *Studies in American Jewish Literature* 17 (1998): 87.

14. See, for example, E. M. Broner's *The Telling* (San Francisco: HarperCollins, 1993).

15. See "On Becoming Female: Crossing Gender Boundaries in Kabbalistic Ritual and Myth," in *Gender and Judaism: The Transformation of Tradition*, ed. T. M. Rudavsky (New York: NYU Press, 1994), 209–228.

Works Cited

Ashcroft, Bill, Gareth Griffiths, and Helen Tifflin. *The Empire Writes Back: Theory and Practice in Post-colonial Literatures*. London: Routledge, 1989.

Bhabha, Homi. "Of Mimicry and Man: The Ambivalence of Colonial Discourse." *October* 28 (Spring 1984): 125–133.

Cixous, Helene. "Sorties: Out and Out: Attacks/Ways Out/Forays." In *The Newly Born Woman*, trans. Betsy Wing. Minneapolis: University of Minnesota Press, 1986.

Glazer, Miriyam. " 'Daughters of Refugees of the Ongoing-Universal-Endless-Upheaval': Anne Roiphe and the Quest for Narrative Voice in Jewish-American Women's Novels." In *Daughters of Valor: Contemporary Jewish-American Women Writers*, ed. Jay Halio and Ben Siegel, 80–96. Newark: University of Delaware, 1997.

Haraway, Donna. *Simians, Cyborgs, and Women: The Reinvention of Nature*. New York: Routledge, 1991.

Horowitz, Sarah. "Jewish Studies as Oppositional? or Gettin' Mighty Lonely Out Here." In *Styles of Cultural Activism*, ed. Philip Goldstein, 152–164. Newark: University of Delaware Press, 1994.

Lerman, Rhoda. *God's Ear: A Novel*. Syracuse: Syracuse University Press, 1996.

Piercy, Marge. *He, She, and It*. New York: Fawcett Crest, 1991.

Rao, Raja. *Kanthapura*. New York: New Directions, 1938.

Roiphe, Anne. *Long Division*. New York: Simon and Schuster, 1972.

——. *Torch Song*. New York: Signet, 1977.

Rosenzweig, Rosie. "Marge Piercy's Jewish Feminism: A Paradigm Switch." *Studies in American Jewish Literature* 17 (1998): 82–87.

Roth, Philip. *Goodbye, Columbus: and Five Short Stories*. Cambridge: Riverside Press, 1959.

Sacks, Karen Brodkin. "How Did Jews Become White Folks?" In *Race*, ed. Steven Gregory and Roger Sanjek, 78–102. New Brunswick, NJ: Rutgers University Press, 1994.

Wood, Joe. "Escape from Blackness: Once Upon a Time in Creole America." *Village Voice* 39, no. 49 (December 6, 1994), 25–34.

17

Restorying Jewish Mothers

JANET BURSTEIN

Because we know from our earliest memories the power and pleasure of "once upon a time," making stories comes as second nature to us all. When we try to explain to ourselves the puzzling behavior of a child or friend, when we struggle to connect the bewilderment of this moment to a future we desire (or to a past that we regret), we make a story. And the story gives shape to material that would otherwise be disturbingly fluid, elusive, resistant to the mind's grasp. The stories we tell one another construct a shared world—especially for children. But for adults too the world becomes knowable largely through the stories that represent it and justify its peculiarities. Thus for individuals and for the cultures that shape and contain them, stories perform multiple functions as they engage, and maybe even delight, the mind.

For Jews, as Victoria Aarons has pointed out, the cultural burden of stories is particularly salient; Jewish storytelling has long been a means of both "bearing witness to the events of the past and of defining the fluid specifics of Jewish identity."[1] Thus in the work of Philip Roth, Delmore Schwartz, and Jerome Weidman, for example, Aarons describes the efforts of protagonists to find their places within Jewish culture and also to define themselves through the agency of the story. The dual questions asked by Roth's Ozzie Freedman in "The Conversion of the Jews" reveal this double quest for both personal and ethnic identity (106, 112); first he asks, "Is it me? Is it me ME ME ME! It has to be me—but is it!" Finally he asks, "Is it us? . . . Is it us?" Roth's later protagonist in *The Counterlife* will insist that both questions can be answered only through storying—creating narratives that both realize and reveal the self as part of its culture.

In general, these dual objectives of storying seem valid for both male and female American Jewish writers. But when they tell stories about parents and children, male and female narratives differ from one another. In fact, if we hold women's storying of filial relationships against Harold Bloom's paradigm for such relationships, the gender-related differences become quite clear even to a nonessentialist reader. A long time ago, Bloom called attention to a phenomenon he called "the anxiety of influence" that complicates the connection between male writers and their precursors—a phenomenon that still seems to shadow the filial relationships that men's stories often tell. Bloom understood what he called "the melancholy of the creative mind's desperate insistence upon priority."[2] As "the hungry generations go on treading one another down" (6), he wrote, male writers "misread" the stories of their precursors in order to "beget" themselves. In art as in life, what Freud called the family romance and its inescapable Oedipal conflict dictate, Bloom argues, that strong sons will fight their precursors through "caricature," "distortion," and "perverse, willful revisionism" (30). They fight because the power of the precursor is so great that it dooms each new generation of men—"whether poets or not" (56)—to the anxious expectation of "being flooded" by it (57): "The precursors flood us, and our imaginations can die by drowning in them." But, he warns, "no imaginative life is possible if such inundation is wholly evaded" (154). Thus, the "strong imagination comes to its painful birth" not by evasion, but "through savagery and misrepresentation" of the stories it inherits (85).

This aggressive scenario is sometimes visible in the work of American Jewish male writers. Herbert Gold's 1961 story "The Heart of the Artichoke" provides a classic example. Gold's narrator sees—too late—the archetypal nature of the battle with his father that followed his refusal to adopt for his own life the plot of his father's story. In retrospect he will be able to realize that when his father stood, menacing, over this rebellious adolescent son, his father's "swaying body knew it loved me as his father had loved him, the woman carrying her child on a belly or breast, the man taking his son only at the eye or the fist."[3] But in the moment, this narrator knows only that he has to fight his father to guarantee his own power.

According to Bloom and *his* precursor Sigmund Freud, these two male creatures fight because fighting is the given of relationship between male precursors and their descendants. According to Nietzsche, Bloom explains, "every talent must unfold itself in fighting" (Bloom, *Anxiety*, 51). And sure enough, the fight itself, in Gold's story, accomplishes the unfolding of the child into the man he became: as they wrestle, Gold's narrator remembers that his father "hugged . . . my ribs, forcing them up—cracking! pushing my hair out, lengthening my bones, driving my voice deep. Savagely he told me his life, wringing my childhood from me. . . . We embraced like this" (299). Like the embrace of Jacob and the angel as they wrestle in Genesis, this fierce contest unites the contenders only by aggression, but their brief union engenders a new adult identity—that will grow mainly by conflict and separation.

One important problem with this mode of male filial bonding, a problem that shows up in many of the male-authored stories that Aarons has studied, is that it produces other long-range consequences as well. For fathers, as Aarons notes, the consequence is "failed expectations." For sons, the filial story becomes what Aarons calls a "saga of guilt" (Aarons, *Measure of Memory*, 172) that begets a profound nostalgia for what has been rejected. Thus Aarons observes in stories by male writers a continuing fascination with the "source of the [son's] estrangement" from his father. In these stories "the past becomes increasingly seductive" (173). For male narrators and/or protagonists, the paternal story begins to hold a meaning that becomes luminous only after it has been rejected, precious only after it has been lost.

Some contemporary critics have assumed this filial dynamic to be so pervasive that they believe it to be characteristic of current American Jewish literature as a whole. Norman Finkelstein, for example, has argued that because of the agonistic relation of strong writers to their precursors—like that of strong sons to their fathers—Jewish writers work in the mode of nostalgia. "To be modern," he says, "is to experience rupture; to be Postmodern is to reflect upon the experience of rupture, and in doing so repeat and further that experience."[4] Contemporary Jewish writers "honor the past *through* rupture" (3), he insists, and then carry it forward in nostalgic recollection.

But rupture and nostalgia don't seem to pervade filial stories written since the late 1960s by American Jewish women. Like male writers, women also revision and transform parental stories. Like male narrators, women often tell of conflict with their parents. But the emphasis in their stories usually falls upon engagement rather than rupture. Perhaps the most powerful example of filial engagement that contains, but is unruptured by, conflict is Vivian Gornick's memoir *Fierce Attachments* (1987). Like Gold's narrator, Gornick's must reject—as a pattern for her own life—the story her parent's life has written. In Gornick's work, the plot of the mother's life is the romance of domestic love. Gornick's narrator rejects that plot. But she grasps at the same time a maternal gift that lies beneath it. The source of this gift is the kitchen window where the listening child first hears her mother turning the calls and cries of neighbor women into stories. This window opens onto an alley in the Bronx where "there were no trees, or bushes, or grasses of any kind."[5] Nevertheless, Gornick remembers it as a "place of clear light and sweet air, suffused, somehow, with a perpetual smell of summery green." Here, she believes, not in the bedroom or the nursery, not at the stove or the sewing machine, is the Jewish mother's garden. Here the child learns to appreciate the interest of women's voices, to feel contempt for the work of cooking and cleaning, and to prize above all things the narrative skill that distinguishes her mother from other women. Mama's "running commentary on the life outside the window was my first taste of the fruits of intelligence," her daughter remembers; like the fairy-tale sorcerer who can spin straw into gold, Mama transforms what is base into something precious: she "knew how to convert gossip into knowledge" (15).

The preciousness of this shared gift will carry Gornick beyond the kitchen window into the life of a professional writer. More valuable to her than the paradigm of domestic romance her mother has wanted to transmit, the pleasure of storying that she has learned from her mother surpasses all other pleasures: "Not an 'I love you' in the world could touch it" (152), she says.

Her relationship to her mother will also include moments of terrible ferocity. But even when she describes physical conflict, language tranforms it into a mode of connection—not severance. For example, when Mama Gornick chases her smart-talking college girl daughter through the apartment and fails to stop at the hastily locked bathroom door, she drives "her fist thru the glass, *reaching for me*" (my emphasis), Gornick says. "I thought that afternoon, One of us is going to die of this attachment" (110). It survives, however, not only this episode but many periodic flashes of competitiveness for control of their joint story. Thus this memoir creates an image of two women sustaining with great difficulty—in war and peace—a complicated intimacy as they walk the city streets, arguing, bitterly fighting, or simply talking together. At the end, laying down a dishtowel as though it were Prospero's wand, Mama Gornick asks: "why don't you go already? why don't you walk away from my life? I'm not stopping you." But Gornick remains "half in and half out" of her mother's house.

These women fight not to vanquish one another, but to carry forward the tricky dialogue in which both can remain engaged. It is this model of intermittent conflict and continuing dialogue—not rupture, guilt, and nostalgia—that seems to engage many American Jewish women writers since the 1960s. E. M. Broner's recent *Ghost Stories* (1995), for example, develops this model. Even after death, the narrator's mother in these stories remains both visible and audible to her daughter. Her reflection appears in the mirror when her daughter combs the wavy hair she inherits from her mother. They argue still about their haircuts. As the daughter observes the weekly ritual of kaddish for eleven months of formal mourning, her mother sits beside her in the synagogue, criticizing, commanding, interpreting, remembering, continuing the cranky dialogue in which they both remain engaged. Like Gornick, this narrator shapes her own life and commitments in ways her mother does not always understand or approve. But she seeks as well the sense of blessing that her mother's approval still carries: "If I am her good girl," she asks herself, "will I hear whispered blessings ruffling my hair, my life?"[6] She confronts in their continuing dialogue their mutual disappointments in one another (124–127). They fight, like Gornick and her mother, about interpretations of their shared past (132–133). But, like Gornick, she hears her mother's story and records it faithfully, without misreading, even though she cannot, would not, relive it. She can't always use her mother's "old words." But this narrator writes them down (66). And she doesn't transform them; she reminds herself when she gets impatient with her mother's digressive narrative style: "It's my mother's story and she will not be rushed" (149). Conserving that story even as she writes her own, this narrator—like Gornick—escapes the double trap of guilt on one hand and nostalgic longing for a rejected parental past on the other. Rejection, estrangement, and supplantation are not the issues for these women, as Broner's narrator's last words to her mother make very clear: "I don't want you to go from me, Mama. Even if you give everything away . . . I don't want you to go away. Stay. I'll listen closely to your whispers" (180). Listening closely, staying instead of rejecting, this writing daughter who both resembles and differs from her mother, whose feminist commitments revise the domestic imperatives of her mother's life, restories her precursor without willfully misreading the maternal story.

In part, the difference these stories describe between rupture and continuing engagement may be psychologically oriented. Nancy Chodorow and others have taught us that women and men relate differently to mothers and fathers in their earliest years in the family. But I think that this difference in the ways male and female American Jewish writers tell parental stories also exists, ironically, because of the silence that Jewish tradition imposed on its women. Traditional Judaism, as we all know, silenced and excluded its women's stories in many ways. But like everything else that human beings try to repress or exclude, women's stories became powerful in exile. And when they found their way into more homely modes of discourse, maternal stories became particularly powerful for American Jewish women writers, many of whom identify their own narrative gifts as part of their mothers' legacies. Like Gornick, Kate Simon, for example, recalls that her Jewish mother at the kitchen window interpreted the neighborhood, making narrative sense of tenement babble, stilling desire for the world beyond the kitchen.

Theoretically, of course, the mother's link to language has come very clear in recent feminist writings. Bella Brodzki writes, "As the child's first significant Other, the mother engenders subjectivity thru language; she is the primary source of speech and love. And part of the maternal legacy is the conflation of the two."[7] The novelist Tova Reich understands the mother's role in this process in this fundamental way: "My mother had been my muse," Reich writes; "She had fed me the words."[8] Here there is neither usurpation nor perverse, willful revision. Instead, as Brodzki suggests, Reich acknowledges language itself as her mother's gift, as the very source of her own power with words.

Connected in this way with language in a child's earliest memory, mothers' voices can empower daughters by showing them how to conceive and articulate themselves as subjects. Thus Kate Simon learns from her mother's stories the power of a narrating persona to give or withhold sympathy from her characters.[9] Indeed, when she remembers that "the voices that filled our world were those of women, the Mothers" (36), she invokes a sub-jective maternal presence powerful enough to shape a child's sense of the world and to "fill" it as well. But not to drown her. The verb's associations with completeness and satiation recall Tova Reich's metaphor of feeding that speaks so directly to these women's sense of verbal empowerment by their mothers.

For some women writers, however, maternal stories can also connect a daughter to the accommodations mothers have made to cultural restric-tions that subdue and devalue women. Violet Weingarten's *Mrs. Beneker* (1967) and Isadora Wing's mother in Erica Jong's *Fear of Flying* (1973), for example, are both complicit in the culture's frustration of active professional women. Marianne Hirsch reports that feminists accuse mothers in our cul-ture of denying "the truth about their own experience of bondage and frus-tration";[10] many stories of the 1970s reveal the shape such denials can take and also the effects on daughters disempowered by stories that mothers either will not or cannot speak.

Filial stories by women, then, can be complicated by the mixed effects upon daughters of the frustrations, deprivations, and restrictions of their mothers' lives. But where some male protagonists fictionalize their father's lives to make a ground for their own stories of self (Aaron's 55–59), women writers like Broner, Gornick, Simon, and many others carry forth the precursor's story even as their own narratives revise it. For example, in the stories of their precursors, the activist Jewish women of nineteenth-century Europe, contemporary Jewish feminists hear not only a call to move into the wide, public world from the cramping pieties of traditional female domestic-ity, but also a fierce cry of rebellion against the ethnic and gendered bonds that connect women with their families and communities. But contemporary activist Jewish women writers revalue the powerful bonds that earlier activists needed to sever.

For Grace Paley's Faith Darwin, for example, activist commitments rise from, coexist with, and even deepen those bonds. Mothering accompanies the activist agenda of Faith's own mother, and sets the activist agenda for Faith herself when the "heartfelt brains" of her son turn her outward from the family to work in a world whose neediness and vulnerability make it seem, sometimes, like yet another (profoundly recalcitrant) child.

Phyllis Chesler politicizes even as she revalues traditional family im-peratives. She brings forward into the light of story the physical experience of childbirth and nursing. Speaking through the body, as Adrienne Rich instructed, Chesler restories motherhood in its most intimate context, surfac-ing the power that lay silent in it for so many generations and thus drawing it into the political arena. The political activism of the European precursors, here, is restoried to accompany the family priorities of American immigrant mothers from whom Paley and Chesler descend.

Rich herself, thinking back through the European activist women with whom she identifies, metaphorically affirms her precursors even as she critiques the specific political causes that failed them. She believes, for example, that the promises of Zionism have been "broken." But she inherits, nevertheless, the first pioneer's determination: "that the life she gives her life to/shall not be cheap/ that the life she gives her life to/shall not turn on her/ that the life she gives her life to shall want an end to suffering."[11] Like Maxine Kumin, who says we carry forth our mothers in our bellies, Rich exploits the trope of childbearing here to suggest that the "unresolved possibilities" of our mothers' lives get stored in us, that generations of women carry forward their maternal precursors like women pregnant with the next generation of children.

Perhaps metaphors of pregnancy and childbirth are inescapable in a study of the ways women restory their mothers. Even Harold Bloom reaches into the experience of being mothered when he wants to imagine a kind of relationship between precursors and their descendants that falls outside the limits of the exclusively agonistic, androcentric system he has created. He speaks, briefly, of a "matrix of generous influence" that is profoundly different from the kind of influence that engenders male anxiety. For him, that "matrix" is illusory. Within it, however, recent stories by American Jewish women are finding their source.

Notes

1. Victoria Aarons, *A Measure of Memory: Storytelling and Identity in American Jewish Fiction* (Athens: University of Georgia Press, 1996), 1.

2. Harold Bloom, *The Anxiety of Influence: A Theory of Poetry* (Oxford: Oxford University Press, 1973), 13.

3. Herbert Gold, "The Heart of the Artichoke," in *Jewish-American Stories*, ed. Irving Howe (Beltsville: New American Library, 1977), 299.

4. Norman Finkelstein, *The Ritual of New Creation: Jewish Tradition and Contemporary Literature* (Albany: State University of New York Press, 1992), 22.

5. Vivian Gornick, *Fierce Attachments* (New York: Farrar, Straus, Giroux, 1987), 137.

6. E. M. Broner, *Ghost Stories* (New York: Global City Press, 1995), 64.

7. Bella Brodzki, "Mothers, Displacement, and Language in the Autobiographies of Nathalie Sarraute and Christa Wolf," *Life/Lines: Theorizing Women's Autobiographies*, ed. Brodzki and Celeste M. Schenk (Ithaca: Cornell University Press, 1989), 245.

8. Tova Reich, "Hers: My Mother, My Muse," *New York Times Magazine* (November 6, 1988), 30, 32.

9. Kate Simon, *Bronx Primitive: Portraits in a Childhood* (New York: Harper, 1982), 4–5.

10. Marianne Hirsch, *The Mother/Daughter Plot: Narrative, Psychoanalysis, Feminism* (Bloomington: Indiana University Press, 1989), 165.

11. Adrienne Rich, *Sources* (Woodside: Heyeck Press, 1983), 19.

Works Cited

Aarons, Victoria. *A Measure of Memory: Storytelling and Identity in American Jewish Fiction*. Athens: University of Georgia Press, 1996.

Bloom, Harold. *The Anxiety of Influence: A Theory of Poetry*. Oxford: Oxford University Press, 1973.

Brodzki, Bella. "Mothers, Displacement, and Language in the Autobiographies of Nathalie Sarraute and Christa Wolf." In *Life/Lines: Theorizing Women's Autobiographies*, ed. Brodzki and Celeste M. Schenck, 243–259. Ithaca: Cornell University Press, 1988.

Broner, E. M. *Ghost Stories*. New York: Global City Press, 1995.

Finkelstein, Norman. *The Ritual of New Creation: Jewish Tradition and Contemporary Literature*. Albany: State University of New York Press, 1992.

Gold, Herbert. "The Heart of the Artichoke." In *Jewish American Stories*, ed. Irving Howe, 270–300. Beltsville: New American Library, 1977.

Gornick, Vivian. *Fierce Attachments*. New York: Farrar, Straus, Giroux, 1987.

Hirsch, Marianne. *The Mother/Daughter Plot: Narrative, Psychoanalysis, Feminism*. Bloomington: Indiana University Press, 1989.

Reich, Tova. "Hers: My Mother, My Muse." *New York Times Magazine* (November 6, 1988), 30, 32.

Rich, Adrienne. *Sources*. Woodside: Heyeck Press, 1983.

Roth, Philip. "Conversion of the Jews." In *Goodbye, Columbus: And Five Short Stories*. 110–114. New York: Bantam/Houghton Mifflin, 1959.

Simon, Kate. *Bronx Primitive: Portraits in a Childhood*. New York: Harper, 1982.

Contributors

EVELYN AVERY is Professor of English and Coordinator of Jewish Studies at Towson University. She is the author of *Rebels and Victims: The Fiction of Richard Wright and Bernard Malamud* (Kennikat Press, 1979), editor of *The Magic Worlds of Bernard Malamud* (State University of New York, 2001), and has written many articles on Jewish American writers. Currently she is editing a collection of essays titled *Divided Selves: Jewish Women Writers in America.* Avery is also the founder of The Bernard Malamud Society, which she now coordinates with Professor Victoria Aarons, and the coeditor of the *Malamud Newsletter.* In addition, Avery serves on the board of *Modern Jewish Studies.*

GERHARD BACH teaches American Studies and ESL methodology at the University of Bremen. He has published widely on twentieth-century Jewish American literature, the culture curriculum, and intercultural education. More recent book publications include *Conversations with Grace Paley,* coeditor with Blaine Hall (University of Mississippi Press, 1997) and *Small Planets: Saul Bellow and the Art of Short Fiction,* coeditor with Gloria Cronin (Michigan State University Press, 1999).

ALAN L. BERGER holds the Raddock Eminent Scholar Chair of Holocaust Studies at Florida Atlantic University, where he directs both the Holocaust and Judaic Studies BA program and the Center for the Study of Values and Violence after Auschwitz. Among his books are *Crisis and Covenant: The Holocaust in American Jewish Fiction; Children of Job: American Second-Generation Witnesses; Judaism in the Modern World* (editor); *Second-Generation Voices: Reflections by Children of Holocaust Survivors and Perpetrators* (coeditor with his wife Naomi), which won the 2002 B'nai Zion National Media Award; *Encyclopedia of Holocaust Literature* (coeditor), which received a Booklist Best Reference Book of 2002 and the Outstanding Reference Source 2003, References and User Services Association of the ALA; and *The Continuing Agony: From the Carmelite Convent to the Crosses at Auschwitz* (coeditor).

Janet Burstein is Professor of English at Drew University. Credentialed originally as a Victorianist, Burstein began publishing in Victorian literature. For the past twenty years, however, she has been teaching and publishing numerous essays on American Jewish writing in journals such as *American Literature, Contemporary Literature, Studies in American Jewish Literature,* and *Modern Jewish Studies.* She is the author of *Writing Mothers, Writing Daughters: Tracing the Maternal in Stories by American Jewish Women Writers* (University of Illinois Press, 1996). In addition, Burstein has published *Telling "the little secrets": American Jewish Writers of the New Wave,* about American Jewish writers of the last two decades (University of Wisconsin Press, 2004).

Harry James Cargas was Professor Emeritus of Language and Literature at Webster University (St. Louis, Missouri) and the author of many books, including *Voices from the Holocaust, Problems Unique to the Holocaust, Conversations with Elie Wiesel,* and *Exploring Your Inner Space.* Cargas was also the author of numerous articles in, among others, *Christian Century, The New York Times, Jewish Spectator, Commonweal, America,* and *Negro American Literary Reflections of a Post-Auschwitz Christian,* and *Shadows of Auschwitz: A Christian Response to the Holocaust.* He was honored for his remarkable humanitarian effort by the Tree of Life Award and five thousand trees planted near Jerusalem in the Harry James Cargas Parkland. He was also recipient of the Eternal Flame Award from the Anne Frank Institute, the Micah Award from the American Jewish Committee, and the Human Rights Award from the United Nations Association. Professor Cargas died in 1998.

Sarah Blacher Cohen is Professor of English at the University of Albany, State University of New York, where she has taught for thirty years. She is the author of *Saul Bellow's Enigmatic Laughter* and *Cynthia Ozick's Comic Art: From Levity to Liturgy.* She is the editor of *Comic Relief, Jewish Wry, From Hester Street to Hollywood,* and *Making a Scene: The Contemporary Drama of Jewish-American Women,* as well as editor of the State University New York Press series on Modern Jewish Literature and Culture and Wayne State Press series on Humor in Life and Letters. She is a prize-winning playwright, with such works as *The Ladies' Locker Room, Molly Picon's Return Engagement,* an adaptation of Saul Bellow's "The Old System," and with such cowritten works as *Sophie, Totie, and Bell, Henrietta Szold: Woman of Valor*, and *Danny Kaye: Supreme Court Jester*. Dr. Cohen has been a humor consultant for the Library of Congress, distinguished Fulbright Professor to Yugoslavia, and a recipient of a Lifetime Achievement Award from the Muscular Dystrophy Association.

GLORIA L. CRONIN is a Professor of English at Brigham Young University, where she teaches African American literature, postcolonial theory, and literature. She is the Executive Coordinator of the American Literature Association. She is coeditor of the *Saul Bellow Journal*, Webmaster and Executive Director of the International Saul Bellow Society, and regularly organizes ALA conferences and symposia. Her book-length publications include: *Saul Bellow: An Annotated Bibliography*, Second Edition (Garland, 1987), Third Edition (www.saulbellow.org); *A Room of His Own: Bellow in Search of the Feminine* (Syracuse University Press, 2000); *Small Planets: Saul Bellow and the Art of Short Fiction* coedited with Gerhard Bach, (Michigan State University Press, 2000); *Zora Neale Hurston: Critical Essays* (Prentice Hall International, 1998); *Conversations with Saul Bellow* co-edited with Ben Siegel (University Press of Mississippi, 1994); *Tales of Molokai* (University of Hawaii Press, 1992); *Jewish American Fiction Writers: An Annotated Bibliography* with nine thousand entries coedited with Blaine H. Hall (Garland, 1991); 1991 Pozner Bibliography Prize; *Jerzy Kosinski: An Annotated Bibliography* coedited with Blaine H. Hall (Greenwood, 1991); and *Saul Bellow in the 1980's*, coedited with L. H. Goldman, (Michigan State University Press, 1989).

ELLEN S. FINE is Professor Emerita of French at Kingsborough Community College of the City University of New York. She is the author of *Legacy of Night: The Literary Universe of Elie Wiesel* (State University of New York Press, 1982), and was coeditor of the Holocaust issue of the journal *Centerpoint* (1980). She has written essays and articles on French Holocaust writers, second-generation writers, and hidden children that have appeared in books and journals both in the United States and in France.

MARIANNE M. FRIEDRICH received her PhD in English and American Language and Literature from the University of Heidelberg. She studied and taught at Washington University in St. Louis, Missouri (Fulbright). She taught at Kent State University, Ohio, and at Webster University, St. Louis, Missouri. Her publications include a book, *Character and Narration in the Short Fiction of Saul Bellow* (Peter Lange, 1995, 1996), articles in journals, and book chapters in *Saul Bellow: A Mosaic, Saul Bellow at Seventy-Five*, and *Small Planets*. Friedrich contributed articles to *Holocaust Literature: An Encyclopedia of Writers and Their Work* (Routledge, 2002).

Her translations include contributions to Simon Wiesenthal's enlarged edition of *The Sunflower* (Schocken Books, 1997).

MIRIYAM GLAZER is Professor of Literature at the University of Judaism in Los Angeles. Her recent books include *Dreaming the Actual: Contemporary Fiction and Poetry by Israeli Women Writers* (State University of New York, 2000), *Dancing on the Edge of the World: Jewish Stories of Faith, Inspiration, and Love* (Roxbury/McGraw Hill, 2000), and, with Bradley Shavit Artson, *The Bedside Torah* (Roxbury/McGraw Hill, 2001). *How Do You Dance Before the Bride?*, her account of the last fifty years of Jewish peoplehood, womanhood, and God, will be appearing soon. She is soon to be ordained as a rabbi in the Conservative Movement.

S. LILLIAN KREMER is a University Distinguished Professor who teaches courses in American literature, Ethnic and Women's Writing, and Holocaust Literature and Film in the Department of English at Kansas State University. She is the author of *Witness Through the Imagination: The Holocaust in Jewish American Literature* (Wayne State University Press, 1989) and *Women's Holocaust Writing: Memory and Imagination* (University of Nebraska Press, 1999). The first text deals with the treatment of the Holocaust in the fiction of ten American novelists. The second focuses on the narratives of women's Holocaust experience by survivors writing from memory and by native-born Americans working from research and the imagination. She is the editor of *Holocaust Literature: An Encyclopedia of Writers and Their Work* (Routledge, 2003), a two-volume reference text covering the work of over three hundred writers. Her articles have appeared in *Modern Language Studies*, *Contemporary Literature*, *Modern Jewish Studies*, *Studies in American Jewish Literature*, *Profils Américains*, *Saul Bellow Journal*, and in numerous critical essay collections.

SUZANNE EVERTSEN LUNDQUIST is Associate Professor of English and Cultural Studies at Brigham Young University. She is the author of *Trickster: A Transformation Archetype* and numerous articles about multiculturalism, Native American literature, and American minority discourse. She is currently finishing two books, *Native American Literatures* and *Learning from Native America*. Lundquist has worked among numerous Native American tribes in Bolivia, Peru, and Mexico as part of her belief that reading and studying minority American literatures also ought to have an experiential component—humanities students should be given the opportunity to apply their learning toward the alleviation of human suffering and humiliation.

BONNIE LYONS is the author of *Henry Roth: The Man and His Work*, coauthor of *Passion and Craft*, a volume of interviews with fiction writers including Leonard Michaels and Gina Berriault, and most recently author of *Hineni*, a chapbook of her own poetry. She has published articles about Philip Roth, Bernard Malamud, Saul Bellow, Delmore Schwarz, Tillie Olsen, Cynthia Ozick, Grace Paley, and other Jewish writers. Her full-length book of poetry, *In Other Words*, which contains forty monologues spoken by women in the Bible (Pecan Grove Press, 2004).

GILA SAFRAN NAVEH is Professor of Judaic Studies and Comparative Literature at the University of Cincinnati. She is the author of *Biblical Parables and Their Modern Recreations: From Apples of Gold in Silver Settings to Imperial Messages*, published by State University of New York Press and nominated for the National Jewish Book Award in the Scholarly Division; coeditor of *The Formal Complexity of Natural Language*, published by Reidel Press; and author of numerous scholarly essays engaging current theoretical frameworks and modern and traditional texts.

HUGH NISSENSON used his prose, poetry and illustrations as narrative elements in his last two novels, *The Tree of Life* and *The Song of the Earth*. He is currently doing the same on a novel in progress called *The Days of Awe*.

SUSAN E. NOWAK, S.S.J., is Assistant Professor of Religious Studies at Nazareth College. She lectures and writes on Jewish-Christian relations, women and the Holocaust, and the impact of feminist theory on interfaith relations. She is coeditor with Alan L. Berger and Harry James Cargas of *The Continuing Agony: From the Carmelite Convent to the Crosses at Auschwitz*.

THANE ROSENBAUM is a novelist, essayist, and law professor, the author of *The Golems of Gotham* (2002), *Second Hand Smoke*, which was a finalist for the National Jewish Book Award in 1999, and the novel-in-stories *Elijah Visible*, which received the Edward Lewis Wallant Award in 1996 for the best book of Jewish American fiction. His articles, reviews, and essays appear frequently in *the New York Times, Los Angeles Times*, and *the Wall Street Journal*, among other national publications. He teaches human rights, legal humanities, and law and literature at Fordham Law School. He is also the author of *Immoral Justice: Cultural Obsession and Popular Discontent in American Law*. He lives in New York City with his daughter, Basia Tess.

Index